BEYOND BELIEF

THE SECRET LIVES OF WOMEN
IN EXTREME RELIGIONS

edited by
Susan Tive & Cami Ostman

SEAL PRESS

BEYOND BELIEF
The Secret Lives of Women in Extreme Religions

Note to the reader: In some stories, names and identifying details have been changed to protect the privacy of individuals.

Published by
Seal Press
A Member of the Perseus Books Group
1700 Fourth Street
Berkeley, California

Library of Congress Cataloging-in-Publication Data

Ostman, Cami.
  Beyond belief : the secret lives of women in extreme religions / by Cami Ostman & Susan Tive.
    p. cm.
  ISBN 978-1-58005-442-3
  1. Women and religion. 2. Religion—Controversial literature. 3. Patriarchy—Religious aspects. I. Tive, Susan, 1962- II. Title.
  BL458.O88 2013
  200.92'52—dc23

                        2012041943

10 9 8 7 6 5 4 3 2 1

Cover design by Erin Seaward-Hiatt
Interior design by Domini Dragoone
Printed in the United States of America
Distributed by Publishers Group West

To all who have trusted me with their stories
and listened to mine in return.
—Cami Ostman

To my parents, who taught me that good conversation
is more important than table manners.
—Susan Tive

Contents

Burnt Offerings

EXODUS

Introduction:

Reflections from the Editors
Cami Ostman and Susan Tive

We met in a memoir writing class taught by author Laura Kalpakian in the fall of 2006. Susan was writing about her years spent in Orthodox Judaism, her difficult divorce, and the disorientation of transitioning out of living an Orthodox life. Cami was writing about how her journey to run a marathon on every continent was helping her find her way after a divorce and a profound change in her relationship with God. As we shared our respective stories—both in class and over coffee or wine outside of class—we discovered surprising parallels in our lives. Both of us had chosen to enter religious communities we weren't raised in. We had each adopted faiths that asked us to eschew many personal "freedoms" and choices most nonreligious women take for granted. Though Cami was not asked to cover her head or stop wearing pants as

Susan was, she was asked to believe that women shouldn't teach men in church and that her husband should be her "head."

Comparing notes further we realized that, despite the differences in our respective religious practices, we could empathize with each other's difficulties reintegrating into the secular world and shared the doubts and second-guessing of our decisions to leave. We understood the self-blame and guilt that comes with leaving strict religion behind. We experienced similar struggles surviving the wistful, nostalgic, and sometimes heart-wrenching emotions that arise from missing familiar community and ritual.

The more we talked, the more we began to ask ourselves, "Why *did* we choose to join such restrictive religious practices?" Even more compellingly, we wanted to explore both "Why did we stay so long?" and "Why was it so hard to leave?" After all, although we each experienced intense emotional and psychological pressure from friends and family to stay, we were not obliged by fear of violence as some women around the world are. What did we gain by staying—what kept us in even through years of serious misgivings?

As we formulated more questions and explored our own answers to them, we began to wonder about all the other women who, like us, had lived or were living through their own version of this story and were grappling with many of the same experiences, emotions, and questions. As our friendship with each other taught us, *women living life inside extreme religions have much in common despite their differences of practice and belief.* Sharing our stories with one another through writing and in conversation helped each of us to feel less isolated, learn from our experiences, and become willing to dig deeper. Realizing that the commonalities of our lives within extreme religion far outweighed the differences of our particular paths inspired us to widen the conversation. We decided to share our stories and give other women the opportunity to tell theirs. Thus, the seeds of *Beyond Belief: The Secret Lives of Women in Extreme Religions* were first sown.

Far and wide we flung our net, asking writers the same core questions we had asked ourselves: Why did you, a modern-day, liberated woman, join a religion that restricted your autonomy? What did you experience inside? What compelled you to stay? What compelled you to leave? How did you leave? What do you miss? How do you make sense of the world without your faith (or with an altered understanding of your faith)?

As *Beyond Belief* began to take shape, the one question we were asked most often by contributors was, "What's your working definition of *extreme*?" It's true that the word *extreme* is an extreme word! For some of our atheist friends, any religion that espouses a belief in any kind of supreme being is extreme. Yet for those who live inside orthodoxy or fundamentalism, what they live is not extreme to them at all: It is quite normal and sensible.

We agreed that we would let women who resonated with the term *extreme* define it for themselves. As editors, it's not our place to pretend we have an objective, unbiased definition of what is extreme that we can apply like a measuring stick to other people's experiences. What we do know is that, looking back on what we put ourselves through at an earlier time, we now see our religious commitments as extreme in comparison to our current lives. We hope you, the reader, will keep an open mind to the stories contained in *Beyond Belief,* and employ empathy as you read, even if certain writers' beliefs don't resonate with your own.

Another question we encountered when we made our call for submissions was, "I was born into a family that practices this religion. Can I still submit a story?" Our answer at first was no, but we changed our minds. Although we originally hoped to find women, like us, who chose to enter their faiths in adolescence or adulthood, we came to understand that, except for some women who risk their lives to leave their religion behind, even those who were born into a particular faith must *choose* to stay in it at least for some period of time (often because the consequences of leaving were, while not deadly, quite huge).

Finally, potential contributors asked us, "I've left a conservative branch of my religion, but I still attend a more liberal church/ synagogue/congregation. Does my experience count as 'leaving'?" Again, our answer was yes. We understand firsthand that faith and spirituality can be in flux. Where we are today may not be where we'll be tomorrow, and so it's best not to judge as definitive where other people happen to be on their spiritual journeys at any given moment.

In fact, it is precisely because we do not consider ourselves judges of other people's experience that we asked our contributors to write "slice of life" stories rather than informative or opinionated essays. It is not our intention to refute or belittle religion. On the contrary, we, as editors, wanted to spark a conversation about the commonalities of women's experiences in restrictive religions. The fact that most of the writers included in *Beyond Belief* have since left or greatly altered their religious practices is a reflection of our longing to hear from those who share the trajectory of our journeys and should not be read as a suggestion that women *should* leave. This book is entirely about sharing experiences in the way women do: by telling stories to one another.

In *Beyond Belief* you will find appreciation and gratitude for experiences of faith side by side with deep resentment and anger. Some writers are still grappling to make sense of their lives both in and out of extreme religion, while others are absolutely clear about how to understand their histories. We have made every effort to include women from as wide a range of religious backgrounds as possible. And while we couldn't include every single religion out there, we are proud of the quality and diversity of writing that has come together to form *Beyond Belief.*

It's our hope that you'll see yourself, your friends, and even a few of the people who irritate you in these pages—and that your curiosity will be piqued and your compassion stimulated. We hope that in reading these stories you will become inspired to enter into open-ended conversations such as the ones we strive to nurture in our own lives.

IN THE BEGINNING

Church Bodies

Naomi J. Williams

1. IN WHICH I LEARN THAT CHURCH TRUMPS EVERYTHING, EVEN ILLNESS

> *This Sabbath is to be kept holy unto the Lord when men . . . do not only observe an holy rest all the day from their own works, words, and thoughts about their worldly employments and recreations, but also are taken up the whole time in the public and private exercises of His worship.*
> —*The Westminster Confession of Faith, XXI:8 (1646)*

Going to church was of paramount importance in my family. Church was so important that we went twice every Sunday, morning and evening, and also Wednesday nights for prayer meeting. One Sunday morning when I was seven, I woke up with agonizing stomach pain and vomiting, and my parents took me to church anyway—that's how important it was.

We lived in Long Beach, California at the time and attended Pilgrim Reformed Baptist Church, a congregation so new and small we met mostly in people's homes. On the morning in question we met at the home of the Wheaton family. They stuck me on a daybed in one of those dark 1970s dens with no books, provided me with a bowl to throw up in, and proceeded with church in the living room. I lay there for an hour, racked with stomach cramps, until a large Siamese cat jumped up on top of me. Terrified of the animal, I hobbled out of the room and into the hallway, doubled over in nauseated pain, until Mrs. Wheaton noticed me. She shooed away the cat and closed me back in the room. To this day, I'm phobic about vomiting. I'm not overly fond of cats either.

Otherwise I liked Pilgrim Reformed Baptist Church. Everyone else's house was much nicer than our downscale apartment, and my younger sister, Mari, and I befriended some of the other girls. And I liked the grown-ups too, particularly the pastor, an Englishman called Ron Edmonds, and his wife, Thaïs. Mrs. Edmonds was Brazilian and had jet-black hair coiffed with meticulous, unliberated perfection. The Edmonds were genteel and never talked down to children. This mattered a lot to me.

But my father, a fractious individual, had a falling-out with Mr. Edmonds, the first of many such estrangements. When I asked why, he said it was complicated, a disagreement between men over how the church should be run. One Sunday morning he woke us up and told us we wouldn't be going to Pilgrim anymore. I cried. He found my grief touching; I remember sitting on his knee while he comforted me. He wasn't a heartless man, my father, however much he pressed his family to extreme religious observance. My mother, a practical and unsentimental Japanese woman, had more moderation. But she rarely overruled my father.

Leaving Pilgrim didn't mean we'd be skipping church, of course. I don't think we took even one Sunday off. But where to go? My parents always disparaged "church-hoppers"—ecclesiastically promiscuous people who cannot commit to a church family but keep shopping around in an endless, vain search for the ideal place of worship. But we did a lot of church-hopping ourselves. My Sunday memories of our post-Pilgrim years in Southern California are mostly of being on the freeway as we drove—and drove and drove—to one church after another. And although we were Baptists, almost all the churches we visited were Presbyterian. *Orthodox* Presbyterian.

2. CONCERNING TWENTIETH-CENTURY CALVINISTS

> *Our first parents, being seduced by the subtlety and temptations of Satan,*
> *sinned in eating the forbidden fruit. . . . By this sin they fell from their*
> *original righteousness and communion with God, and so became dead in*
> *sin, and wholly defiled in all the faculties and parts of soul and body.*
> —*Westminster Confession, VI:1–2*

The churches we attended belonged to a subgroup of Protestants who call themselves Reformed. *Reformed* here alludes to the Protestant Reformation and describes a motley ecumenical category that includes Baptists, Presbyterians, Dutch Reformed, Brethren, and even the occasional Episcopal outliers who see the Puritans as their spiritual forebears and point fondly to a 1646 document called the *Westminster Confession of Faith* as a summary of their core beliefs. They are, in a word, modern-day Calvinists.

Christians of most stripes believe in some concept of sin. But

Calvinists go for *total depravity,* the belief that people are entirely incapable of right action without God and deserve His wrath simply by virtue of being alive. In tandem with this bleak diagnosis is the doctrine of predestination, by which only those elected by God from before time will be saved from eternal damnation. I won't dwell here on the myriad ways in which this peculiar and anachronistic set of beliefs played on my mind as a child. Suffice it to say that I lived with a level of terror—of death, of Judgment Day, of not being one of the elect—that years later would prove a bonanza for more than one therapist. I was also one of those hideous children who casually told playmates that they were going to hell.

For Christians of the reformed persuasion, like my parents, adherence to these Calvinistic tenets was far more important than broader denominational labels like Baptist or Presbyterian. The Orthodox Presbyterian Church was, and may still be, one of the largest networks of reformed churches around. That's why, after the blowup at Pilgrim, we often ended up with the Orthodox Presbyterians.

I was not very clear on all this back then, of course. I remember more than one playground conversation that went something like this:

"What religion are you, Naomi?"

"Baptist."

"Oh, do you go to First Baptist?"

"No. We go to a Presbyterian church."

"But you said you were Baptist."

"We are."

"So why don't you go to a Baptist church?"

"Because the Presbyterian church believes more what we believe."

"Doesn't that make you Presbyterian?"

"No."

"That makes no sense."

"I can't really explain it. So what religion are *you?*"

"Catholic."

"Oh. Too bad. You're going to hell, you know."

3. ON BAPTISM

> *Baptism is a sacrament of the New Testament, ordained by Jesus Christ,*
> *not only for the solemn admission of the party baptized into the visible*
> *Church; but also to be unto him a sign and seal of the covenant of grace.*
> —*Westminster Confession, XXVIII:1*

The only difference I could see between the Presbyterians' and Baptists' beliefs was baptism. My father told me that church government was another point of departure, but at age seven I couldn't quite grasp that. (Years later I would come to appreciate this difference when the actions of a dictatorial Baptist pastor and his henchmen elders, accountable to no one, nearly destroyed my family, but that's another story.) There was also a cultural difference I could sense even as a young child, and that had to do with volume. The Baptists were louder. Louder and more theatrical in the pulpit, in their singing, in their professions of faith. Presbyterians, on the other hand, practiced their dread faith with a certain polite restraint.

But baptism was clearly the distinguishing field mark. Baptists baptize by immersion and reserve the Sacrament for professing believers only, while Presbyterians, like most other Protestants, baptize by sprinkling, and administer the Sacrament not just to new Christians who haven't been baptized previously but also to the infant children of Christians.

The logic of the Baptist position, articulated by my father, seemed unassailable to me. In the Bible, John the Baptist baptized converts, not converts and their babies. And this was no misting of houseplants; it was a manly Sacrament, performed in rivers. People got wet. Of course no Orthodox Presbyterian believed that baptizing infants conferred salvation. The children of believers were as depraved and hell-bound as the most unchurched pagan of those humid places where missionaries went. But the Presbyterians argued that infant baptism demonstrated the parents' public commitment to raise their children in the truth.

Baptism was a problem for me. I wanted to become a Christian. I prayed for this every day. And although I knew baptism wouldn't save me, it seemed a convincing proof of one's election. But I had never learned to swim and couldn't even put my face in the water. Hell, I was afraid of taking *showers*. How would I ever endure baptism by immersion? If we were Presbyterian, I would've been baptized as an infant and that would've been that. What rotten luck to have been born to Baptist parents!

I did have occasion to be thankful that at least we weren't Brethren. Once during those church-hopping years we visited a Brethren church while they were baptizing a large crop of new Christians. The Brethren, like Baptists, practice believers' baptism. But they do *triple* immersion. The baptizee goes under three times, once for each person of the Trinity.

The service was interminable. And one of the baptizees, a girl not much older than I, had obviously never learned to swim either. She spluttered and gasped each time she surfaced and tried to say "Wait!," holding up her arms, heavy in soaked and clinging baptismal robes, to resist the pastor. But he kept pushing her down again: "In the name of the Father,"—*dunk*—"the Son,"—*dunk*—"and the Holy Spirit"—*dunk*. People around us tittered, but I was swallowing hard, trying not to cry.

It was a relief to return to the dryness of the Orthodox Presbyterians after that. They were a friendly lot, the OPs, frequently inviting us to their homes for lunch after the morning service. Our doctrinal differences rarely came up, but when they did, it was always good-natured.

"One day a Presbyterian pastor runs into his friend, a Baptist pastor," began a joke told at one of these gatherings. "They begin to talk about baptism.

"'What if a person gets in the water only up to his feet?' the Presbyterian asks. 'Would that count?'

"'No,' the Baptist minister says. 'You have to go in farther than that.'

"'How about up to his knees?' the Presbyterian asks.

"'No,' the Baptist says. 'That wouldn't count.'

"'Up to the hips?'

"'No, no, no.'

"'To chest level?'

"'No.'

"'How about the chin? That's almost all the way in.'

"'No.'

"'Up to the eyes.'

"'No,' the Baptist insists. 'You have to get the top of the head wet.'

"'The top of the head? That's what matters?'

"'Yes.'

"'Well, we're in complete agreement!' the Presbyterian pastor declares. 'We get the top of the head wet too!'"

4. OF FAMILY DEVOTIONS

God is to be worshipped everywhere, in spirit and truth; as, in private families daily.
—*Westminster Confession, XXI:6*

Many evenings after dinner, my father would call us together for family devotions. Lasting about half an hour, it usually included a Bible reading, some catechism, and a closing prayer. It was torture, especially for Mari. We had to memorize our fair share of scripture verses—in the King James version, of course. Worse was having to memorize the *Westminster Shorter Cathechism.* This document, completed in 1647 by the same good people who brought us the *Westminster Confession,* consists of 107 questions and answers about doctrine presented in gorgeous seventeenth-century English. I can still perfectly recall questions 1 and 4:

Question 1: What is the chief end of man?
Answer: Man's chief end is to glorify God and to enjoy Him forever.
Question 4: What is God?
Answer: God is a spirit, infinite, eternal, and unchangeable, in His being, wisdom, power, holiness, justice, goodness, and truth.

My father spanked us if we failed to correctly recite the assigned passages. I had a knack for on-demand, short-term recall, and avoided getting hit. My sister was often not so lucky.

5. TREATS OF INDIGNITIES SUFFERED AT VACATION BIBLE SCHOOL

> *God gave to Adam a law, as a covenant of works, by which He bound*
> *him and all his posterity to personal, entire, exact, and perpetual obedi-*
> *ence; promised life upon the fulfilling, and threatened death upon the*
> *breach of it; and endued him with power and ability to keep it.*
> —*Westminster Confession, XIX:1*

The summer after I finished second grade, my parents sent me and Mari, who'd just finished first grade, to Vacation Bible School. It went for one week, meeting two or three hours every weekday evening at the OP church in Garden Grove, one of the many places where we'd occasionally worshipped. Mari and I had to carpool with an OP family we didn't like very much: April was snotty, Andy bratty, their mother meek, and their father quiet except when he exploded with violent rage at one of his kids.

The theme for the week was God's Law—always a crowd-pleaser with the elementary school set. The hymn for the week, which April and Andy's parents made us practice in the car, was #450 from the Trinity Hymnal, the official hymnal of the OPC:

> *Most perfect is the law of God,*
> *Restoring those that stray;*
> *His testimony is most sure,*
> *Proclaiming wisdom's way.*

> *O how love I thy law! O how love I thy law!*
> *It is my meditation all the day.*
> *O how love I thy law! O how love I thy law!*
> *It is my meditation all the day.*

Bible stories illustrated the theme throughout the week: the stalwarts who followed God's ways, no matter how repugnant or illogical—Abraham, who showed God he was willing to kill his own child; Moses and the Israelites, rampaging their way as instructed through the Promised Land; the brothers James and John, who abandoned their father, Zebedee, at a word from Jesus. Counterexamples were also presented for our edification. Look what could happen if you didn't obey God! Jonah, swallowed by a whale; Ananias and Sapphira, who dropped dead after lying about money in church; and poor Achan, who couldn't resist sneaking forbidden war booty into his tent and was stoned and burned to death along with his entire family.

Mari and I were in different classes for the week, and we both had problems with our teachers. An aide in my class had big, bleached blonde hair. She wore short skirts, low-cut knit tops, perfume, and makeup. She had a distinctly un-Presbyterian name—something like Deena. But this was the clincher: she didn't know the Bible stories. I finally accosted the head teacher and told her Deena did not seem like a Christian.

"Well," the teacher whispered back, "she's *not* a Christian."

"She's *not?*"

"We thought helping out with Vacation Bible school would be a great way for her to be introduced to the Gospel," the teacher explained. "Can you please pray for her?"

"Oh. Okay," I said, but I was appalled. What were they thinking, foisting an unbeliever on unsuspecting kids? What if she, you know, led us into error?

But at least Deena was nice, whereas Mari's Vacation Bible School teacher told her that she wasn't coloring correctly. At home this was met with more outrage than my news that one of my teachers wasn't even a Christian. Mari was a very talented artist. I give my parents credit for this: they took their total depravity seriously and harbored no illusions that Christians were better or smarter than other people. They gave Mari to understand that this woman who'd criticized her drawings was an idiot. "Pay no attention," my mother said. "She doesn't know what she's talking about."

Though my notions of Presbyterian common sense and courtesy were sorely tested that week, they were somewhat restored after class on the last day. On our way to the parking lot with Andy and April and their parents, Mari said she needed to go to the bathroom. The classrooms were locked up already, but someone directed us to the main building. Mari didn't want to go alone, so I went with her.

The heavy double doors shut behind us, leaving us alone at one end of the long, dark, silent sanctuary. We hurried to the bathroom and finished as quickly as we could, then rushed back to the doors we'd come through, but the doorknobs wouldn't budge. We pressed our small bodies against the double doors but nothing happened. It was Friday night, everyone was leaving, and we were locked in the church.

I have some memories of trying to be brave at times when I knew Mari was scared, but this isn't one of them. I panicked, and Mari followed suit. We cried and banged on the doors, screaming for someone to let us out. The staid Presbyterian interior, so lacking in inspiration on Sunday mornings, was, in complete darkness, as terrifying as the most Gothic cathedral.

Eventually the pastor of the church came in through a side door and rescued us. "Look," he said, his seminary-trained voice low and soothing, "all you have to do is press on the bar. See?"

We hadn't realized that the wide metal bars spanning the width of each door would open them. We may not even have seen them in the dark. He opened the door, and outside a whole bevy of OPs was clucking about how they'd been *trying* to tell us what to do but we'd been so busy carrying on that we couldn't hear. The pastor shushed them and took Mari and me back in the church, gently insisting that we open the door ourselves, to see how easy it was, so we'd never have to be that scared again.

Seven years later, an American Airlines DC-10 crashed shortly after takeoff at O'Hare, killing that kind pastor and 270 other people on board. I've since learned that that bar he showed Mari and me how to use, so common on industrial doors, is called a panic bar.

6. IN WHICH I LEARN THAT CHURCH TRUMPS EVERYTHING, EVEN DEATH

> *The bodies of the unjust shall, by the power of Christ, be raised to dishonor; the bodies of the just, by his Spirit, unto honor, and be made conformable to his own glorious body.*
> —*Westminster Confession, XXXII:3*

In April of 1973, when I was finishing up third grade, we moved to the East Coast in order to attend a particular Reformed Baptist church, and our church-hopping days ended. But in the months before we left California, my parents more or less settled on one OP church. This congregation convened, of all places, in a mortuary in Cerritos. The building was shaped like a boxy *U*, with the main entrance and a spacious lobby at the bottom of the *U*, the chapel along the right side, and on the left a wing of small rooms, very nicely furnished, that we used for Sunday School classrooms in the morning. The children liked the lobby, which had an indoor koi pond. We were forbidden to touch the water, but most of us, at some point or other, dipped in a finger or shoe, and a few of the more intrepid kids managed to touch a fish.

The place looked very much like a church, and most of the time we could forget that the building had other uses. But there were occasional reminders, like the evenings we had to wait for a memorial service to conclude in the chapel before we could go in for our evening service. And there was the time one child (I think it was Andy) reported to the wrong classroom for Sunday School and spent some minutes sitting by himself next to an open and occupied casket before one of the adults discovered him.

Then there was the awful smell. This happened rarely—twice, that I specifically recall, both times in the evening. It assaulted us as soon as we entered the lobby. Bitter and cloying, the stench traveled straight up our nostrils and deep into our heads. It corresponded to no previous experience of smell—not to bathroom smells or garbage smells or to any of the industrial odors of Southern California. The nauseating stench of unchanged water in a vase of cut flowers that have died—it was like that, but much, much worse.

"Ew! What is that smell?" the children all asked. One of the mothers said it was a dead fish from the indoor pond, and no one contradicted her. Mari and I knew this wasn't true. We'd spent the earliest years of our life in Japan. Dead fish did not smell like this. We knew it, and so did all the other children. We knew what the smell was, knew it in an instinctive, olfactory memory of the collective unconscious way. This was the stench of death. *Human* death.

Incredibly, no one would leave. The service would proceed as scheduled. Ladies clapped handkerchiefs to their faces. The men sat upright in pews, manfully inhaling, faces green. The grown-ups instructed us not to complain. I figured out that if I breathed in and out through my mouth I wouldn't smell anything, but there was something sickening about this too, as if I were ingesting death. We sat there, enveloped by the stinging perfume of human decay, hissing through the hymns, all of us watching the clock and waiting for deliverance. *The chief end of man is to glorify God and to enjoy Him forever.* Were we having fun yet?

Why couldn't these people, who had not the slightest hesitation about telling their children that they would burn forever in hell when they died, be honest about the real-world manifestations of physical death? Here, surely, was the real "end" of man—dead, breaking down into volatile organic compounds, a mortician's project. Talk about a powerful object lesson. But all we got by way of explanation was dead fish.

I was a logical child, a legalistic child, a self-righteous pain-in-the-ass of a child. So I wondered: If Ananias and Sapphira were struck down dead by God for telling a lie in church, why were all of our parents still alive? But I did not say this aloud. By age nine I already suspected that much of what people said—even Christians, even parents, even Reformed Baptist and Orthodox Presbyterian parents—was not to be relied on. But I also understood that they could not help themselves. They may have been elect of God from before time, but they were still, after all, totally depraved.

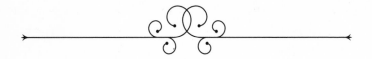

Direct Line to God

Cami Ostman

The oldest of us is Donny. He's twenty-two, and even though this is only my second time meeting him, I'm already enamored. The first time we met was at church, the one time I visited with Hope a few weeks ago. Donny's got this black hair styled up in a stray-cat-strut swirl and milky white skin, smooth—and warm, I'll bet. His eyes are so blue I have to look away when he greets me at the door and says, "Come on in." His gaze makes me blush. Donny's roommate, Ted, is beautiful in his own right, with sandy hair and hazel eyes that sparkle when he says your name, but he doesn't have that edgy, forlorn expression that Donny wears. I'm a sucker for forlorn. It runs in my family.

At only fourteen I'm the youngest in the group. I'm even younger than my best friend, Hope, who is also fourteen but whose birthday is almost a month before mine. There are thirty of us in all, but I know only Hope and Donny and Ted so far. After Donny invites us in, Hope makes her way around the room greeting everyone. I take a seat in the circle next to a girl with extra-white hair, thick glasses, and eyes that flutter around like she couldn't hold them still even if she tried. She's an albino; I can tell because you can practically see right through her skin. She says Hi and It's nice to meet you and My name is Hedda, what's your name? I tell her and then we look away from each other and pretend to study the carpet.

Donny and Ted's place is in the basement of somebody's house and it's super ugly. The rug is don't-look-too-close-or-you'll-find-gross-stuff-down-there maroon and the walls are paneled with wood. Hanging next to the front door is a velvet picture of Jesus holding an electric guitar. The picture glows in black light. I know this because as soon as everyone is seated, Donny plugs his own guitar into his amp and turns down the lights. Only one lamp stays on and it has this pulsing, buzzing bulb that radiates a purple luminosity—I love that word, *luminosity*. Anyway, the velvet Jesus becomes brilliant and his red guitar shimmers—Donny's that is, not the guitar in the Jesus picture. Jesus's guitar disappears when the lights are low and turns into a shepherd's staff. It's cool.

Even though the apartment is small and cramped and smells like mold, it's the only place we can all go out of adult earshot. Since Donny and Ted are the youth pastors at Hope's church and are considered adults, the main pastor has given his approval for youth group to meet here. I'm glad because if my mom found out I was going to church, she would flip a switch. This way, I can go to church service without lying, exactly.

Donny leads us through about five choruses. I don't know the words, but I think it's awesome the way everyone sings like they're singing love songs, with their eyes closed and swaying. Only, I'm a little embarrassed when kids start raising their hands in the air like they're reaching for something they can't quite get to, even on their tippy toes. I'm not sure where I'm supposed to look. They seem like they're doing something private, like when you touch yourself at night, but they're doing it here right in front of everyone. I close my eyes, too, so no one catches me watching.

The guitar gets really quiet. Donny picks out a gentle melody, and I open my eyes. He's got his eyes open too, and he sees me looking at him and winks. I'm totally in love with him even though I'm pretty sure I'm not supposed to be since he's the youth pastor. Closing my eyes again, I suddenly hear somebody near me talking quietly in what sounds like a foreign language. Hope told me about this. She says it's called "tongues" and that it's a sign that God lives in your heart when He's given you the ability to talk in a foreign language you've never learned. She says it might be an earthly language that somebody can translate or it could be a heavenly language—the language of the angels—so you can pray things to God that you don't even know you're praying.

This is why I've come tonight: to get the gift of tongues. Hope says I'll feel better if I have God's special prayer language. Although I'm skeptical, I could really use a direct line to God because the way I've been praying in my own Baptist church isn't changing anything. In fact, things are getting worse. Two weeks ago, my mom put me on restriction for raising my eyebrows when she accused me of being more interested in my Baptist friends than I was in our family. I only raised my eyebrows because it was such a ridiculous thing to say, but she sent me to my room and told me I was never to go back to that "cultish brood" again. They were making me "contemptuous and disrespectful." She came up to my room later and saw me reading my Bible, which flew her off the handle for good. She nabbed it away, right out of my hands, and stalked out of my room, slamming the door behind her.

I'm hoping that if I get God's special prayer language, my mom will let me go back to church and that maybe she'll even come with me and get saved herself. That's why when, after the singing stops, and after Ted reads from the Bible about how "bad company corrupts good morals" and then tells us the story about how he actually *stopped* drinking when he turned twenty-one because God told him to, I start to get nervous. Hope told me it's always after the "message" that God baptizes people in His Holy Spirit. That's what you call it when you start to speak in tongues. It comes from the Bible story about how the flames of the Spirit came down from heaven on the heads of all the believers at Antioch and they all started talking in foreign tongues.

I'm sitting next to albino Hedda when Ted finishes speaking and I'm looking around for flames, which I imagine look like holograms, like those cartoon images projected on the mist at the late show in Disneyland. But then Donny goes, "So, like always, we're prepared to pray for anyone who would like to receive the Holy Spirit tonight."

And Hope pops up her hand and she's like, "Oh, Cami wants it, I think. Right, Cami?"

Donny looks at me, and I can hardly even stand how blue his eyes are. "Pull your chair into the center of the circle, Cami." All twenty-nine pairs of eyes are looking at me and I'm completely mortified of course, because I know that half of them are looking at this gigantic pimple I have nestled beside my right nostril. But I also really want to get the baptism of the Holy Spirit because I need the direct line to God that everyone else in the group has, so I go ahead and pull my chair into the middle of the room.

I don't really know what to expect, but Hope is next to me

saying, "Don't worry about anything. This'll be really great." Once my chair is settled squarely in the center of the room, everyone stands and circles around like they're all looking at a cute little puppy or something. It's pretty weird to have so many people standing that close to me. I have trouble getting a breath. In my family we're not very touchy-feely, and I'm not sure how it's going to be to have my whole body covered with hands. But it's not so bad. Some kids kneel around me and grab my ankles, my shins, my knees. Other kids stand behind me and put a palm up against my back or my shoulder. Pretty soon, most of me is covered. Hope puts her hand on my head and runs her fingers through my hair the way she sometimes does at school during play practice when we're all sitting backstage giving each other back rubs before Mrs. Doling arrives to get things started.

Once all the kids are in position, Ted starts to pray, really quietly at first. "Thank you, Father; we praise you, Father," he's saying. I'm always wondering about making God into a father. Ever since I memorized the Lord's Prayer last year at my own church, which starts, "Our Father, which art in heaven," I thought it was funny that the pastor was always talking about having a personal relationship with our "heavenly Father." It's not that I don't know some dads, like in my neighborhood or from friends at school, who are pretty involved and spend a lot of time with their children. It's just that most dads are sort of busy. And if you took my dad as an example, some don't even live with their families, so the whole personal-relationship-with-a-father comparison eludes me. But since the Bible is the word of God, I'm not allowed to argue, so I just keep my mouth shut.

Anyway, Ted is whispering this whole series of phrases and so is everyone else. Since I've only been born again for a short time and it happened in a Baptist church where no one prays out loud unless they have to, I'm not used to talking at the same time that someone else is praying, but here they all talk quietly simultaneous-like. I keep my head bowed.

Next, Ted starts praying louder, "Dear Holy Spirit, we just invite you to totally overtake our sister, Cami, and completely overwhelm her with your presence and give her your gift of tongues and help her feel you in her life daily and make her become a blessing to everyone around her."

"Yes, Jesus," someone says. And another person says, "Please, God." And I open my eyes just a little and there's Hedda with her brow crinkled up, praying so hard I almost worry she is going to get a headache.

I don't know what everyone is expecting will happen, but they keep up the quiet, short little aspirations of praise for a long time. Hope keeps running her fingers through my hair, and I start thinking about how she knows everything about me—well, almost everything. Hope knows that my parents don't pay much attention to me. My mom most of all because she spends a lot of her time in her bedroom with her new husband while I take care of my younger brothers. Hope knows my dad lives in a little trailer outside my grandmother's house and that he snorts cocaine sometimes; Hope even came with me to see my dad once, just to see if he was okay. Hope knows that tonight I had to tell my mom I was going to her house to study at her kitchen table and that at my house we don't even have a kitchen table—only a coffee table in the living room where everyone eats, and it's always cluttered with dirty dishes so you can't really do your homework there. Hope agreed with me that it wasn't lying for us to come here tonight because we did spend ten minutes at her house studying for our college-prep English test.

But there are also things Hope doesn't know—things I don't tell her because I know everyone in my family would kill me if they found out I said something. And she likes this about me, that I can keep secrets. She always tells everyone, "If you have something that's totally exploding inside you that you have to say out loud but you don't want everyone to know, you can tell Cami because she can keep a secret like nobody's business." And it's true. There are things about my family I'll take to my grave.

Anyway, we all pray for a really long time. And nothing is happening, so I start to feel guilty that everyone is spending so much time trying to convince God to let me talk in angel tongues. Plus, their hands are getting sweaty on my back and legs. But I want this direct line to God because after this meeting I have to go home, and when I get there my mom is going to be boiling mad at me since I accidently left a little Gideon's New Testament on the bathroom counter. If she finds it, she'll know I smuggled it into the house after she took the first one away. I remembered that I'd forgotten to put it back in my coat pocket only after I got to Donny and Ted's and now I'm hoping my new prayer language will help me convince God to make sure my mom miraculously doesn't see it.

I open my eyes and turn my head to see if I can make Hope look at me. She's already got her eyes open and she leans over and says, "It's okay, sometimes it takes awhile, just start moving your mouth. God will take care of the rest."

I'm super glad she's there. I bow my head and concentrate. In my heart, I pray, "Okay, God, help me out here."

Nothing happens for another long time. I start to feel really bad, like maybe God isn't that interested in me, or maybe I'm not really born again. Maybe—even though I walked down to the front of the church and said the Sinner's Prayer with my Baptist pastor—maybe I don't believe in God quite right. And then I start to get kind of freaked out because if that's true, then my name still isn't written in the Book of Life, and also God won't help me by fixing the troubles in my family.

My chest gets really tight and I wonder what Donny is thinking because, even though there isn't any chance for us since I'm fourteen and he's twenty-two, I want him to like me and he probably won't if I'm not really saved. With everyone pushed in around me praying (but probably secretly wishing God would get on with it), I hyperventilate a little. I can't quite catch my breath. This happens to me a lot, but it's never happened in front of people before.

Hope sees what's going on and she whispers in my ear, "Just take a breath, Cami. God loves you. You just have to start moving your mouth."

Ted raises his voice above the hushed praises to pray loudly now, "Father, it's time. Give our sister your gift. Give it to her now." I figure I should at least do my part, so I start to move my mouth—opening and closing it really fast and swishing my tongue around inside.

Suddenly out comes this long, incredible string of syllables. And it keeps coming and coming. My heart starts thumping hard, but I'm shy about the sound of it so I'm doing it almost silently, but Hope is watching my mouth and she says, "Do it louder, Cami." So I up the volume just a little bit. It's for real; I'm totally speaking in tongues. And the sounds just keep flowing out like you can't believe.

Hedda hears this and says, "She's got it." Then everyone starts cheering. I stop speaking and then start up again to make sure it's real. It is. One girl who has been sitting on her knees in front of me even starts to cry and to hug my calf. They all start applauding and hugging me and saying, "Thank you, Lord."

After several minutes everyone quiets down and goes back to their seats. I do the same, but I'm in a daze—like I'm high, even though I've never been high, so I'm only guessing. The rest of the meeting is hazy as I keep thinking that now God can answer my prayers because I can tell Him what I don't even know I need. We sing a few more songs and then everybody eats the treats that Hedda's mom brought when she dropped her off.

LATER THAT NIGHT, HOPE'S dad, who is also excited that I got my prayer language, drops me off in front of my house. My mom and stepdad and brothers are all watching TV and they don't notice when I come in. I say hi, but they're fixated on their police show. It's a rerun, and they love reruns in my house—I don't love them so much, but it's mostly what we watch. So I just step over the clutter on the living room floor and make my way to the bathroom to see if my New Testament is there or if I'll be in royal trouble when my mom's show is over. There it is, in exactly the same place I left it when I took it out of my pocket. Nobody has noticed it. My new prayer language must already be working! So I stick the Bible back in my pocket, tell God thank you, and go upstairs to my room to study for my English test.

Beaten by Devotion

Huda Al-Marashi

When my mother was a young girl in Baghdad, her family made yearly pilgrimages to Karbala, the town where Prophet Muhammad's grandson, Imam Husayn, was killed in the seventh century AD. On the anniversary of his death, a day known as Ashura, Mama wrapped herself in a long, flowing black *abaya* and made her way through Imam Husayn's gilded shrine. There she sat on Persian rugs and listened to passionate retellings of his martyrdom that made her cry.

When I was a young girl in Monterey, California, my extended family made yearly pilgrimages to a run-down 1960s church in South-Central Los Angeles that had been converted to a mosque. We told our teachers and bosses there was a death in the family, never mentioning the death occurred well over a thousand years ago. With our bags tied to the roof rack and eight of us squeezed into a car designed for seven, we crossed three hundred miles of interstate, listening to tape recordings of religious services that made my mother, uncle, and grandfather weep, their shoulders bobbing up and down with each sob.

My siblings and I did not cry. Our Arabic vocabulary was limited to the domestic, and my family's tapes were not only garbled from use but full of words to which we'd had no exposure. My father did not cry either. I'd seen him cry only once, when he found out one of his sisters had died, and that had been only a short, angry burst of tears. My stepgrandmother pulled her face behind her *abaya* because sometimes she cried, but sometimes she didn't, and holding back tears at a time like this was not a sign of strength.

Shia Muslims believe the tears we shed in the name of our ill-fated imams (those spiritual leaders we believe are the rightful successors of the Prophet Muhammad) are blessed and rewarded. They are not to be comforted or contained. These tears were, in fact, the motivation for our journey. We traveled to this mosque precisely because the speaker was a prominent religious scholar, a descendent from the Prophet's family known by the title of Seyyid, and even better known for his ability to evoke the soul-cleansing cry my elders craved.

But first we had to endure the hot car, cramped seating arrangement, and a series of stops for gas and stretching. Halfway there, we pulled up to a Carl's Jr. on a desolate patch of desert highway littered with proverbial tumbleweed. My father ordered coffee, onion rings, and fried zucchini—this just to officially make us customers before my step-grandmother put out her spread: kabobs she fried that morning, pita bread, and a bowl that held iceberg lettuce, whole tomatoes, and a knife. I stared at the table too embarrassed to eat the sandwich my stepgrandmother offered me.

Born and raised in America, I knew it was wrong to bring your own lunch to a fast-food establishment. I knew it was even worse to wash for your daily prayers in a public restroom. As we poured handfuls of water on our faces and arms and then wiped our wet hands along our heads and feet, I saw women trying not to stare, throwing us glances as they washed their hands, sneaking one extra look as they walked out the door. And I knew, when we stepped outside to pray in the parking lot, the locals of Lost Hills, California would think we were the crazy practitioners of a strange religion.

In spite of this, when it was my turn to pray I put on the white cotton *chador* that covered me from head to toe. Dressed in what looked like a ghost costume, I bowed and prostrated on the state map Mama used to cover the gravelly asphalt. To object would have brought on a different kind of shame. Instead I prayed quickly, my *chador* billowing up in the hot wind, my uncle calling out, "Slow down." I prayed that no one was watching.

At the mosque, the church's pews stood against the walls of what had once been the nave. An enormous chandelier, donated by the Iraqi owners of a crystal shop, hung in its center, and a curtain stretched across the area that had been the altar, dividing the men's section and the women's section into drastically dispro-portionate parts.

At the door designated as the women's entrance, I balked at the space. The elders sat shoulder to shoulder on the pews pushed against the wall, and the floor was covered with women and children, sitting cross-legged, knee to knee. I pointed out the obvious: There is no room for us. But Mama would not be swayed. We added our shoes to the growing mound by the door and waded through the sea of women and children, stopping to regain our footing in the spaces between their bodies.

My stepgrandmother soon found room on a pew. Mama bent down to greet and kiss the people she recognized from our yearly visits. At home, Mama was a busy suburban mother juggling work and nursing school, but here she was someone else entirely, more Iraqi, more Shia. From under her scarf and *abaya,* she spoke to us in Arabic as if English had not conquered her tongue as well as ours. "*Sallemi,*" she prodded us along to greet her friends with the traditional "*Assalmu Alaikum,*" followed by a kiss on each cheek.

Mama had relatives in the area that had arrived earlier. They now pulled their purses into their laps to make room for us. Then the Seyyid's voice carried over the partition, at first didactic and then afflicted with the weight of the tale on his lips. Mama stopped her crying and urged me to pay attention. "If you listen," she promised, "you'll understand."

I hated being told this. We had been making this journey for years now, but the only things I knew about the story of Imam Husayn were the things Mama had told me in English. I knew he and his family had been on their way to Kufa when the reigning caliph's army had intercepted them. In one day, Yazid ibn Muawiyya's men killed Imam Husayn's valiant brother and handsome nephew, his thirsty six-month-old son, dozens of his followers—all this before beheading the imam himself and setting fire to the camp where the men's sisters, wives, and daughters awaited their return.

Knowing this outline was not enough to help me decipher the narrative within the mournful dirge the Seyyid recited, the poignant details that made the women around me sob and slap their thighs. The only thing I recognized were the names that floated out of the Seyyid's sermon like clear little bubbles, but I longed to understand more. I wanted to know what could be so sad it made people cry every time they heard it year after year. When Mama told me parts of the story, I felt sad, but I never burst into tears. I didn't know if it was something about how the story was told in Arabic or if it was something about the people listening to it. Did Iraqis cry easier? Was I too American to cry? Or maybe the tears were age related? Maybe only adults cried?

I studied the faces around me, hoping to find all the young people in the crowd dry-eyed. I'd almost confirmed my assumption when I spied two sisters in tightly wrapped headscarves huddled at their mother's feet. They had tissues in their hands with their heads bent down. I couldn't tell if they were trying to appear as if they were crying or if they actually were. I strained to get a better look and discovered that one of them had tear-stained cheeks. I was crestfallen. How come she understood when I didn't?

My jealously, however, was fleeting. The Seyyid concluded his sermon, and I heard the rustling sound of the microphone changing hands. Soon another speaker would recite a series of call-and-response chants that our congregation would keep time to by beating on their chests. My thoughts wandered to the year before when a small group of women had attempted the *latmiya,* a lamentation ritual Mama said she had not seen since she'd left Iraq. That night, Mama had moved in circles, her hands flying up to her face in rhythm with the chant being recited. The faces of the women around her reddened from a combination of tears and slapping. Together their hands made the sound of a unified clap. When she motioned for me to join her, I shook my head. That circle belonged to the women who understood Arabic, the women who were real Iraqis. But as the evening wore on, I had regretted my decision to sit on the sidelines. I'd hoped she'd ask me to join her again, but she didn't. Now I wondered what I would do if they assembled for the *latmiya* again.

As soon as the recitation started, Mama took my hand and brought me into the circle. I was relieved she did not ask, that I did not have to choose. My heart pounding, I watched her for a hint as to what I should do. When she started to move, I copied her, bending so that my hair spilled forward while slapping my forehead with both hands. The movement of my hair brought relief from the crowd's heat, a small breeze on my sweaty neck. The muscles in my back warmed and loosened as we moved in circles around the room. Bend, slap, stand, and step.

On my third revolution around the room, something amazing happened. I understood. After years of attending services in an incomprehensible fog, one line opened up my world. The speaker called out, *"Abd wallah, Ya Zahra, ma ninsa Husayna."* At first it was nothing more than a tight knot of language, but after the third or fourth time of repeating it, that knot unraveled into distinct, intelligible words, "I swear to God, O Zahra, we will not forget Husayn."

Shia legend had it that Imam Husayn's mother, Fatimaaz-Zahra, attended every *majlis,* or gathering, where the name of her martyred son was mentioned. These words were being spoken to a presence among us. Each time we repeated them, the cries of the group grew louder, and the women in the circle no longer stepped, but jumped, bringing their hands high up into the air and then pulling them right down on the top of their heads. I jumped with them, beating each side of my head with my hands, and before I knew it, I was crying with a mix of emotions. Relief to have understood, overwhelmed by the power of the words on my tongue. I was promising a mother that I would not forget the death of her son.

A realization surged through me. Many of these women had known the pain of Fatimaaz-Zahra firsthand. The Gulf War had just ended, and there wasn't a woman next to me who hadn't kissed her father or brother good-bye without wondering when she'd see him again. For the first time, I understood the Shia adage "Every day is Ashura. Every land is Karbala." Daily, the martyrdom of Imam Husayn played out in someone's life, somewhere in the world. This was especially true in Iraq, a country whose modern history was marred by tragedy and tyranny. I thought about Manal, standing across the circle from me. At the height of the Iran-Iraq War, armed soldiers had stormed into her uncle's home, accused them of being Iranian sympathizers, and deported her right along with them. She never saw her parents again.

This thought made me cry even more. Each time I brought my hands up to my face, I slapped myself a little harder. The tender skin on my face stung, but it was a good hurt. Just a small burn. A little reminder of how lucky I was to know only such inconsequential pain.

When the *latmiya* was over, the women fanned their *abayas* to cool down and moved about the room, exchanging hugs and kisses with the wish "May God accept your prayers."

Mama came over to me, sweaty and out of breath. When she kissed me on the cheek and whispered, "I am proud of you, *hababa*," a bud of warmth bloomed within me. I was a good girl.

Mama's elderly aunt motioned us over to the pew where she sat. Leaning on her cane, she said, "When I see you with your daughters, I think of Zaynab and cry more." Mama squeezed my hand. She was honored by this comparison to Imam Husayn's sister, the hero of Karbala, the one who had condemned her captors for the injustice done to her brother in a fiery speech, the one who had held the first mourning assembly in his name.

The following day, we reconvened on the men's side for a special ladies' session. Stretched across the walls were black banners with Imam Husayn's name painted in bold white Arabic lettering.

At the front of the room and just behind the chandelier in all its incongruent splendor was the Seyyid's chair, raised on a platform and covered in black fabric. This space was not expansive by any means, but it felt ample and generous by contrast to the women's side. The older women spread out along the pews, their bodies relaxed; children ran in every direction.

Right away I joined the circle of women, waiting for the recitation to start with their headscarves dropped to their necks, their *abayas* open so that they draped on either side of their bodies. Our speaker, an elderly women in a crinkled scarf, pulled toward herself the microphone positioned in front of the Seyyid's chair. At the start of her reading, two women from the edge of the circle stepped into the center; depending on the speed of the chant, they either bent forward and brought their hands up to their faces or jumped from side to side, bringing their hands down on top of their heads. Sometimes they turned around and faced the women in the outer circle, stopping in front of each woman to make a guttural "huh, huh," noise that acted as an invitation to match their fervor and energy. Although I was too afraid to go in the center of the circle, Mama wasn't. She led the women in the outer circle until she got tired and had to retreat to its edges.

At times, I looked over at the other women, those standing outside of the circle and lightly beating their chests, those sitting on the pews and crying quietly. I wondered what kind of woman stayed on the sidelines. Within our own tradition, these lamentation rituals were surrounded by controversy, and I wondered if the women looking on were not as devout, or if they did not believe in the *latmiya*, if they thought the practice was too extreme. I wondered what it said about me that I was standing there. I thought about my teachers, my friends from school, my friends who were Sunni Muslims. What would they think if they saw me standing here, beating myself? But as we moved in slow, deliberate circles about the room, I was surprised that something so mournful, something so cult-like in its outward appearance, could feel so beautiful to the insider. The women's silky black *abayas* flowed with their every movement, making their bodies appear as if they were dripping in sadness. Their faces, red from tears and the marks their hands left on their cheeks and foreheads, spoke of things too powerful, too gray to explain. Yes, love and devotion to the imam had brought them to the edges of this circle, but their bodies, now given the permission to speak, had so much more to say.

In this circle, we were witnesses, people with the power to keep a tragedy alive for more than a millennia. The Shia may have been the historical losers, our desired successors never assuming power without it ending in bloodshed, but we were also the masters of memory, victorious in our ability to give relevance to our past. It struck me as something every atrocity deserved, a group of people who would honor their suffering for the ages.

When the session concluded an hour later, my back ached from the repetitive bending forward, and my tight muscles told me something of why not everyone participated. But at the same time, I felt a satisfaction that canceled out the hurt. I did not understand all the words that had been chanted around me, but I had participated in a tradition larger and grander than my teenage self.

My satisfaction was short-lived. Instead of kissing and hugging me as she had the night before, Mama took my chin in her hands and said, "What did you do your face?"

"What do you mean?"

"Your face," she said, feeling gently under my eye.

"What about my face?" I asked.

"You gave yourself a black eye. You know you're not really supposed to hit yourself?"

"Really?" I said, touching my hands to my cheekbones, trying to feel what Mama saw. But the only thing I felt was the sting of tears. I was afraid to say more. I was afraid I would cry for misunderstanding so much.

"You're supposed to bring your hands up to your face but when you get there you just tap."

I felt flush. I thought hurting yourself was the whole point.

Drawn by the commotion, a small group of women formed around me, each one of them offering a piece of advice as to how to perform the *latmiya*. I fought away tears until I picked up on something in the tone of their advice. It was pride. Mama stood next to me, explaining what had happened, and she had a pleased air about her. She shook her head with an almost imperceptible smile, as if to say, "Look what she's done in the name of Imam Husayn."

Watching Mama with the women around her, I realized the power of that little mark. It announced to the community that I had stood with Mama during the time of the *latmiya*, that I cared about my religion, and that I wanted to learn more. It proved I was different from the girls who had sat at the back of the room and whispered with their friends. I felt pure, good, obedient. Even though I didn't recognize the girl that had been spinning in the center of the room moments before, I liked her. She belonged.

Baptizing the Annas

Caitlin Constantine

I gather my scriptures and wait for my Sunday School leaders to finish the morning lesson on the importance of faith in our daily lives. Once the Young Women's class is over we head to Sacrament meeting, the most boring part of church, where we are required to sit silently for a whole hour listening to our elders drone on like dial tones about gratitude and prophecy and blah blah blah. We're only thirteen. How can my friends and I be expected to pay attention to church stuff for three hours every single Sunday?

Just before we are dismissed, Sister Armstrong stands up and makes one last announcement. "I have some exciting news," she says, grinning. "Our class has been selected to perform baptisms for the dead at the temple."

I stop packing up my belongings and blink at Sister Armstrong. *Baptisms for the what?*

I had converted to the Church of Jesus Christ of Latter-day Saints more than four years earlier when my father married my stepmom. Her family had been Mormons since the church's earliest days. Because I was nine the church proclaimed I was old enough to make my own decision—they wouldn't baptize me right away like my younger siblings. I had to take weekly lessons for months just as if I were an adult. Much of what the missionaries taught me was confusing, but I wanted so badly to be a Mormon—and, more importantly, to be part of my new family—that I just nodded and agreed, as if I understood everything.

It was no wonder that every week still brought new surprises about my adopted faith. Most things, like tithing, taking the Sacrament, and missionary work are like normal parts of any church, but "baptisms for the dead" sounds positively grotesque. Before I can stop it, my mind conjures images of decaying bodies floating in a baptismal font, bits of flesh and gore breaking free from the corpses as they are plunged underwater. I shudder.

"For those of you who don't have temple recommends, you'll have to make an appointment for an interview with Bishop Carlson." She continues smiling beatifically at us. "What you'll be doing is very important. You'll be giving people who died without hearing the Gospel a chance to return to Heavenly Father's side one day."

After we are dismissed, the other girls get up and leave, already chatting and laughing, as if Sister Armstrong has just announced another car-wash-and-hoagie-sale fundraiser for Girl's Camp. Their voices drift in from the hallway and I briefly consider joining them, but I linger in the room. Mustering up my courage, I slowly walk over to Sister Taylor, who is putting her teaching manuals and Scriptures in her big shoulder bag. I sit down next to her. Sister Taylor is the leader of the Beehives, our young women's group, and

I spend more time with her than with any other leader. I trust her to answer my questions without making fun of me.

"Uh, Sister Taylor?" I stammer. "What exactly does Sister Armstrong mean by 'baptisms for the dead'?"

Sister Taylor puts one last notebook in her bag and calmly looks at me. "It means we do baptism by proxy." I must look even more confused because she continues. "We do them in place of people who have died. You will be baptized on their behalf. It's how we give others the chance to accept the Gospel even though they weren't able to do so when they were alive."

Although I still don't understand the "by proxy" part, I am somewhat relieved. Instead of sharing a pool of filthy water with a bunch of rotting corpses, I'll be immersed in sparkling clean, chlorinated water just like my own baptism, but this time I get to do it inside the temple.

THE TEMPLE IN SALT LAKE CITY has towered over my life for as long as I can remember, even before I was baptized a member of the church. It radiates holiness and virtue, from its white spires that shimmer in the sunlight to the golden statue of the Angel Moroni calling upon the faithful below. The temple isn't just physically imposing; it also looms large in my future life. When I marry, the ceremony will be within its walls. When I have a family, I will be sealed to them for all time inside. Without the rituals performed in the holy temple, I would be forever cut off from the Celestial Kingdom and from living alongside Heavenly Father for all eternity.

The closest I've ever come to getting inside the temple is walking through the grounds during Christmastime and admiring the millions of lights that decorate every spire and towering archway. Being baptized for dead people will be my first chance to penetrate this most heavily guarded sanctum. I feel a delicious thrill of excitement.

But before I can explore the enticing secrets of the Salt Lake Temple, I have to obtain a "temple recommend" by passing an interview with Bishop Carlson. Because I've known Bishop Carlson since the days when the most complicated decision in my life was picking the color of my Trapper Keeper, I figure it won't be a big deal. Bishop Carlson is a rotund grandpa of a man perfectly suited to play Santa every year at the ward Christmas party. He calls his wife, Louise, "Squeezy Weezy" and sometimes he falls asleep on the stand during Sacrament meeting. He once helped me catch, clean, and cook a trout at Girl's Camp. I adore him.

No one ever talks about what it takes to get a temple recommend, so I'm not sure what to expect at my interview. I arrive at my appointment with Bishop Carlson a few days after Sister Armstrong's announcement. His small office is stuffed with a desk the size of a raft, so I have to turn sideways to get to a chair. The walls are covered with framed prints of Joseph Smith and Jesus. I know these pictures well; every home—including my own—displays them prominently in living rooms and entrances. In the standard-issue portraits, both men radiate sainthood, with the same ruddy pink cheeks and piercing gazes that seem to look right into your soul. A photo of the Salt Lake Temple also adorns the scant wall space. I look at it longingly as I take my seat on the opposite side of the desk and primly fold my hands in my lap.

Bishop Carlson welcomes me into his office with a few minutes of small talk and looks at me with his kind, twinkling eyes. "I'm going to ask you some questions," he says. "I need you to answer truthfully, okay?" I nod. He picks up a piece of paper, peers at it through his bifocals, and clears his throat.

"Are you sexually pure?" he asks, his voice suddenly businesslike.

I stare at the coarse brownish-green carpet, dumbfounded. Am I *what?* I don't know what I expected him to ask me about, but this is *not* it. Bishop Carlson's eyesight is bad, but is it so bad that he misses my pink eyeglasses, my too-short pants, my bony knees and elbows? Even if I wanted to be sexually impure, I doubt I could find someone who would be willing to help me out.

I manage to croak out a yes. He makes a note on a piece of paper, and I wonder if my answers are going in a file somewhere. He moves on to the next question.

"Have you ever used alcohol or drugs?"

I shake my head, no. I can't bring myself to look at him, even though it occurs to me that he might take my lack of eye contact as a sign of guilt.

"Have you ever touched yourself? Have you ever smoked? Have you sinned?"

He recites his list of questions in a bored monotone. He probably asks these questions every day. No adult or teenager in the community is spared this indignity, I'm guessing. Does everyone else feel this embarrassed? Does anyone else think it's weird to be asked to share such personal information? Does anyone tell the truth?

I sneak a quick glimpse at the photo of the temple, white and pure and tall enough to reach Heavenly Father, and remember why I am doing this. The temple better be worth it.

I take a deep breath; my eyes never leave the floor. "No," I say, "I have never touched myself." "No, I have never done drugs, I have never used alcohol." "No," I say, "I have never sinned." This last statement is a lie, but I haven't committed any of the Big Sins, like murder or premarital sex, so a no seems justified, even though lying is a sin itself. I sidestep this moral quandary and keep answering the way I know I am supposed to, just to get Bishop Carlson past the sex questions. I'm sure that Heavenly Father understands my plight and won't hold my dishonesty against me.

Soon we move on to more familiar territory, where my years of Sunday School and Sacrament memorization ensure I am well versed. When Bishop Carlson asks about church doctrine, I finally lift my head and look him directly in the eye. I've made these same statements in public many times: while bearing testimony in front of the ward, giving talks during Sacrament meetings, and taking part in testimony meetings during youth camp. This part is easy.

"Yes, the Church and the Book of Mormon are true," I tell him. "Yes, Joseph Smith was the true prophet of Heavenly Father." "Yes, my testimony is strong and, yes, I am a faithful believer."

Bishop Carlson checks off the last item on his list. He pulls out a small card from his desk and signs it, then tucks it into a file folder on his desk.

"See you at the temple," he says, smiling. I grin, relieved that I have proven my worthiness.

NORMALLY, I LIKE NOTHING better than to spend my Saturday mornings burrowed between the sheets, but on the Saturday of temple work, I fly out of bed the second my alarm clock starts shrieking. In the next thirty minutes, I shower, eat, and put on my prettiest church dress, a long yellow one with mauve poppies. I check my makeup and sling a backpack filled with toiletries and clean underwear over my shoulder and walk to church.

When I get to the meetinghouse, a group of teenagers is standing around on the lawn near the parking lot, waiting for the youth leaders to arrive in their minivans. I join my best friend,

Andrea, on the lawn, and we regard each other with sleepy nods and yawns. The minivans arrive and we climb in, claiming the backseat for ourselves.

A half hour later, our convoy pulls into downtown Salt Lake City. We park a few blocks away and walk through the dewy spring morning to Temple Square. By this time we are wide awake. Our jokes and laughter echo down the empty streets at this early-morning hour.

The temple grounds are nearly vacant. The only signs of human life are the attractive lady missionaries, who serve as ambassadors to the small armies of camera-wielding tourists who will stop by the visitor's center later in the day. We bypass the visitor's center as our leaders guide us into a small building at the base of the temple. A thrill quivers in my chest as we enter; this building is for members only.

We cram inside the lobby of the building and are greeted by a group of temple workers dressed entirely in white. White dresses for the women, white ties and shirtsleeves for the men, white hair on every head that has it. An army of old, white-haired temple elves. A Young Men's leader hands a stack of temple recommends to an older man behind a desk. Andrea and I stand in the back whispering while we wait for the adults to finish their business. A temple worker finally gestures us to follow him.

We march through a labyrinth of hallways that smells dank and moist, like the locker room at school. The sound of fluorescent lights buzzes overhead as we pass temple workers driving golf carts. They all greet us with the same cheerful smiles. Through endless tunnels we walk for so long that I wonder if we are lost. Finally we climb a short staircase and pass through a set of heavy wooden doors into a beige waiting room, furnished with outdated furniture and filled with church-issued literature and Books of Mormon. I feel a pang of disappointment; I expected more from the temple.

We move on to a room filled with rows of tall shelves piled high with stacks of neatly folded white cloth. Each of us takes a turn at the counter, telling the temple workers our size. They disappear into the shelves and come back with armloads of more white cloth. Our next stop is the locker room, where we change out of our Sunday best and into our temple wear.

The first garment I put on is a jumper that is meant to serve as underwear. I'd rather wear my own—how could my simple cotton briefs from JCPenney do any harm? But I follow the instructions I've been given and put on the jumper. It billows like a sail and the crotch hangs down well below my knees. I have no idea how many women have worn this over the years, and I'm sure I don't really want to know.

The next item of clothing in my stack is a white jumpsuit made out of stiff canvas; it reminds me of something you'd wear to work with toxic chemicals or at a nuclear power plant. I pull it on over my saggy old-lady underwear and zip it up the front. When I let go, the neck of the hazmat suit droops and exposes my nonexistent breasts. I am mortified. I bunch up the collar of the suit in one hand and grab my backpack with the other, then shuffle dejectedly through the locker room. On the way out, I catch a glimpse of myself in a full-length mirror. A wretched girl stares balefully back at me. She doesn't look like someone about to take part in one of the most sacred rituals of her religion; she looks like she's going to a costume party dressed as a deflated Stay-Puft Marshmallow Man.

Another temple elf steers me into a cavernous room where wafts of chlorine and dense warm humidity greet me. Still clenching the neck of my suit, I find a seat with the girls at the end of a marble bench along the right wall. The boys sit on the other side of the room. With a furtive glance I note that everyone else looks just as ridiculous as I do. I lean back against the wall and take in my surroundings.

I am sitting in the most opulent room I've ever been in. My feet rest on slabs of cool white marble shot through with streaks of gray. The wide staircase that leads up to the massive baptismal font is constructed from chunks of the same marble. The font is a giant bowl at least twenty feet around, carved with grapes and ivy leaves. It rises from the floor on the backs of twelve shiny, golden bulls, each one as high as my shoulders. I feel like I have walked into the pages of my Roman history textbook, leaving Salt Lake City and the twentieth century far behind.

At my own baptism I was submerged in a narrow hot tub tucked behind a divider in a classroom at the meeting house. As I gaze at the gleaming bulls and rub the smooth cool marble with my feet, my baptism feels shoddy in comparison. Then again, at least I *wanted* to become a member of the Mormon Church. I can't say the same for the dead people on whose behalf I await my turn to baptize.

Soon I hear my named called and step gingerly up the marble stairs, careful not to slip. At the lip of the font I see Brother Douglas standing in the waist-deep water, waiting for me to join him. I descend into the warm, crystal-blue water, my hazmat suit unfurls, billowing around my body as it swirls in the water.

Bishop Carlson and another elder from the ward sit in a pair of padded folding chairs on a small platform overlooking the font, a small television near their feet. Another, larger television faces the middle of the font. The men are dressed in white. But, unlike the smiling temple workers, these elders look serious. Even jovial Bishop Carlson looks somber and preoccupied as we begin.

Brother Douglas takes my hands and positions them so I

am holding his arm. I remember my grandfather holding me the same way when he baptized me four years earlier. I let go of the collar of my hazmat suit and let it fall, exposing my thirteen-year-old chest. I pray that the elders are truly as righteous as they are supposed to be.

Brother Douglas holds his free arm over my head, then says the same words my grandfather said:

"Having been commissioned of Jesus Christ, I baptize you in the name of the Father, and of the Son, and of the Holy Ghost. Amen."

But instead of saying my name after "I baptize you," Brother Douglas reads a name and a date of death from a list on the television. Then he lowers me into the water. A second later, he brings me back up. I have just enough time to wipe my eyes and nose before he puts my arms back in place and says the same words again, this time with a new name and date of death, and back under I go.

Name after name I go under the water and come back up, each time with a new name and date of death.

Head above the water. More words. New name. Back under the water.

After the final baptism, I stand quietly trying to catch my breath so I can walk out of the font. I am dizzy and my nose burns with chlorine. Only now do I realize that I have just been baptized for a dozen women, all named Anna, who lived and died in the 1600s.

Who were these Annas? I wonder. *Are they now Mormons? What about their own religions?*

Brother Douglas shakes my hand and thanks me, and I walk up the stairs on the other side of the font, still a bit dazed. A temple worker hands me a towel and a rectangle of white polyester with a hole in the middle that she calls a shield. She tells me to put it over my head and wrap it around my body when I am done showering. As I make my way back to the locker room, I am flooded with questions. Why would Heavenly Father make eternal salvation dependent on a few sentences and a dip in a hot tub? Can't He just look in our hearts and know? But there's no time for my questions. There's still one more ceremony to go through to secure the salvation of those just baptized. They have to be confirmed, too. I get dressed and make my way to another waiting area where I pick up a pamphlet about the temple and halfheartedly page through it.

When I hear my name called I am once more led into a different room, where the same three elders who baptized me are waiting. They direct me to a big leather chair and gather around, gently placing their hands on my head while they confirm me, over and over again, once for each Anna. Their hands are heavy and the leather is slippery. I struggle to keep myself upright and try to ignore the newly formed questions swarming my mind.

WHEN WE LEAVE THE temple it is late morning. Hundreds of long-dead people are now members of the Church of Jesus Christ of Latter-day Saints. The souls of a dozen women named Anna are one step closer to living with Heavenly Father forever in the afterlife, or so I am told. Outside, hundreds of living people stroll around the temple, gazing up at its sacred spires. The sun has brightened the thin city air, and as we walk to the van I feel the warmth on my damp hair. I try to stop thinking about baptisms for the dead and listen to the cars and people passing by.

The donuts and orange juice we eat on our way home taste

better than I imagine possible. After we finish, Andrea and I make plans for our sleepover later that night. We talk about what movies we will watch and how late we will be able to stay up. I think about which pajamas I want to bring and what we'll do in the morning. As we leave the city I watch the landscape turn from gray to brown, and I think about anything but the Annas of the 1600s.

Uniforms

Leah Lax

"Okaaayy!" That was a twentysomething bearded rabbi at the opening orientation for the Live and Learn Sabbath Experience, rubbing his hands together as he addressed the crowd. Dallas's Shearith Israel synagogue was hosting the Lubavitcher Hassidim from Brooklyn, Jews who still lived by the old Code of Jewish Law. The men, like this rabbi, wore beards and yarmulkes and black-and-white clothes. Their wives, somewhere in the background, were in long skirts and long sleeves, their hair covered with wigs or scarves. We were among the attendees he was addressing, me and my friend Ana. It was 1972, and I was sixteen. I was immersed in college plans, intent on graduating early, moving out to make my mark in the world.

We all sat in rows of folding chairs at one end of the social hall. It looked like about fifty of us had shown up for the weekend-long program. I figured most in the crowd were there for the same reason we were, had come like tourists to see Hassidim in action, and that many were probably members of the synagogue hosting this event.

We were to sleep over in Sunday School rooms and experience an orthodox Sabbath, follow all the rules. Which explains why Ana and I had both come in costume, that is, in the women's dress code we'd been handed when we registered: skirt length to the calf, sleeves at least to mid forearm, closed neckline, and pantyhose. I rarely wore a skirt, preferring my jeans or red overalls, but it was important to me to get this right.

Going make-believe orthodox with Ana for a weekend was like a game, one that was playful but also serious. There was a soaring spirit feeling I wanted out of religion that I imagined I could find— somewhere—and I believed the Hassidim were all about that spirit. Transcendence, Ana called it. A leap above, to God.

Ana was a college student at SMU (Southern Methodist University), two years my senior, and I wanted to follow her, would follow her, anywhere. I had first met her two years before when I had cut Sunday School class at our liberal, social-minded Reform Temple and wandered the halls. Since I'd been small I understood that my mother sent me and my sisters to Sunday School only to sit among the children of her peers and create an impression of our family's propriety. That was our job. We were to exemplify good behavior as the teachers talked at us about do-good theology, while at home cockroaches ran up the walls and my mother slept through her drugged days and our mentally ill father spent his time in the living room recliner grinding his teeth away and reading every word in the newspaper, including the classifieds. Now in high school, I still went to Sunday School, but I had taken to skipping the classes.

One Sunday, I found Ana leading a group of singing kids on her guitar, her soprano voice floating above the rest with a lovely lilting vibrato. When I got home, I looked up her number and started calling her every day like a pesky little sister, and even though she said I called too often, it didn't take long for us to become friends. We may have been an odd pair given our age difference, but Ana said I was deep and fearless, and I was simply smitten. She didn't seem to notice. I'd often find her waiting near my school bus in the morning in sunglasses, long brown hair feathered in the wind, the top of her convertible down, radio blaring. Skipping school was an easy decision.

Together we were taking a different look at Judaism—reading books and experimenting with the rituals that our modern synagogue spurned, trying on and exchanging ideas and identities like costumes in a backstage dressing room. Others of our friends were affecting a hippie air or carrying around *Quotations from Chairman Mao* or *The Communist Manifesto, Siddhartha,* or *Dune.* Regardless of our various current identities, we all had the same vocabulary, using words like *materialism* and *establishment* to mean our parents' pettiness, *heavy* and *peace* to indicate a value of rising above the small-minded adults. It wasn't a big jump from there to religion. Our religion. Ana's father was a composer of Jewish liturgical music, and it seemed important to her to figure out how to reframe the religion that she lived with day-to-day in her family. I was happy to examine it with her, side by side.

On the days that I skipped school to be with Ana, we would wander, shop, chatter over Chinese food about our reading and our dreams. Spending the weekend with the Hassidim was just another costume to try on, one all the more appealing because we did it together. Besides, we had planned to go camping, but it looked like rain.

The rabbi standing before us had long white strings hanging

over his belt at either hip that I thought curious. His full beard was reddish, he wore a large black yarmulke on his already-balding head, and he was pale. Three other men about the same age stood behind him, all dressed in the same black and white, all seeming a bit on display and mildly self-conscious about it, arms clasped behind, looking out at the crowd. "Before we get started," our rabbi announced, "here are the Sabbath rules."

Ana grinned. "Game rules," she whispered.

He had quite a list: The Sabbath begins tonight at sundown and is over tomorrow night after sundown. Set the lights in your rooms before the Sabbath begins and don't touch the switch until it's over. No writing; no using a car or telephone. Do not use or touch anything that requires electricity. Don't tear anything—cloth, paper, or other material. No scrubbing or washing, whether it's an object or one's own body, so better not to brush teeth; no showers, no hot water or soap, but it's okay to rinse off in cold water if you must.

There were murmurs, but little apparent surprise—none of the laughs or shaking heads I had expected. It seemed many here, unlike me, were familiar with the Sabbath laws. A few asked informed questions: Isn't it allowed to get a child to turn off the light if I forgot and left it on? I'm a doctor, so doesn't that mean I can use the telephone for my work?

But they all sounded a little meek before rabbinic authority, as if the rabbi owned Jewish Law. I felt that way, too. He owned us as well, for the time being, even if that was voluntary. Only one question sounded incredulous. "We can't tear anything, but surely," the woman said, "you can tear toilet paper?"

We couldn't. We had to prepare that in advance.

"We're Jews," I whispered to Ana. "But I didn't know any of this stuff."

I was both leery of rules and attracted to them. My mother was incredibly inconsistent, would suddenly decide she had rules we should have known, even if she'd never revealed them to us. Her anger for not following them would come like a shot out of nowhere, a demand, we knew, to make her happy. There was love at stake for us bound up with those unknowable rules. I was always uncertain around my mother, trying to please, never getting it right. In high school as well, there seemed to be unwritten rules among the girls that made being one of them my endless social failure. There I was in my overalls, longing for my girlfriend and dreaming at night that I was a boy, watching mystified as the other girls pretended to be women, girls I'd known a long time who didn't seem themselves anymore as they touched up their makeup in the bathroom mirrors and swished around boys. I couldn't figure out their rules either, and I wanted to.

"Here's our schedule for the evening," the rabbi said. "In a few minutes, the women are going to light the Sabbath candles. When they say the candle blessing, that's when Shabbos begins. It is our women who inaugurate the holy Sabbath."

Our women. The phrase swept me solidly into the group, into a reassuring and rare sense of belonging. But it also sounded as if these strangers owned us. But then again, by "our," didn't he just mean "Jewish"? So wasn't I already in? I was confused, conflicted. Both attracted and repelled. Our women.

"Oh, and one more thing," the rabbi said, like an after-thought. Then he glanced sideways and swallowed. "Throughout . the Sabbath, the women and men will participate separately."

I looked up.

"This is the modest way," he said. "Separate is Godly." For the rest of this timeless Sabbath, the women were to sit separated from the men at meals and behind a partition at prayers. We would gather in designated areas; pray apart, with low voices; eat apart.

So much was coming at me so fast. Out in the world, there was a budding feminist movement: Bella Abzug in Congress in her hats, the Equal Rights Amendment making its slow movement state to state, women burning bras on television. But at this event we had stepped into a different society apart from all that. I supposed this gender divide was no more strange than all the other new rules. Maybe, I thought, this was just like summer camp orientation, reasonable enough that we would be subdivided into groups with different activities. In any case, I liked that I had just been deemed a woman and thus an adult.

The rabbi talked on about Jewish women lighting Sabbath candles all over the world, about how Jewish women have been doing the candle ritual on Friday evenings for thousands of years. He called those women noble and important. Images of this simple simultaneous act of lighting candles played in my mind, the little flames lit by women around the world, always at sundown, flickering shadows on dining room walls, covered heads bowed over centuries. That was solidarity, global, historical—a true sense of belonging. The rabbi said that we women brought light to the world.

He paused and gave us a long gaze, then raised his voice for dramatic effect. "It is time," he said, "for the women to inaugurate the holy Sabbath." He gestured toward a long table at the other end of the hall set with unlit candles. He turned and stretched out one arm as if we women were honored guests he was ushering through a doorway into his own home. But it also seemed we had no choice.

Around me, the sound of women rising, a rustle and movement, gathering of pocketbooks, murmurs, the click of heels. Our new mission was an important one. Together we would light those candles and create a peaceful island of time, a Sabbath Island, for our People. And so Ana and I glided away among the women, leaving the men behind.

Near the kitchen was a single narrow table with many little brass candlesticks and a pile of matchbooks at one end. Ana's eagerness made me smile. We all gathered around the candle-covered table, maybe twenty of us.

"I can do this one. It's basic Sunday School," Ana said.

"I feel weird," I murmured back.

Ana took a book of matches from the pile and lit two candles, then covered her eyes with her hands and recited the Hebrew blessing. But this faux kind of female-ness we were taking part in was yet another set of rules that I couldn't begin to intuit. Shyness settled over me like a veil.

Then, standing there deep within that female group, I was suddenly grateful for this rare sense of belonging among women. Here we were, all immersed in the same moment in the same prayer, the same ritual. I, too, took up a matchbook. Struck a match. A sizzle rose up, then a blue and yellow flame. I also remembered what I'd been taught in Sunday School. Hold the flame to the wick, I thought, until it burns small and strong on its own. Recite the blessing, hands over eyes. *Baruch atah adonoi elohenu.* Then I stood surrounded by the others' whispers, magnetized to them among their wafts of perfume, tiny swaying movements, Ana's sleeve brushing my arm. Before me was a horizon of wavering little flames. Maybe, I thought, maybe we were more than just blips in history, more than statistics. We could be women who, as the rabbi said, had just changed the world with the strike of a match.

We could mean something. Because, like God, we could create a day.

WHEN I WAS SMALL I was afraid of the dark. One night, I woke up terrified in the black night. I wanted my mother. Once out of bed, unable to see in the dark, I waved jerking, trembling hands in front of me for obstacles and somehow found my way into the hall-way. All along the hall, I knew, were the huge canvases my mother had painted; we lived in her narrowed, cluttered chaos edged in her tilting planes of color, although in the dark the colors were only memory. I groped my way past my sisters' rooms, curling my toes as I crept, wide-eyed and blinded. A lurch, then a halt, fingertips guiding me as they brushed the stippled wall.

The wall ended at my parents' doorway, and without it as my guide I was in a void, breathing hard. I dropped to my knees and crawled forward like a blind infant, particles and fibers in the musty carpet pressing into my palms. At the end of this long journey I met the drape of my mother's bedcover and stood with a rush. I became a toddler, moving sideways inch by inch around her bed, holding on.

I fully expected my mother to send me back to my room, but she muttered and moved over—no open arms or caress, but I could stay. I slept then and dreamed, but even though I had gotten myself to where I wanted to be, the boy I was in my dream was still looking for his mother. In the morning, I woke with that need for her, the wish for her love a sharp place in my throat. I suppose I have always been compelled to set out clueless through the dark for new places while at the same time looking for safety, heading away yet hoping against logic that in the end I would find I'd come home.

FOR THE SABBATH EVENING prayer service we moved to the other end of the social hall, where they had set up more rows of chairs in two sections with a partition down the middle.. The women were to sit on the left. We took a seat.

Another Hassidic rabbi introduced himself as Rabbi Geller and explained that he was in charge of the weekend. He was a short, dark-haired man who bounced as he spoke. Then he positioned himself squarely in front of the men. Soon the men started reciting the Hebrew prayers out loud and very fast, not at all together, sometimes breaking out into joyous deep-voiced song.

I knew enough of the Hebrew alphabet to know that reading it is phonetic. One can sound out the words without understanding anything. Still, I was surprised that so many of the men could participate so fluently. "Wow," I whispered to Ana. "They are really going fast."

"You think anyone understands what they're saying?" Ana said.

"At that speed?" I said. "I wouldn't even understand if it were in English."

The male cacophony fell over us like a startling rain. We were not to mix our voices in prayer with the men, not to raise our voices. A few of the women read from their prayer books. The rest of us sat quietly and waited for the service to end.

I was becoming restless. There were two Hassidic women in the row in front of us. I knew they were Hassidic because they were wearing wigs in addition to their modest clothing. In those wigs it seemed almost as if they were in a play, in costumes filling the roles of being women. One was older, in a blonde nylon wig. The other had a sleepy thumb-sucking toddler glued to her lap. Both sat up with a self-conscious propriety that I took as elitist. They, too, whispered their prayers. Around us, whistling streams of air from more whispered prayers became audible in tiny moments between the men's songs.

I put the prayer book down on the seat next to me and shifted in my chair, tugging at my skirt. I was bored, disconnected from the prayer service, and because of this disconnect the old sense of feeling myself an outsider loomed again. I got up. I told myself I wasn't rejecting anything, that it was just as if I'd been browsing the booths at a fair and wanted to move on and see more. Ana was still enjoying the old melodies when I slipped out.

LATER, AT DINNER, the men and women sat on opposite sides of the room. The tables were covered in white and laden with enormous trays of kugels and salads, dishes of eggplant, carrots, eggs, pickles, and thick hand-cut slices of challah. There was a head table across the front connecting the two sides where Rabbi Geller and others of his group were assembling into a line of black coats, beards, and black hats.

The image of Rabbi Geller and his friends was starting to make sense. Maybe it was the repetition, each of them the same, the message projected again and again. Outside of this room, the Vietnam War was grinding on. Every night there were men on television looking purposeful and serious in identical uniforms.

"Look at those guys at the front," I said to Ana.

She rolled her eyes. "Fashion statement," she said.

But now their Hassidic garb spelled out a statement of mission to me. They were God's elite corps. "It's not about fashion," I said to Ana. "And it's not a costume."

"No?" she said.

"It's a uniform," I said. "They are soldiers for God."

Ana's eyes laughed.

But the self-assuredness that comes with internalizing clear rules, and the nobility of purpose that comes with a sense of mission, were just beginning to take form inside of me. Besides the uniforms' clear message, the Hassidic rules were defined, even written down—so unlike what I had encountered up until now. And their rules seemed to promise an almost maternal Godly love. Sitting there at the table, I didn't think this as much as feel it: Unlike with my mother, and unlike in school, where I didn't know how to be what other girls called a "woman," here maybe I could get the rules right. I was excited by the newness of it all, by the possibilities.

RABBI GELLER STOOD UP holding a silver goblet of wine and began to sing the Sabbath kiddush wine prayer. I recognized the tune, even though I knew it from my tone-deaf father, who remembered it from his Brooklyn childhood. When I was small and my father was well, he sang it to me in a one-note monotone, sitting on my bed before I slept. Something about those quiet moments in low light would start him talking about his immigrant parents and their old Jewish ways, the songs and habits they had brought from Russia. My grandparents had both died, both gone. In a way, so had my father. But he told me on those long-ago nights of how his mother had polished the silver wine goblet and candlesticks every Friday and set out the challah under a white cloth, preserving a steadiness and order that had been lost in our family before it got to us. Then he would stretch out beside me and sing old show tunes. You say potato. I say potahto. Let's fall in love.

I lifted my chin and sang the kiddush along with the rabbi.

We were served an enormous meal. I was long past full, sleepy, lulled.

After the meal, a quiet moment. Rabbi Geller then sang a moving meditative and wordless Hassidic song in a melodic minor key. He had a rich tenor/baritone voice that made me think of a cello, and he sang with his eyes closed, *Na nana na*.

Gradually, others leaned back into their chairs and joined him, even hung their heads back as they sang. Some closed their eyes. Ana did the same. The tune wandered, lingered, sad and searching. Laced with Ana's soprano, the voices slowly rose and filled the room, ebbed and swelled, rolled over us in waves. The song became a separate place of great feeling.

I, too, closed my eyes and sang. As I did, the tension I normally carried rolled out of my fingertips. I relaxed into the waves, let myself be carried. Communal song wrapped me in warmth and security like a human prayer shawl.

Suddenly, the rabbi came to a halt. Everyone grew quiet. I opened my eyes in the dead silence to find he had put up his palm like a stop sign. "A woman's voice is a precious jewel," the rabbi announced in a slow and careful voice. "Of course a jewel shouldn't be flashed around. A jewel should be kept in a safe and treasured place. That is why women are not to sing in public."

I woke up then, to find myself just a woman, and deeply embarrassed for projecting my voice. Ana shook her head. But, I reasoned, we were being honored with this enforced silence. It was supposed to be an honor. Still, I looked down at my hands.

When Rabbi Geller began again, only the men joined him. The singing grew, and grew, until the rabbi raised his arms, urging them to get out of their uptight secular selves, and the men all rose, full of righteous spiritual energy, willing and eager now to let themselves go. For God. They danced as one, a roomful of singing men, stomping feet and dancing rhythm.

We stood at the side of their exuberant closed circle dance as they jumped and sang, hands on shoulders and backs. Faster and faster; the whole place filling with zeal. Shirttails came out. Ties were pulled off. How they danced! Some of the Hassidic men took off their long black coats, tossed them aside, and rejoined the fray, white strings flying at their hips. Mouths open, singing, singing, voices going hoarse. Faces red and beaded with joyous sweat. The whole room reverberating in deafening song.

Ana's face was lit, absorbing the electricity, and I forgot about being silenced. I tapped her arm and gestured at the dancing men, nodding at them with my chin and smiling, smiling at the scene and the fervor, carried away by the irresistible Hassidic confidence in their own rightness and goodness, this demonstration of Godly joy. In my mind, I was in the middle of those dancing men, my hand on a sweating back, feet swept up in the beat, singing out loud, all of us bound together by a single pulsing rhythm of faith in exclusive and holy intimacy. This was where I belonged. Yes—I was one of them, among them, not a woman on the sidelines. I had escaped everything. It's true, I thought, exultant. You can lose yourself in God.

LATE THAT NIGHT, in spite of the rules that forbade musical instruments on the Sabbath, Ana spread out her bedroll on the floor and sat on it cross-legged to play her guitar. She picked at the strings quietly, singing to herself. Behind our closed door, I reasoned, we weren't exactly singing in public, so I sang with her. We became a little bolder, raised our voices, harmonized.

Then, a knock on the door. Ana's hand fell flat on the strings. We eyed one another.

But there were no Sabbath police at the door. It was just a girl about my age who introduced herself as Janice—small-boned, her brunette hair fine and straight. She had come from Fort Worth with her mother for this event, knocked because she had heard us singing.

I welcomed her, and once I closed the door, we had our voices again. Janice's singing was clear and fine. We sat and sang in three-part harmony, all of us cross-legged on an open bedroll. Ana led on guitar with me leaning toward her, our eyes locking in the tune.

THE NEXT MORNING I woke early but skipped the morning services. Ana was still sleeping. Near the coffee urn I met Seema, the Hassidic woman with the blonde wig I'd noticed at the prayer services. "What's your name?" she asked. She sounded like an official greeter.

"Lisa," I said.

"And what's your Hebrew name?"

I had recently asked my mother that question, because it was a blank to be filled out on the registration form for this weekend program. My mother had rolled her eyes. "We're Americans," she said, with all the vehemence of a first-generation American. It seemed Hebrew names from the Old Country didn't fit that view. But I managed to get the story out of her: how for social reasons she had wanted my name announced from the pulpit at the temple after I was born, how she'd been told by the temple secretary that, in order to do that, I had to have a Hebrew name. "So the rabbi just gave you one," she said. "We were never going to use it, anyway, so it didn't matter what it was."

"And?"

"It's Leah." She said the name with obvious distaste.

"Lay-ah?" I said.

"That's how the rabbi pronounced it."

"It's Leah," I told Seema, proud that I knew the pronunciation. "Why?"

"That," Seema said, "is the name of your Jewish soul." She turned then to the table next to the coffee urn, put a blueberry Danish on a paper plate, and offered it to me, touching my shoulder with the other hand, an intimate gesture, as if she'd known me for years. "Have something to eat?" she said.

I accepted the plate as if it were an invitation into an elite society, an exclusive club. How could I not step in? I had a moment of guilt about my non-Jewish friends, how they would be excluded here without a Hebrew name and Jewish pedigree to give them entry, but still I nibbled the sweet dough, and before we parted I had accepted Seema's offer to teach me more. She would call, and I could come to her home to spend a Sabbath.

It was like this: Seema smiled at me, touched my shoulder. Said I belonged. In that moment, with the touch of her warm hand, my few conscious objections seemed to fade into irrelevance, as if her warmth, her smile, her touch dream-launched me into weightless flight that would float me right into Hassidic arms.

Seducing God

Joshunda Victoria Sanders

My mother's devotion to her faith had taught me to chase after God—from the small Catholic churches in Philadelphia, where I was born, to the cathedrals of New York City. We lived in many places when I was a kid: shelters for homeless families and battered women and the homes of distant relatives or friends, not landing in our own apartment until I was thirteen. But no matter where we lived, Mom made sure we were always within walking distance of a Catholic church.

Maggie, the mother of five children (of which I was the last), was a black and Cherokee Indian woman with high cheekbones and reddish-brown skin. She had been raised in a traditional Southern family as an orphan, since her own single mother had died when she was young. In 1976, her youngest boy, Jose, had been struck and killed by a bus when he was twelve years old. I was born in January 1978.

I was his namesake. "A miracle," she said often. "A gift from God."

Her God, though, was white, like the majority of congregants in the churches we attended. At home, she collected pictures of a pale-skinned Jesus—his Sacred Heart beaming red and gold—and his mother, the Virgin Mary. Her collection of religious artifacts from items she'd purchased in the St. Patrick's Cathedral gift shop included calendars bearing smudges of her maroon lipstick where she kissed Jesus's likeness.

Maggie wore a safety pin of about a dozen small medals bearing the figures of saints that she affixed to her bra each morning. For years we woke early to attend 7:30 AM mass. Witnessing her fervency, coupled with the realities of our challenging life, complicated my own relationship with God.

I loved God the way I loved Maggie—deeply, but with skepticism.

Her distant God had given us to each other, I reasoned. And our complex mother-daughter relationship—shaped by her borderline personality and bipolar disorder—mirrored my relationship with Him.

I tried to make sense of Maggie singing His praises from the front row of cathedrals from state to state as we went hungry and usually asked priests or rectors for subway tokens or dinner money. I was acutely aware that we were poor black women in a world that favored a white male God and white skin. *How could we possibly be made in a white God's image?* I wondered. Were we really like the cursed children of Cain, destined to be slaves because God made it so? And if He really loved us, how were we, His children, allowed to suffer so much?

As my racial identity and pride as a young black teenager

developed in the inner cities and poor ghettos of New York City in
the 1980s and 1990s, I wrestled with these questions, but I never
asked my mother how she reconciled her love for God with the realities of race and class that we lived. Given her mental health, I questioned the God she clung to, an almighty presence who inspired
unquestioning loyalty even in the absence of assistance with our
struggles. She believed God spoke directly to her, even in loss. I
didn't know what to believe.

While Maggie pursued Catholicism as relentlessly as she pursued everything else—at the cost of alienating herself from her
Baptist aunts and sisters—I secretly sided with my aunts. It felt
unhealthy to me for black women to worship white saints, especially
since the spheres we traveled in were replete with brown waves of
people, in Harlem, in Manhattan, in Queens, in Brooklyn.

The faith of my aunts was derived from their personal relationship with the resurrected Jesus Christ who died for our sins, not
the mysterious Trinity and its pale emissaries that my mother worshipped. In the Black Baptist Church my aunts attended, sweaty,
well-dressed bodies praised the Lord with their raucous, joyous
hymns for hours. This made more sense to me than Maggie's brand
of Catholicism, but though the music and ceremony was rapturous,
it still didn't feel right for me.

I badly needed a belief system that built me up, not one that
reinforced my sense of unworthiness.

THE NATION OF ISLAM had long been on my radar. In Philly,
where I was born and raised for the first part of my childhood, I
spent hours playing on the steps outside my grandmother's house,
which faced a number of white, wooden storefronts that opened to

reveal streams of black men in clean, pressed suits with copies of *The Final Call* newspaper tucked under their arms. Of course, I didn't know that those newspapers beckoned their readers to follow Elijah Muhammad or forgo eating pork and other foods that the Nation connected to slavery. But I could sense that, behind those white doors, community was happening in a way that didn't happen for me in my family.

My mother and I moved to New York when I was six. There I saw men who looked like those I'd noticed in Philadelphia, but there were many more of them, especially in Harlem. On the boulevard named for Malcolm X, men walked in the charismatic leader's spiritual footsteps. I noticed them gathering on street corners, selling newspapers for $1. Sometimes one of them would pull a boy my age dressed in baggy jeans or a long T-shirt out of foot traffic as he headed toward McDonald's or the Apollo Theater and ask him if he knew he was a king, descended from the Original Man: a black god whose history had been erased by America's racism.

I had no idea what these bits of conversation meant, but I noticed the intent way each black boy listened to his elder, his posture straightening during the lecture. The promise of renewal and leadership, I realized later, must have edified black boys and men, since it was directed toward helping them survive a world that disproportionately incarcerated them, arrested them, castrated them, and brutalized their bodies and self-esteems.

When I was twelve I read *The Autobiography of Malcolm X as Told to Alex Haley.* The story of Malcolm Little, the hustler who became El-Hajj Malik El-Shabbazz, or Malcolm X, fascinated me. Both reading this inspiring text and then seeing Spike Lee's striking biopic *Malcolm X,* which came out soon after, initially gave me a sense of solidarity with another nomad, one who had survived childhood trauma to go on to become influential and powerful. In the montage at the end of Lee's film, the children who repeated "I am Malcolm X" gave voice to something brewing inside me—a sense that, even a generation removed from his, I too could be like Malcolm X. In young Malcolm Little, whose mother, Louise, had struggled with depression as mine had, I saw myself.

I was growing up in a cult of two—me and my bipolar, unmedicated, and very Catholic single mother. Our universe was one of violent manic episodes, when she would curse and punch me randomly and without provocation, punctuated by peaceful moments, when she would let me rub her feet after a long day. Malcolm X had also been bullied—by racism, madness, and poverty, both where he grew up and before he went to prison. Instead of allowing the pain of his past to destroy him, he found faith to persevere. It was a faith I craved.

My world was shaped by the trauma of homelessness and the idea that any door we closed behind us might never again open; we'd been evicted so often that, by the time I was a teenager, I'd lost most of my childhood possessions. This continuous loss had been too much for me to process as a child, but when I read how Malcolm Little had watched his childhood home set ablaze by the Ku Klux Klan, I had an intimate understanding of what it felt like to see everything one once considered safe consumed by real or proverbial flames. That kind of loss is confusing and isolating for children, but in this shared experience, I felt closer to the young Malcolm. If he were alive, I was sure we could share battle stories.

But what Malcolm X and I had most in common was a firm belief in God. Through his conversion from Christianity to the Nation of Islam, Malcolm was transformed from a hustler bent on survival by any means necessary into a powerful, charismatic leader.

His conversion was embedded with deep racial and class pride, as evidenced by his teachings promoting black men as gods on earth. In him, I saw a template for how to climb out of what seemed like insurmountable circumstances, and to do so almost entirely by faith alone. Because my understanding of God had been shaped by the Nation's theological polar opposite, the Catholic Church, I wondered if I could find more conviction converting to the Nation of Islam once I was no longer living with my mother.

The connection I felt to Malcolm X and his conversion story launched me into a quest to find a secure, sacred place for myself, some sort of structure with boundaries, strict boundaries even— since my childhood had almost none. It was a journey that would continue for several years until I learned for myself what being a part of the Nation of Islam really meant. After I finished reading the Malcolm X autobiography, I mustered the courage to tell my mother I didn't want to go to mass with her anymore. I was not brave enough to venture to a mosque in Harlem by myself, but I started reading *The Final Call* when it was offered to me on my solitary treks around New York City.

LIFE IN NEW YORK was chaotic. Over the course of six years we lived in four of the city's five boroughs, in a series of halfway houses, shelters and welfare-subsidized apartments. My mother's mental health never seemed to get better, despite her faith and prayers. During her most terrifying manic episode, she became furious at me in the middle of the night after a phone call to my boyfriend lasted too long. She hurled herself on top of me and put her hands around my throat after striking my back and shoulders with her thick fists. "I wish I'd never had you," she yelled. "I'll kill you."

The same hands that she used to caress the rosary, each bead delicately, lovingly held while she said her prayers, were clasped around my throat, trying to squeeze the breath from my body. "I'll kill you," she repeated, as tears fell from the corners of my eyes onto the bed.

Like all her other outbursts, after a matter of minutes—or was it an hour?—Mom eased off of me, worn out from the demon that possessed her. She wept, contrite, rocking back and forth, mascara running down her face from sweat and tears. "I'm sorry. I love you so much. I'm so sorry."

I ran away, only to return soon after, determined that I would strike back if she ever hit me again. I was fourteen, and on the brink of suicidal depression; the only thing that kept me from succumbing was that I earned an academic scholarship to an all-girls' boarding school and left to attend.

At the Emma Willard School, a four-hour bus ride from home, God was evident to me in the bucolic beauty of my new surroundings. When I wasn't studying, I stole away from my dorm to walk near a creek on the edge of campus, or to feel the crisp breeze of upstate New York on my face while I jogged on a tucked-away path. I felt God, but in an undefined and unreachable way.

By the time I finished high school, I had not stepped foot inside a church in four years. I feared I'd lost the possibility of knowing a God who could understand me and guide me. I thought I'd try to live without Him.

IN MY OWN WILDERNESS of lost faith, I found a glimpse of order. I started college at Vassar, studying political science, Africana studies, and English literature. My second year, I dated and fell in love with a popular basketball player and dreamed of marrying him. I felt my life was coming together, until I realized that he'd slept with some of my friends. Then I began to fall apart.

By this time, my mother had moved just across the street from campus, which only added to my anxiety. I had been striving to find something or someone safe to belong to, but for all my efforts I still had no waiting container ready to hold me. I took to accosting my liver with vodka and cranberry juice that I drank from half-liter plastic cups. And though I'd learned to cling to books and studying in times of distress, as the months passed I grew more and more tired of trying to keep myself motivated to rise above the abuse and trauma of my childhood. I had reached my spiritual nadir. The only club I was a part of was the invisible network of other lost souls. I wanted to either end my life completely or totally change it, and I didn't know where to look for help. I knew I needed God, but nothing in my religious history directed me in trying to find Him.

EVENTUALLY, DURING SPRING BREAK, I took a trip to Columbus, Ohio, and coincidently reconnected with Charlie, an old DJ friend who upon our reacquaintance presented himself as a practicing member of the Nation of Islam. Charlie was over six feet tall, with skin the color of banana pudding and brown-amber eyes as wide as spoons. I was so smitten with him that I wrote him love poetry, comparing us to the actors Ruby Dee and Ossie Davis. We were both music fans, and sang and rapped along with our favorite Jay-Z songs. We could talk for hours about life and music.

Almost every black man I'd ever known or known of—famous or not—had been touched or shaped in some way by the Nation of Islam, and its primary edifying principles that black men are actually gods and that they could break free of the oppression and the disrespect of racism through submission to Allah. Charlie was no exception.

He had the most peaceful face I'd ever seen. He had a precision about him that I envied: His Timberland boots were free of scuffs or dirt, as if he placed them back in the shoebox they came in each night; the half-moons of his perfectly manicured nails were dirt-free. And in accordance with Muslim law, he did not eat pork or drink alcohol.

"Your diet sounds really difficult," I said to him one night. We were sitting in his truck in a parking lot outside the studio where he produced music. The windows were open halfway and the night air reached our faces like its own seductive song.

"It depends on who you're doing things for," he said back. "When we do things for men, they're hard. When we do things for God, that's the ultimate honor."

There was God again, I thought, butting into my life without really saving me from anything. I felt I had honored God just by surviving my life so far. How could a hard life become easy just because one leaned on God? My mother had lived in poverty for years, all the while praising God's name. I nodded at Charlie's perspective, though. How could I argue with what he believed, and with what seemed to have transformed him so thoroughly? Perhaps the difference was that the God Charlie worshiped was more like us: black, flawed, trying to be better.

The peace Charlie had found was the serenity my life was missing. More than that—he had a spiritual context, an anchor in a community of other black people that seemed to ground his faith.

Once spring break was over I had to leave Charlie and return to Poughkeepsie. We were physically separated, but we stayed in touch through phone calls that became increasingly infrequent. I could not get him off my mind, though. I couldn't shake the feeling that, like Malcolm X—despite growing up in an environment overshadowed by police and in a society ready to cast black men as violent, aggressive pariahs—Charlie had found a moral compass through faith that offered a path not predestined to dead-end in prison.

A COUPLE OF YEARS later, it was, in fact, prisoners who solidified the void in my life I was beginning to think only Allah could fill. As part of an independent study during my junior year, I met with a group of men in a prerelease program at Green Haven prison. A group of about six of us—mostly black women—went weekly through the dull, cool corridors of the prison, passing wives and girlfriends and children who had been waiting for who-knows-how-long to get inside. On the other side of metal detectors and unfriendly guards—who warned us not to touch the prisoners in any way, not even to shake their hands—we were led to community rooms to advise these men on transitioning to life outside.

Each week as we endured this procedure I felt my own sense of fear, grief, and constraint. The confined prison space felt as cramped as my impoverished childhood had been. I was supposedly better off than they were, because I had been lucky enough and determined enough to study my way into elite schools. But was I really?

One thing I knew for certain: Whichever God had granted me grace, whatever He looked like, whatever religious path I might need to take to find Him, I knew that He had been present for me, because I was not in a prison like the barred bricks and mortar I visited weekly. I looked forward to those trips because they were a reminder of the other possibilities that existed for me as a young black person in New York's poor neighborhoods. Growing up I had dated drug dealers and once even offered myself up as an unlikely volunteer to help sell illegal guns. The desire to escape poverty often made me forget ethics or the law. Though I was now in a position to help these men, still, in my soul, I felt more connected to the prisoners than to many of my privileged white classmates.

A couple of the men we met with wore kufis, caps that look like crocheted hats, which are common Nation attire in prisons. Once, after a session, one of these men told me I was beautiful. "You would be even more beautiful as a sister in the Nation," he said.

"What do you mean?" I asked.

"One day, you'll find out," he answered. Somehow I believed he knew something I didn't.

And perhaps he did. Not long after his prediction, I spiraled downward again in my own prison. Mine was not physical but emotional, the walls made up of childhood pain, the pain of my breakup, and my subsequent self-abuse, which leaked from my pores in morning classes where I sat, hungover, unresponsive to questions after only two hours of sleep—that is if I went at all.

Unable to free myself from depression, and terrified that Maggie's mental illnesses were manias that I'd inherited, I tortured myself thinking that maybe if I had been a more submissive, proper woman, I would have spared myself God's wrath. Slowly, I started thinking that it was possible that Charlie, the Malcolm X I admired, and even the men at Green Haven prison, were indications that their same discipline and salvation was accessible to me too.

Maybe, just like the man at Green Haven had insinuated, if I were a "sister," covered by Allah's protection, my life could be different. I imagined I would be able to sleep well at night, that I would be able to enter true intimacy and love with ease. The presence of a god like Malcolm X's God, one that I could feel and understand, that made more sense to my world, might liberate me—both from the cult of two I'd experienced with my mother and still carried with me and from the tortures of the too-much freedom that led me to such hard living. I wanted a container for my many emotions, a boundary that would make me feel safe no matter what chaos came my way.

With this hope and my continued longing for community and a true black religious life driving me, I bought a Qur'an—and a headscarf. I reread Malcolm X. I stopped hanging out with my drunken friends. I wanted the black man's God that Charlie knew, that the men from the Green Haven prison knew, and that the suited men in Philadelphia and New York, and Malcolm X knew. I would pursue their God. I would seduce him with my faithfulness.

Show Me the Way

Elise Brianne Curtin

I met Amber last year, just hours into our freshman year at Wagner College, a small school in Staten Island, New York. We clicked instantly, and as the twilight of our first evening together faded into darkness, we stumbled down a moonlit path that ran along the edges of the tennis courts behind our dormitory, clumsily making our way to the kegger in the woods hosted by a bunch of thirsty frat boys. It didn't take much for the two of us to start slurring our words and showing skin, dancing in the moonlight to the beat of a boom box blasting through the darkness. She reminded me of my friends back home. One wild night led to a slew of them, and we became inseparable.

But that was last year. Now, it's the beginning of sophomore year. Amber and I have been away from each other for over three months. Summer is shifting into fall, and I'm changing, too.

"YOU LOOK LIKE AN old lady," Amber had scowled at me earlier as she scrunched her unruly ringlets, her painted lips pouting. She was dolling herself up for a party; I was sitting in a chair in our room with a journal on my lap, a cup of tea in my hands, and a serene smile on my face. Later, she called me, drunk and laughing, and tried to get me to come out and join her. "Come on, Elise, *please!* You're seriously going to hole up in there all night and pray?" A guy's voice interrupted and sneered, "What? Are you reading your *Bible?*" I hung up the phone and at first bit back the tears, but then let them fall, my head in my hands.

Hours have passed, and the tears are still streaming down my cheeks. I'm lying in bed, burrowed into the top bunk of our dorm room, pulling my ice-blue penguin sheets and well-worn comforter up to my chin. My mind is racing, chest is heaving, fists are clenching, body is shivering. Words are escaping my lips in a fervent whisper, over and over again—*Show me the way, the truth, and the life.*

Just moments ago, Amber staggered in and collapsed on the bottom bunk. I want to climb down and nudge her awake so we can cry together, like we did in the final throes of freshman year, when she was reeling from a recent fling and I was doubled over and sobbing in her lap because a Brooklyn boy broke my heart.

Doesn't she realize I'm still here? I'm still me, just . . . different? But whatever that closeness was that we shared, it's gone now.

I close my eyes and struggle to conjure the soul-searching me who created this mess, hoping to unearth a satisfying explanation for why I'm losing my best friend. In my mind's eye, I wander away from here, to the golden fields and wooded trails of my hometown. To memories of the trees towering over me and the crunch of twigs and dirt beneath my feet. To my dog, Spy, running freely by my side. Sleeping on a blanket in my parents' backyard, watching the silhouettes of the trees sway in the moonlight, listening to the leaves rustling and the choir of crickets chirping their rhythmic rhapsodies. Staring into the stars as they shimmered in the blackened sky, my shoulders pressed against the cool, hard ground, I had pondered and wondered about all sorts of things. *Who am I? What am I? How am I? Why am I?* I voiced my ruminations aloud, in what felt like prayers, and waited for someone to answer me. And in those sweet stargazing spells, I communed with what I came to know as God.

"I am the way, the truth, and the life," I murmur. The first words of Jesus Christ I'd paid attention to in years. I grew up going to Episcopalian church services and Sunday School, but I'd decided a long time ago that God and Jesus and Santa Claus and the Easter Bunny were all lumped into the same category of lies adults tell children to keep them wondering and guessing and believing in power structures and mythical characters that have the capacity to influence and dictate good, moral, and socially acceptable behavior.

But when at the peak of my solitary summertime explorations I came across a copy of the holy book in my parents' living room, I was spellbound. After skimming the pages and landing on the way-truth-life verse, I just sat there at the kitchen table, staring long and hard at those words, soaking them in like light-deprived skin takes in the sun's healing rays. Reading Plato's works in my freshman-year philosophy class had gotten me meditating on things like truth and love and the unseen realms. But until that moment, it hadn't occurred to me that the biblical savior of the world might have some answers as to how to deepen my understanding of them.

Jesus claimed to know *the* way, *the* truth, and *the* life, so I wanted to know *Him*—to sit at His feet and drink Him in: His words, His ways, His everything.

I started tapping the shoulders of people who claimed to know this Jesus fellow. My mom, my grandma, my mom's pastor, my grandma's proselytizing Christian friend. I even tried talking directly to Him—Jesus, the son of God—a few times. I scoured the Internet. On a whim, I wrote to a convent, expressing my interest in becoming a nun. Then I wrote to an obscure group of Essenes, hoping they would invite me to commune with them in the mountains. No one responded.

And then it was time to go back to school.

Just a sign—something, anything to show me that I'm not alone, that I'm not crazy. Burying my face in my blanket, I breathe slowly, deeply, and say it one more time as I drift into sleep.

Show me the way, the truth, and the life . . .

THE NEXT MORNING, I wake to a roaring so loud it sends shudders through my body, our dorm room, the whole building. I bolt out of bed.

There's commotion outside. Amber and I run to the lobby of our floor, which has a wall-to-wall, floor-to-ceiling window overlooking lower Manhattan. What we see through that window has us wide-eyed, our mouths agape, stunned, speechless.

One of the two World Trade Center towers is ablaze. Within seconds of our arrival, we see a plane fly directly into the other tower, exploding in a massive cloud of smoke and flames. "What the hell was that?" a latecomer to the lobby cries. "A bomb?!"

"No, a plane. It was a plane," someone answers. "Didn't you hear it? It flew right over us!" I rub my eyes, still groggy with sleep.

What's happening? I stand there, my feet planted, transfixed by the catastrophe unfolding before me.

My already cloudy vision begins to blur. Memories of my late-night pleadings flood my mind. *Show me the way, the truth, and the life.* Is my desperate and weepy appeal for God to speak to me, to reach out and show me why I'm here, actually being answered somehow, in all of *this?*

"Jamie. I've gotta call Jamie," Amber says hurriedly. I snap out of my internal musings and follow Amber to our room. Our friend Jamie's boyfriend is an intern in one of the towers. Amber gets her on the phone, and she's hysterical. We run up to Jamie's room; Nicole and Jackie, our other friends, are already there. The TV is on. Jamie is on the phone, trying to get ahold of someone who knows something about her boyfriend. The stunned reporters on the TV screen don't know what to say; they keep replaying the scene we just watched in real time. *Who? What? How? Why?* These are my questions, but nobody has the answers.

We sit and wait for close to an hour. I'm getting a headache from listening to the news correspondents repeat themselves ad nauseam. I wish they'd just leave the cameras on and shut up. And then, just like that, one of the towers falls—as in, plummets to the ground. My mouth drops. "Oh my God, the tower. Fuck, it's going down!" Nicole cries. Jamie groans and covers her mouth with her hands.

Echoing through the hallways are the sounds of people crying and yelling, doors opening and closing, footsteps rushing to and fro. "He's not there today? He's okay?" I hear Jamie asking of whomever is on the other end of the line. "Oh, thank you. Thank you." She heaves a sigh of relief as she hangs up the phone, her pretty blue eyes spilling tiny droplets as her skin regains some of its original color.

A girl pops her head in the room. "They're having a vigil at Trautmann Square," she tells us, and then ducks out and disappears. We don't know what else to do, so we grab our things and go.

Outside our building, the collective confusion is palpable; the campus is fraught with fear. Terror washes over and through me, suspending me in its awesome grip. I feel faint and dizzy, barely able to focus on putting one foot in front of the other as I merge with the mob of students rushing toward the square. I stop to steady myself, and a surge of something more powerful than panic rises inside me, allowing me to regain composure. Concern and compassion for those who are across the water, in that mess and dying, flood my system. *What can I do? What can I do? Dear God, show me the way.*

We arrive at Trautmann Square. The sun is shining. The air is still. A smattering of our fellow students is gathered there with us, spread out along the cobblestone walkways bordering the square. Sheets of paper with prayers and songs are being passed around. Someone is playing bagpipes; their mournful crooning weaves its way through the spaces surrounding us. The swirling sounds diminish and a priestly voice is asking us to honor the fallen with a moment of silence. The speaker quotes the words of a well-known scripture: "Yea, though I walk through the valley of the shadow of death . . ." I look around me. Most people are holding their handouts, focusing intently on following the words printed on the papers as they are read aloud. Others are simply staring into space, their eyes glazed over. Some are crying and holding one another; still others are talking in hushed voices. I am soundlessly absorbing all I see and hear, feeling frozen and powerless, longing with increasing intensity for God to show me my role in the midst of this chaos.

The crowd begins to sing. I am struck by the earnestness in two female voices emanating from my right. I edge my way closer to them. The woman nearest to me notices and moves in my direction, holding out her copy of the hymns so I can sing along. I gratefully accept.

When the song is over, the priest clears his throat. "I'm sorry to be the one to break this news, but I've just received word that the second tower has fallen. Let us once again take a moment of silence to honor the lives of those lost in this tragic event."

Murmuring voices and shuffling feet. Then, silence.

The vigil comes to a close, but I don't want to leave. Students are commingling and milling about, and I can't shake the feeling of wanting to *do* something. "We're going back. You coming with?" Amber asks.

"No, no. Go ahead without me," I respond, determined to make myself useful.

I watch my friends walk away, and then turn to face the women standing next to me whose voices were so stirring. One is young and pretty, with straight brown hair and clear blue eyes: big and bright, warm and inviting. "Wow, this is something, isn't it?" she says.

I'm half shaking and half nodding my head. "Yeah, sure is . . . " I recognize her as someone I've seen around campus. Her eyes, luminous and sparkling, are not easy to forget.

She smiles at me with a smile that lights up her whole face, takes my hand in hers, and says, "I'm Sandra."

"And I'm Sofia," says the other woman, the one who shared her handout with me. She's petite, with a somewhat unsettling intensity flashing in her eyes and tight black spiral curls falling wildly about her face; she speaks with a strong accent that sounds Latin American to my sheltered suburbanite ears.

"Elise," I smile, too warmed by their presence to be intimidated.

Sofia's gaze softens a bit. "You know, we're a part of this really great church, the Church of Christ, and we're having a service tonight if you want to come along."

"Really? I'd love to!" I exclaim. *Maybe this is God's answer to me!* Unable to hide my enthusiasm, I almost reach out to hug them, but stop short.

Sophia laughs. "Well, good. It's not too far from here, but do you need a ride? I'll be on campus all day so you can just come with me."

"Sounds like a plan," I say. I feel so sure God has led me straight to these women, I impulsively spew out my story of summertime salvation-seeking and of last night's brokenness, how I was up for hours begging to find the way, the truth, and the life, and how meeting them isn't just a coincidence; it's an answered prayer!

"I just wish there was something I could *do,*" I say at the end of my sudden burst of chatter.

As if on cue, a voice rises from across the square. A man is holding a megaphone on the steps of the Student Union. "For those of you who are wanting to help, I just spoke with the American Red Cross. This is a national emergency, so the best thing any of us can do right now is stay put and stick together and, if you can, give blood."

I can do that, I think. Though it hardly seems like enough.

LATER THAT NIGHT, I climb in the passenger seat of Sofia's car. Minutes later we're pulling up to a small church in a residential neighborhood. THE UNITARIAN CHURCH OF STATEN ISLAND, the sign on the front lawn reads. Sofia catches me looking at the sign and quickly explains, "The International Church of Christ doesn't believe in owning buildings, so we rent from the Unitarian Church." *Sounds fair enough.* I nod my head and take in the rest of my surroundings. The building is quaint and cottage-like, with a brown brick exterior and antique-looking stained-glass windows. I watch as people of all ages and colors gather outside, greeting one another with loving embraces. A rush of warmth softens my insides, and I happily surrender myself into their arms, hugging and even kissing on the cheek some of these beautiful strangers.

The sounds of singing and clapping draw us into the sanctuary. "Soldiers of Christ, arise, and put on your armor . . . " The tiny church barely holds the congregation. Sofia guides me through the bustling bodies to an open pew. Sandra with the bright blue eyes is standing at the front of the room, leading songs with a group of singers, their voices blending and harmonizing in angelic accord. She sees me in the crowd and smiles. I smile back as I clap and sway with the others, basking in the tightly knit glow.

The music dies down, and the singers find their seats. A young man steps into the hollow of the pulpit. He is tall and good-looking, with commanding eyes and a disarming smile. He's dressed in street clothes, and he carries himself like someone who spends a lot of time on stage. "Let's bow our heads and pray," he says. "Father God, be with us now . . . "

His words muddle and melt in my ears. "That's Mike," Sofia leans in and whispers when he finishes praying, "the minister." He's unlike any preacher I've ever seen, and his intensity captivates me. "When I saw those towers go down, something inside of me broke," he's saying. "All those souls, all those people suffering and dying without knowing the truth. It's time for us to wake up. . . . God needs us now more than ever—to step up and spread Jesus's message, to take up the sword of truth and the helmet of salvation. To seek and save the lost. . . . " His emphatic proclamations hit the spot. I wipe my eyes, discreetly. My body is quivering.

Sofia wraps her arm around me. The trembling subsides. We lock eyes. Hers are soft, brimming with tears, brilliant flecks of green glimmering in her dark brown irises. She squeezes my hand. The music is starting up again. "I prayed, yes I prayed. I prayed, oh I prayed. I prayed, yes I prayed until I found the Lord. My soul just couldn't be contented . . . " The voices of the congregation swell with conviction as they sing. The lyrics are simple, so I join in.

In this moment, as my voice merges with the masses until I can hear it no longer, I am clueless as to the eventual significance of this small act. There's no way for me to know that in becoming one with this group of believers, I am signing up to spend six years of my young adult life in a fantasy land where God speaks through microphones using seemingly perfect preachers and their wives to persuade their devotees to do as they're told. Or that I will soon be challenged to cut myself off from my friends and family who do not agree with my new ways of thinking and being and believing; or that in the not-too-far-off future I will marry a man I've never even kissed—all for the sake of upholding the sanctity of the way, the truth, and the life of which Jesus allegedly spoke.

No, right now, all I know is I *believe*—I believe God is with me, and that he led me here. I believe I have found a way to *do* something, not just for my own lonely and searching soul, but also for those around me, and especially for the ones who lost so much on this tumultuous day.

"I found, yes I found. I found, oh I found. I found, yes I found. I finally found the Lord . . . "

Swan Sister

Yolande Elise Brener

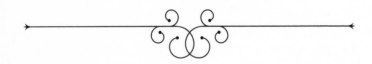

My elder brother, Adam, was the most constant person in my life. In our earliest years, we changed homes often, and our father left when I was three and Adam was five. But Adam was always there. I could always lean on him or hold his hand, and I loved him fiercely.

I held tight to Adam for comfort and because I longed to find out what he meant when he teased me, saying "I know something you don't know." Adam knew how to make people happy just by smiling and letting the world roll over him. I have always been more serious than he, even as a little girl. I wanted to do something great, to sacrifice my life for something bigger than myself—like Joan of Arc did, or like the sister in the Six Swans fairy tale, who spent six years silently sewing stinging nettle suits to turn her swan brothers back into men. In morning sermons at my Church of England school I learned about Jesus and wished I could love unconditionally with such passion that I could heal the sick and raise the dead. My greatest childhood desire was to meet Jesus someday.

By the time I was sixteen I got accepted to art school and moved to London to live on my own. As Jesus had not turned up yet, I continued to follow my eighteen-year-old brother in his search for the truth, which had turned serious by this time. I accompanied Adam when he ate vegan food with Hare Krishnas and took wafers and wine with Catholics; I stopped short of following him only when he began fasting with Franciscans. Finding no religion adequate, and aided by hallucinogenic drugs, Adam concluded that he was Christ himself.

Shortly after Adam realized his divine mission, he turned up in my London flat and announced there was a global conspiracy against him. Even as he stood at my door I noticed there was something different about him. His clothes hung loosely off his bony limbs and his eyes searched above my head as if he were being hunted. "Listen to the radio," he said. "It's talking to us. They're in the television too. Nothing is an accident."

I turned the radio off while Adam looked suspiciously at my window.

"They're in the walls," he said. "They know where we are."

By his shaking, nicotine-stained fingers, the small scratches on his arms and face, and his unsettled eyes, I could see that Adam was in trouble. I had never seen mental illness before and it shocked me. He was the same person on the outside but so changed inside that I was frightened for him.

As befitted the self-proclaimed Son of God, Adam took up residence at our local Church of England chapel. He curled up in the wooden apse, the stained-glass windows casting blue shadows of saints across his face. The vicar, switch-thin and pale in his dog collar, spoke with my mother about exorcism but decided on eviction instead. Several pink-cheeked police officers removed Adam to Heatherwood, a shrubbery-bound hospital in Ascot, twenty-five miles outside of London. But soon, Adam was discharged back to my mother's house only to begin his cycle again. Sometimes he would disappear for months at a time and then reappear with mysterious bruises and cuts. Several times he turned up in jail or in hospital, and I was always relieved when he finally came home.

Not long after one of his releases, I took the forty-minute ride to visit Adam at our mother's house. We went for an afternoon stroll into the nearby Runnymede Forest, and by twilight we had walked deep into the woods. We didn't talk much but occasionally stopped to look at an interesting plant or to identify what kind of animal or bird was scurrying away. We both loved nature and I savored this time together, relaxing and sharing, listening to the soft voices of the leaves in the breeze and the slowly settling earth under our feet. As children we had often wandered together along the Thames or across the fields beside our mother's house. I never felt more at ease than when I was in nature, and being with Adam right then was as comfortable as it had ever been.

When we reached a point where I was sure we were lost, Adam suggested we build a fire. It made no difference to him whether we knew where we were going or how long we would be there. The air was taking on a chill, and if it weren't for the moon lighting our way through the ancient foliage, we would have been in total darkness.

Adam expertly built a fire in the shape of a pyramid and filled it with dry leaves and twigs. The flames rose quickly and cast a flickering orange light across his somber face. I reflected on how, as a child, Adam had been so carefree. He would run around the bonfires we built in our garden in the autumn, waving sparklers and climbing a nearby oak to get a better look at the world. Now as I watched him, I wondered where all his exuberance had gone and felt sad that I could do nothing to help him retrieve his former self.

Out of the silence, Adam sighed and looked toward me. "Sometimes I think I can only get better with you," he said.

His words seared like burning black embers in the pit of my stomach, while the cold night air began to bite at my fingers and nose. I knew he was sick, but Adam's faith in my ability to help him scared me. How could I stay here with Adam and take care of him? I yearned to give my brother the stinging nettle suit that could set him free to live a life like other men. I imagined him with a wife, laughing and playing with children of his own. But as much as I wished for this, I didn't know how to weave that fairy-tale ending. And besides, I had my own life to attend to: My new boyfriend, Richard, needed all of my attention to overcome his ambivalence about our relationship, and then there were my studies. I wanted to make a go of my own life, too.

"How long do you want us to stay here?" I asked, wondering if we would find our way out through the night-darkened trees.

"Forever," he said.

"I have to go back to London tonight, Adam," I said, fearing that if I didn't return, Richard would end up spending the night with someone else. I couldn't let that happen.

Resigned, Adam extinguished the fire with a layer of damp leaves. His six-foot frame bent and stretched with the gentleness of an oak. As the last flicker of fire glinted in his moss-colored eyes, I turned and walked back out of the woods and down the hill.

Later that night, as my bus pulled away, I watched Adam's lanky form shrink into the distance, the moon still glowing above him. I didn't know when I would see him again. My hunger for the nobility of the swan sister was matched only by my desire for the intimacy I was building with Richard. Between brief moments of satiation was an almost constant yearning. I felt as brittle and disposable as a doll.

FOR YEARS ADAM CONTINUED the cycle of hospitalization or incarceration, followed by escape. When he was free, he sometimes grew his hair and beard long like Jesus. At other times, he shaved his head and wore white robes like a Buddhist monk. Occasionally I encountered him on London's street corners meditating, dancing, or begging—and, each time, the sight of him so vulnerable made my heart ache. During this period, I worked hard at my life. I graduated from East London University and attended a postgraduate film course at Saint Martin's. I cowrote and made a film with Richard, then made two more films with other friends.

One of these films would indirectly change my life. It was a documentary called *Soul Searching* and was about what the human soul might look like if we could see it. An interviewee we spoke with for the film was a German man named Roderich, a teacher at the Principle Life Study Centre in London. I had no idea what the Centre was or what its members believed. I only knew that when we arrived to interview Roderich, an international group of wholesome-looking young people invited us to stay around after our conversation and discover the true meaning of life. My friends were suspicious, so we left right away. But I was curious. Something about Roderich and the young people at the Centre tugged at me, and I promised myself I'd return.

A week after we finished editing *Soul Searching*, I saw Roderich passing out business cards in front of a minimart on Charing Cross Road where I had often encountered Adam meditating in his robes late at night. Roderich stood under the same streetlight where I had last seen my brother just a few days earlier. And although Roderich looked nothing like Adam, and wore a beige trench coat and a secret agent hat instead of Adam's signature white flowing robes, to me he represented something I was missing—or someone. With his prominent brow, jutting cheekbones, and chapped lips, Roderich looked determined, as if his mission was so important that he had not stopped to even drink water for days. (I later learned he had been fasting for a week.) His dedication impressed me, and I felt amused at God's sense of humor leading Roderich here to the last spot where I had seen Adam. Despite my friends' derision of Roderich, I could not help but feel drawn to him. My stomach tingled at the sight of him there, a spiritual teacher who potentially held answers to my deepest questions. I had to speak to him. Excitement and fear sparred in my chest as I felt something profound was about to happen.

"What a coincidence to see you here," I said as I approached. "We've just finished editing *Soul Searching* and we ended the film with one of your comments—the part where you said the soul wasn't something hovering around in space, but what exists within the love we share with each other right here and now."

Roderich moved more directly into the beam of the streetlight and gazed at me.

"You must come to study," he said in his carefully measured English. "I have many more things to say to you. This is a sign from God that you meet me here now."

"I'll come soon," I laughed nervously, actually not intending to do so. I wasn't sure I wanted to be alone with him in his mysterious study center. Still, something about this man, his German accent, his tattered devotion to his post in front of the market, and the way he looked at me, drew me in.

"Come tomorrow," said Roderich. "Tell me what time and I will meet you at the Centre."

THE NEXT DAY, I turned up at the Study Centre at 1:00 PM. Roderich led me to a room where I watched a short video that basically introduced me to the idea that following my own desires wouldn't make me happy because, as the Bible says in Galatians 5:17, "The flesh lusteth against the Spirit, and the Spirit against the flesh: and these are contrary the one to the other: so that ye cannot do the things that ye would."

The words in the video resonated with me. As I thought about it more, it struck me that my own desire for my boyfriend had interfered with my more spiritual desire to help my brother. I longed for the strength to make more selfless choices in my life.

After the video finished, Roderich invited me to discuss it with him. We walked up a spiral staircase to a pink-and-white room with tête-à-tête round tables and bright windows. As we started talking, Roderich expressed such interest in me that I found myself pouring my heart out. Among the many things I told him, I shared that I didn't know what love was, and that I did not understand why people lost their minds.

"My brother said that he could only get better with me," I said, searching Roderich's face for an answer to the question that haunted me: Could I help Adam?

"When your brother says you can make him better, he is right," said Roderich. "If you dedicate your life to God, He will heal your brother."

My heart thudded against my ribs so hard that I felt the vibrations right up to my throat. Could I take back the selfishness of the night when I had walked away from Adam in the forest? My decision that night ate at me constantly. Could I fulfill my dream of seeing my brother happy and free the way I remembered him as a child? My eyes clouded over as I struggled not to cry, but Roderich didn't look away.

The mysterious German's gray eyes bore through to the back of my head. I had never experienced such intense focus from a man who clearly was more interested in my soul than my body. When Roderich spoke to me, he looked only at my face and seemed to have all the time in the world to listen to me. I began to feel that the Study Centre was home to a different and purer kind of love than what I had known.

For the next ten days I returned to the study center. I watched videos about the purpose of Creation, the fall of man, and the parallels of history. From these videos—which were based on a philosophy called the Divine Principle—I learned the Study Centre's answers to the big questions posed on the ivory business cards the members handed out in the street. Is there a spiritual world? Does true love exist? Why do the innocent suffer? Will Christ come again? I loved the Divine Principle theory, which says we are all destined to live for the sake of others and create perfect, everlasting families. I felt I had been leading a selfish life, and I longed to turn that around. The possibility that I could actually do so filled me with new hope.

By only my second visit to the Principle Life Study Centre I started to feel an infusion of bliss while watching the videos. When I put on the headphones and listened to the lectures, I felt like angels were holding their hands above my heart and hugging me with pure loving energy. After years of yearning for intimacy, I started to imagine that I could experience ecstasy even without touch.

By the third day, I felt safe only within the doors of the Principle Life Study Centre. The moment I walked inside, I felt sated and complete. When I left, I felt alone and separate from those still inside, who were quickly becoming my surrogate family. It was as if an invisible thread bound me to the Study Centre and pulled me back whenever I stepped away. The people inside were innocent, open, and interested in me as a soul—not because they wanted anything from me. They didn't care if my films were good or if I was an accomplished artist or if I was pretty. These new friends liked me purely for my heart. They saw me as a vessel who could carry out God's will. Inside, I didn't have to strive; outside my life consisted of an unfaithful boyfriend, a brother I couldn't heal, and, with the completion of *Soul Searching,* the dissolution of creative connections with friends I had been working with for the past two years.

I started to feel that if I could do what God wanted me to do, I would no longer be judged by Him or by other people, because I would no longer have to figure out the difference between right and wrong. God would tell me through His words and I would simply follow.

This, I believed, was my chance to save my brother as he had asked me to do that night in the forest. And—with all my connections so tenuous now—this was my opportunity to belong to a new family, one that would never reject me, as long as I followed the rules. The feeling of relief was enormous.

On my tenth day of studying, I learned the answer to the Centre's most important question: Will Christ come again?

The answer? Yes. He already has come. In the book of the Revelation, an angel came from the East carrying the seal of the living God. Therefore, the Messiah would arrive in the East, in an Asian country. We were told he could not appear in Japan because the Japanese had started too many wars, nor in China because they were Communists, so he would come to Korea. Actually, he had already come to Korea.

While it seemed like a jump in logic that the Messiah was living somewhere in Korea, I had read from studying the Divine Principle that the human heart—when connected to God—could possess a "knowledge" greater than logic. And as the mindless ecstasy I felt while watching the videos was as powerful as any drug I had tried—and having no explanation for this other than the possibility that what I was learning was true and right—I chose to suspend my disbelief.

Anyway, what did I have to hold on to outside of these new teachings? If believing the Messiah had returned to Earth via Korea was all I had to do to become a better person and save my brother, I could do that. I could put my questions and my logic aside.

AFTER A WEEK OF study, I asked Roderich how I could do God's will. What did God require of me?

"Give up everything you own, Yolande. Come and live with us. Pray for your brother every day, and the spiritual world will heal him."

These were exactly the words I needed to hear. It was as if I had swallowed a large effervescent tablet, like a slot machine was wrought into action. I gulped and felt the fizz fill my chest as my cogs began to turn. Now I knew my purpose. I was eager to leave behind my life of striving for the trappings of success in a world that changed whenever I began to understand it. I wanted to give up art and romance—which now seemed like myths to me—and live my life for the sake of others. Here was my chance to become the fairy-tale swan girl who saved her brother through years of pain and sacrifice. I believed God had prepared me for this moment of decision since girlhood. I believed I had been exposed to my brother's suffering so I would become determined to work toward the healing of all the world's mentally ill. Didn't Jesus tell one young man if he gave everything to the poor he would find "treasure in heaven?" I loved the concept of giving everything away, of just being a raw human available to do the will of God. Besides, if what I'd been learning was true and we had to create the Kingdom of Heaven on Earth in three years, there was no time to hesitate.

"I've decided to move in," I told Roderich the next day.

AFTER AN INTRODUCTORY WORKSHOP the following day, my membership was approved. A day later I arrived at the church center with just a small duffel bag. Within eleven days of accepting Roderich's first invitation to study, I'd left behind my brand-new apartment along with all my ambitions, friends, and family. On inspection by my elder sisters and Spiritual Father, most of the contents of my bag were discarded, since my clothes weren't modest enough and my books "belonged to Satan." Thus, stripped down, I began my new life.

EACH DAY FOR ME as a new initiate was scheduled from early morning until lights-out. I awoke at 5:00 AM to catch a bus at 6:00 that carried me from our house in West London to a 7:00 AM meeting across town in the Study Centre. After each meeting, I was sent out to beg for money until 7:00 PM. In our morning sermons, I learned that every penny given to God was a penny snatched from Satan, and that we should use any means necessary to procure as much money for God as possible. "Any means" included "Heavenly Deception," or even stealing if we could do it without being caught. Acquiring money was how we supported the building of the Kingdom of Heaven. Even though I knew the church had multiple businesses, it never occurred to me this money might actually help pay the substantial bills of the church's real estate around the world.

My devotion to the church and my desire to save my brother kept me going all day every day with barely any breaks. From my starting point at the Study Centre each morning, I asked for contributions from everyone I encountered as I moved about the city. Carnaby Street and anywhere in the London Underground were particularly lucrative spots. While holding out my *One World* magazine, I asked every person who passed me for a donation for homeless children. Although this line wasn't strictly true, I justified the "homeless children" claim by telling myself that all people were homeless children until we created the Kingdom of God on Earth.

We were allowed £2 each day for lunch, but in order to save all my earnings for the church sometimes I took discarded fruit from a street market, and once I took a bag of chips from a garbage can.

Every night before going to bed, I took a cold shower to punish myself for having lusted after men in the past. Some nights I was so tired I fell asleep in the middle of my bedtime prayers. One such night, a sense of ecstasy awoke me deep in the middle of the night. As my sisters slept around me, my heart radiated with love that pulsed in and out simultaneously. The sensation was so powerful it seemed to beam like a floodlight to the farthest corners of the room. I believed this was God's love—and proof I was in the right place. My last thoughts before falling asleep again were prayers for a healthier, happier world, and for my brother to be cured.

Roderich said God gave me this feeling to encourage me to continue living this life, and I felt sure he was right. For once in my life, I was never alone. I was working toward a better world. Moment by moment, I became more attached to my new persona and more divorced from my old self. I now wore garments that covered my neck, arms, and legs for modesty, and shaved my head to evict the spirits that my House Mother told me were clinging to it. I gave myself to all of this wholeheartedly.

ALTHOUGH I HAD LEFT my old life behind, I was reminded of it at times. Occasionally when I was out begging I encountered friends I used to know. I ignored them completely and walked around the streets of London in a state of spiritual bliss, certain that—with each penny I received—I was transferring the world's power back to the good side.

Once, an old friend saw me begging. She approached me but I turned away. In despair she fell down and grabbed my ankles.

"Yolande, don't go back to those people," she pleaded. But by then I was certain I was one of "those people"—and my past friends and family were not a part of my new life.

I walked away from my friend, ignoring her tears, believing her to be trapped in a Satanic realm to which I, thankfully, no longer belonged.

SINCE EARLY CHILDHOOD, I had longed for a fairy-tale world where families lived happily ever after and even one small girl could change reality for the better. The girl in "The Six Swans" stayed silent despite the burning nettle stings she received while sewing her brothers' suits. In the years to come, I too would withstand pain without a word of complaint. I would overlook shocking facts about Reverend Moon and the Unification Church. I would strive to give up my personal desires, expectations, and beliefs. And I would stay the course, making allowances for divine necessity, certain that my brother would be healed. My only concern during all this was my fear that, like the girl in the story, I wouldn't finish in time—and that Adam would be left with one snowy white wing hooking him to his enchantment forever.

BURNT OFFERINGS

Turning Twelve

Lucia Greenhouse

*"My little daughter lieth at the point of death: I pray thee,
come and lay thy hands on her, that she may be healed;
and she shall live."*

*. . . And [Jesus] took the damsel by the hand, and said
unto her, Talitha cumi; which is, being interpreted, Damsel,
I say unto thee, arise. And straightway the damsel arose, and
walked; for she was of the age of twelve years. And they were
astonished with a great astonishment.*

—Mark 42:5 (King James Version)

I sat perched on a high stool in Aunt Helen's kitchen, pulled my
brown hair back into a ponytail, and waited, senses heightened,
as Uncle Jack meticulously prepared to pierce my ears. He placed a
white hand towel over my shoulders, like a barber might. He zipped

open the black travel case holding his sterilized surgical tools, and methodically set them on the counter. He ripped open a new package of rolled sterile cotton, tore off two small pieces, and soaked them in a bowl of rubbing alcohol to swab my left earlobe, then my right, before promptly discarding the barely used cotton ball onto a specially designated dish. The process of using two cotton balls seemed at once both impressively expert and a tiny bit silly. How dirty could my earlobes have been?

Uncle Jack was tall—six foot seven—with astonishingly blue eyes and close-cropped hair of indeterminate color. His skin was nicely tanned. He wore a pale pink golf shirt and khaki slacks with a needlepoint belt that Aunt Helen had probably stitched for him. On his feet were the same black Gucci loafers with the horse-bit buckles that my dad always wore.

My uncle, Harry Alvin Johnson, MD—whom everyone called Jack—was a plastic surgeon, which I knew from my cousin Mimi meant that he made ladies' boobs bigger and teenagers' noses smaller and once sewed a girl's ear back on after her horse bit it off. He also pierced all his nieces' ears when they turned twelve.

On that particular spring day shortly after my twelfth birthday, I didn't pause for even a moment to wonder how it was that I was permitted to have my ears pierced, although today, decades later, it is something of a conundrum. What puzzled me at the time was the fact that my uncle, a plastic surgeon, was on one side of me, preparing to pierce my ears, and my mother was on the other side of me, acting as his assistant, swishing the shiny new gold post earrings in a dish of alcohol.

It struck me, all of a sudden and possibly for the first time, that there might be something a little complicated about my uncle being a plastic surgeon and my mother, his sister, being a Christian

Scientist. Actually, it struck me as maybe *very* complicated. After all, not only was Uncle Jack a surgeon, but my mother's father, "Bops"—long dead—had been a family physician, and my grandmother, who now sat beside me, holding my smaller hand in her much larger bejeweled, powdery soft, knotty hand, had been a registered nurse way back when.

And we didn't believe in doctors.

Maybe—*maybe*—almost everyone in the whole world went to doctors? Maybe we Ewings were weird? I eyed my mother skeptically, eyebrows raised, but she stood there casually and obediently swishing around the gold earrings in a dish of rubbing alcohol—sterilizing them—even though I knew from Christian Science Sunday School that there was *no such thing as germs.*

Mom just smiled back at me, as though my expression were one of anticipation.

Which it sort of was. What had started as puzzlement turned accusation became anticipation, then fear. I saw the syringe. My uncle pointed it straight up in the air and flicked it with his middle finger, and a little drop of clear liquid spurted out the end of the long, sharp needle. I had only seen this move executed on *Marcus Welby, M.D.,* because we never went to doctors, not even for annual checkups. (*Marcus Welby, M.D.,* was forbidden viewing in the Ewing household.) My heart raced.

For years I had been captivated by the forbidden: St. Joseph Aspirin, peeing into Dixie cups (which my cousin Mimi told me about), and doctor visits with reflex tests (the ones with the rubber hammer to the knee) and tongue depressors and saying *aaaah.* But now, the moment had arrived for me to be seen—or treated, sort of—by a doctor. Suddenly, that needle spurting upward sent my wandering curiosity straight back to the safety of the familiar.

A little voice whispered in my head. *There is no life, truth, intelligence, or substance in matter.*

Grandma gave my hand a squeeze. "Are you scared?" she asked.

I shook my head, no, but I was. My throat clenched and I tried to swallow. I knew from Sunday School that if I was afraid, I could quote the Bible or *Science and Health,* and my fear would go away.

The Lord is my shepherd, I shall not want . . .

The problem was, whenever I thought of the twenty-third Psalm, my eyes got watery. If I were to carry on with *He leadeth me beside the still waters,* I might soon be crying. I switched back to *Science and Health with Key to the Scriptures* by Mary Baker Eddy, to the Scientific Statement of Being.

"All is infinite Mind, and its infinite manifestation, for God is All-in-All."

Uncle Jack approached me with the syringe.

"What are you doing?" I asked, my posture retreating.

"I'm numbing your ears with Novocain."

"Will it hurt?"

"You'll feel a pinch. But then, after a few minutes, you won't feel anything. That's when I'll pierce your ears."

I felt the pinch, and then a sting. Uncle Jack hadn't mentioned anything about stinging. I squeezed my eyes shut and returned to my mental recitation.

"Spirit is immortal Truth. Matter is mortal error . . . "

A few minutes later, Uncle Jack pulled and tugged at one ear, then the other. I felt—or rather, I heard, but didn't feel—a popping sound.

"There you go, Lucia, you can take a look, " he said, pointing to a mirror on the far wall. He winked at my mother.

Sliding off the high stool, I approached the mirror as though I were balancing a book on my head.

On the wall I saw my toweled shoulders covered in thick blood dripping from two very large needles—poles, really—sticking through my earlobes. I gasped, horrified. I felt my stomach turn.

"Jack, you bully," Mom said.

I'm sure my uncle thought it was a funny joke, but I wasn't laughing and neither was Mom.

"Come on back," he said, sheepishly.

Within seconds, Uncle Jack inserted the earrings into the holes made by the poles, and snapped on the backings. He took a few more alcohol-drenched cotton balls to clean up my bloody ears, removed the towel from my shoulders, and sent me outside to show the boys.

My little brother, Sherman, and my cousins, Harry, Steven, and Sargent, were taking turns going off a bicycle jump they had constructed on the driveway. I asked if they wanted to see my newly pierced ears, but they didn't. My cousins had seen puffy lobes before, and Sherman was far more interested in the jump. I asked if I could have a go. After ignoring me for a few more loops, Sherman reluctantly gave me the bike he was using. I headed toward the ramp of the jump at full speed.

What happened next is a bit of a blur. I was flat on my back. Above me I could see, in the foreground, Uncle Jack squatting on my right, holding my wrist and looking at his watch. On my left, my mother kneeled. Her eyes were closed, and her lower lip was firmly pinched between her teeth. Between Uncle Jack and Mom, directly behind me, stood my grandmother, with one hand over her mouth. I heard her utter the word *concussion*.

Uncle Jack asked how I felt, and he ran his fingers over my forehead and scalp. I winced. My head throbbed as he found the bump at my hairline above the right eye. Mom opened her eyes and gazed off into the near distance. I could tell from the way her head bobbed very slightly that she was deep in prayer, affirming the Truth about Man's God-given perfection. When one of my cousins told Uncle Jack that the handlebars of the bike had given way as I went off the jump, and I had launched headfirst into the concrete, it became apparent to me that it was *my* God-given perfection my mother was affirming.

My mom's focus turned to me, and my eyes filled with tears. I felt sick to my stomach and, oddly, like I had done something wrong.

"Would you like to go home?" Mom whispered gently.

I nodded, and started to sit up, which was a bad idea because everything turned topsy-turvy, like it used to in the fun house at the Excelsior Amusement Park (which for me was never much fun). I returned to lying on one side, my hands serving as a pillow for my cheek, the pebbles digging unpleasantly into them.

Grandma turned away from me and said something to Aunt Helen, who had finished scolding the cousins for the bicycle ramp. Uncle Jack and Mom had words—but I heard none of them. I wanted the bad feeling to go away and thought closing my eyes would help. It didn't. It just made things worse.

"You okay, Loosh?"

Sherman, not quite ten, knelt beside me and uncharacteristically took my hand in his.

Eventually I did get up, and we returned to Mom's station wagon and drove home. I got to sit in the front seat, which should have felt like a privilege but didn't. I put my head in my mom's lap and she drove one-handed, rubbing my back with her right hand. Sherman and Mom sang the five verses of "Oh, Gentle Presence," which we all knew by heart, and when they got to the last line, "and

Mother finds her home and heavenly rest," we were pulling into our driveway. I felt a little better.

Mom settled me in my parents' room, in the high four-poster bed with the pretty canopy. Then she excused herself to call Dad from the phone in his adjacent study. I heard fragments of her end of the brief conversation: Ears pierced. Bike jump. Tumble. *Concussion.*

I knew from the silence that my father was probably correcting my mother, reminding her not to use such a word.

"Mm-hmm," my mother said, "Yes."

She hung up the phone and dutifully dialed again. I listened for each rotation of the dial—short for low numbers, long for the higher numbers, the *zzzzzzz* of the dialing much faster than the clicking of the return—and wondered whom she was calling.

"Mary?" she said, "It's Joanne Ewing."

It used to be that we called Mrs. Hannah whenever we had a "little problem," but ever since Dad himself became a Christian Science practitioner, he handled all but the most serious matters that arose in our family. Mom and Dad must have been worried about the possibility of . . . that *word* . . .

Physically, I didn't actually feel all that bad. My head hurt—but it was only a dull ache now, unless I touched the bump with my fingers. Then it stung. If I turned my head quickly, I felt seasick. So I tried not to move.

My mother didn't use *concussion* with Mrs. Hannah. She gave her most of the other details though, about the bicycle jump and the handlebars and the ear piercing by Jack. After a few minutes of silence (in which Mrs. Hannah was praying and instructing, and Mom was listening, and I was imagining what the worst-case scenario might be for a *concussion*), Mom called out to me from the next room and asked me to pick up the phone on the nightstand.

"Hello, dear," Mrs. Hannah said. She had the voice of a Disney character, high, nasal, and singsong. Hearing it made me feel sad again.

"Your mom tells me you took a little spill?" she asked sweetly.

"Yes." My throat ached as I tried to sound brave.

"Can you tell me what you're working on in Sunday School?"

I had to think about that. I had no idea, to be honest. But she would never know, nor would she check with my teacher, so I gave her a plausible, made-up answer.

"The seven synonyms for God?" I offered.

"Very good. And what does Mary Baker Eddy say are the seven synonyms for God?"

That was easy. "Principle, Mind, Soul, Spirit, Life, Truth, and Love."

"And what is the Truth about you, Lucia?"

"The Truth is, I cannot be hurt."

"You're absolutely right. Why is that?"

"Because I am the perfect reflection of God. And God is perfect. Therefore, I am perfect."

"That's right. You can hold fast to that thought, Lucia. Have you learned Mrs. Eddy's definition of Man?"

I closed my eyes, to search my memory, but that made me feel gross, so I opened them again. I was pretty sure I knew the definition, but not positive.

"The . . . compound idea of . . . infinite spirit?" I said.

"Very good. That's the first part. And what else?"

"The . . . spiritual image and likeness of God? The full representation of Mind?"

"That's right. Do you know what that means?"

"I think . . . it means . . . "

If I told Mrs. Hannah that it meant I could not be anything but perfect, I'd be giving the right answer. But I couldn't get the words out; they just wouldn't come. Out of nowhere, I felt utterly exhausted. Holding the phone to my ear required an effort I simply couldn't make. I let the hand piece of the phone go so that it rested on the pillow a few inches from my ear. Mrs. Hannah's voice became the squeak of a mouse. I felt strangely far away from myself. I tried to concentrate on Mrs. Hannah's voice.

"Mrs. Eddy says: "When an accident happens, you think or exclaim, 'I am hurt!'" Your thought is more powerful than your words, more powerful than the accident itself, to make the injury real. Now reverse the process. Declare that you are not hurt and understand the reason why, and you will find the ensuing good effects to be in exact proportion to your disbelief in physics, and your fidelity to divine metaphysics."

It struck me as odd, suddenly, that our practitioner—and Mom and Dad, and every other Christian Scientist I knew—used the present tense when quoting Mrs. Eddy, as though the founder of Christian Science were still alive. But Mrs. Eddy was dead.

Or maybe she *wasn't* dead. I mean, I *knew* she was not dead—because in Christian Science, there was no death. But, I was sort of confused. If Mary Baker Eddy wasn't dead—because there's no death in Life—then that meant Abraham Lincoln was also not dead. Right? I wondered if Mrs. Hannah would say, "Abraham Lincoln says . . . " if she were quoting him. Or if she would say, "Abe Lincoln said . . . "

"Lucia?" Mary Hannah asked.

"Yes?" I said, jolted back to the present.

"The Scientific Statement of Being?"

Together, we recited it, which required no thinking.

There is no life, truth, intelligence, or substance in matter. All is infinite Mind, and its infinite manifestation, for God is All-in-All. Spirit is immortal Truth. Matter is mortal error. Spirit is real and eternal. Matter is unreal and temporal. Spirit is God, and man is his image and Likeness. Therefore, man is not material, he is spiritual.

WHEN DAD GOT HOME from work that evening he carried me to my own bedroom, like he used to when I was a little girl. He made a show of it—all handsome and movie-star-like—and that alone cheered me up. But I didn't touch the dinner Mom brought me on a tray. I wasn't hungry.

I pinched the lobes of both ears (which now ached a bit) and marveled at the return of sensation. I knew from Sunday School that there was *no sensation in matter*. But, what about my earlobes? The Novocain had made sensation in my ears disappear. And then, after the Novocain wore off, I could feel them again.

And what about Abe Lincoln? (And everyone else who ever lived? Except maybe . . . Jesus?)

Was he *really* still *living?*

Nothing made much sense.

And what about concussions? What if I had one? Could I die from a concussion? Should Mom and Dad have taken me to the hospital?

The next morning at breakfast I felt perfectly fine. I sat at the kitchen table, eating my breakfast of Quisp cereal with one hand while the other hand gently twisted my earrings one rotation each. My ears were sore and unpleasantly crusty, but I *adored* my earrings. They made me look so much older than I had the day before.

Dad bounded down the stairs, singing, "Oh what a beautiful morning," and then he was standing behind me, affectionately squeezing my shoulders.

"You've had a beautiful demonstration," he said. "If you like, you can come with Mom and me to next Wednesday's Testimony Meeting and share it."

I wasn't sure I wanted to. I fiddled with one of my earrings.

"Would you like to?" Dad asked.

I knew it would mean a trip to Baskin-Robbins. I looked up at the ceiling, pondering the offer.

"And you know, now that you're twelve," Dad added, charmingly, "you can join the Mother Church."

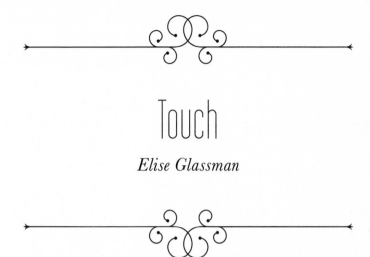

Touch

Elise Glassman

"Ready to go?" My mother stood between me and the library checkout counter.

Startled by her sudden appearance, I shifted my armload of books, moving the top book to the bottom of the stack I'd prepared for checkout. My sister and I were homeschooled and Mom had to approve everything we read, even books by Christian authors.

She picked up the top book. "Another detective novel? I sure hope there's no swearing in this one." Last week I'd had to return Agatha Christie's *The Murder at the Vicarage* because she'd opened to a page where Hastings uttered "goddamn." She moved on to a collection of Greek plays. Soon she'd get to the bottom of the pile, to The Book. I felt sick to my stomach. If she opened it, if she read what I'd just read—

My sister Maggie ran up. "Mom. The meter maid's coming."

Mom said, "Oh dear—well, go ahead and check out. We'll see you at the car."

That night, after Maggie turned out the lamp on her side of the bedroom, I stayed up reading The Book: *Deenie,* by Judy Blume. It was, without a doubt, a book my mother would never have allowed me to read. But it drew me right in, with its easygoing prose describing the nonchalant grittiness of growing up in a city, and Deenie getting dragged by her mom to modeling jobs. And then boom— here was Deenie, in the bathtub, touching herself. My hands went cold as I read. I felt my pulse pound in my ears. How did someone else know about this? I did this, too, I touched myself, but I had no idea other girls did it. Reading about Deenie and her "special place" made my face hot with shame. I read the passage again and again. Did touching myself make me a bad Christian? Would I go to hell? I hadn't planned on searching out The Book at the library and sneaking it home, but here it was. Now, lying in bed, I held The Book with one hand and, with the other, I slipped my fingers into the waistband of my underpants and stroked the warm, liquid place between my legs.

MY FATHER WAS THE pastor of an independent Baptist church, my mom the pastor's wife, which meant she was like the First Lady, an unpaid figurehead who helped with her husband's ministry—she picked up nursing home residents for church, coordinated potlucks, sewed costumes for Christmas plays, typed up the handouts for the occasional funeral. Our parents homeschooled Maggie and me and our little sister because they believed they were supposed to obey the Bible literally, to "train up a child in the way he should go." They were certain they could do better than the godless Bellingham public school system, not to mention the local Christian schools, with their Christian rock music and boys with hair down over their ears and girls in sweatpants during P.E.

So Monday through Friday, from eight to three-thirty, my sisters and I went to school right in our own living room. Homeschool was where I learned that the Earth was six thousand years old and the fossil record a secular tale aimed at eliminating the Lord from Creation; I learned that modern art and jazz encouraged promiscuity and drugs, that human emotions would always betray me, and that having high self-esteem meant that I was prideful and setting myself above the Lord. I learned that my body was a skin sac of wantonness and betrayal, and that doing what I felt like doing, what felt good, was the worst sin of all because our only goal as Christians was to do the Lord's will. And while going to church and praying and reading the Bible and denying myself might not feel good, it pleased Him and so it was enough, it was the only thing; it was everything.

This isn't to say that we didn't get out of the house sometimes; we went on field trips to museums and the salmon hatchery, and once a week Dad conducted P.E. class at Cornwall Park. I was as much of a jock as any chunky four-eyes in a split skirt could be. I did have a decent jump shot and a solid right hook, and once in a while, dribbling down the cracked basketball court in my slick-soled Keds, I forgot about the slip hiking up around my waist and the teenagers smoking and watching from the picnic benches and lost myself in the game.

One time, after I sank a pair of free throws, a guy called, "Nice guns, Amish Baller," and his friends laughed, smoke curling out of their pierced nostrils, and I realized how ridiculous I must seem. A part of me wished I could hang out with those kids and smoke and casually make snotty remarks, but I knew that with my Sears glasses and zits and calf-length skirts, I'd only be a target for humiliation. Imaginary people—in my books, in my daydreams—were the only people I trusted. I knew their faults and follies and dreams and they could never say or do anything to hurt me.

"Sɪs. Wʜᴀᴛ's ᴛʜᴇ Sᴘᴀɴɪsʜ word for *Bible*?"

I looked up from my American Lit test. Maggie and I were sitting at the dining room table. I could hear Mom in the other room, giving our little sister a spelling quiz: *"Bursar." "B-u-r-s-a-r." "Succumb." "S-u-c-k-u-m."*

"Biblia," I said, watching her scribble. "You better pass your test. Dad said we can't go to the youth rally in Prosser this weekend if we don't all get As."

She tossed her hair, silky and blonde, whereas mine was broomhandle brown and frizzy from a recent Toni home perm. "We'll go. Sis, we *have* to. Rob and Aaron will be there."

I agreed with her. We *had* to go. Every independent Baptist teenager in Western Washington would be there. But it was far from a done deal. Although Maggie was a decent student, Mom always graded her more severely than she did me. I wondered sometimes if it was because Maggie was so pretty and sunshiny, so unlike Mom and me—we were dark haired, serious, reserved. It was very possible that our parents had decided to teach her humility.

Anyway, we were going to have to partner up if we wanted to get to Prosser. "Concentrate," I told her, seeing that she was staring off into space. I'd spent most of the past weekend lying on my bed and fantasizing about Aaron, even though I was afraid I'd be far too shy to talk to him. We'd met Rob and Aaron—best friends from a church in Renton—at a rally last year. Rob was brash and dark haired, and most girls, including Maggie, thought he was cute, but I liked tall, skinny, funny Aaron.

"Girls, no talking in there," my mother called from the other room.

I looked again at my test. I'd been counting on the usual true/false softballs, and now I was staring at a page of multiple-choice, fill-in-the-blank, and essay questions.

"What's the word for *church*?" my sister whispered.

I sighed. "Um—*iglesia?*" Why hadn't I studied my American Lit harder? I'd started to buckle down last night, had settled on my bed with my notebooks and some pretzels. Then I'd gotten distracted—again—by The Book.

My parents had never said much about sex, except that God wanted us to remain virgins for our future husbands. I'd taken to examining encyclopedias and health textbooks at the library, looking at drawings and trying to imagine the mechanics of it. What did Aaron's penis look like? Would he want to touch me with it? Last night I'd read The Book until Maggie fell asleep, and then I'd turned off the light and hugged my pillow, pretend-kissed it, imagined that I was a princess and Aaron a handsome prince. I'd reached into my panties and stroked my wet center and felt all my worries about tomorrow's exams melt away in a wash of pleasure.

Deep in my fantasy, I hadn't heard my mother come into the room for prayers. Suddenly she was standing over me, praying softly, "Dear Heavenly Father—" I froze, eyes squeezed closed, hoping she couldn't see the mound of my hand tucked between my legs. Only after she said "Amen" and went away did I realize I'd been holding my breath. The warmth between my legs had cooled. I felt like crying. Rolling onto my side, I tucked my hands under my pillow, my fingers stiff and smelling like myself.

Concentrate, I told myself now, and looked again at my test. I took a deep breath. "In *Pilgrim's Progress,* compare Christiana's pilgrimage to Christian's, and for extra credit, show where similarities may actually . . . " *Blah blah blah.* I couldn't concentrate. I was going to fail, and it was going to be God's punishment for sneaking dirty books home, for not studying, for thinking bad thoughts about Aaron, for allowing my hands to roam and ravish my body.

"Mom!" Maggie called. "May I go to the bathroom?"

"You may be excused. Leave your test facedown on the table."

As soon as Maggie left the dining room, I was up. I grabbed the American Lit Teacher's Edition off Mom's stack of books at the end of the table and flipped to the key in the back. On my wrist I wrote answers: ABBAD, DCABA, and so on. I scanned "What to look for" on the essay questions and quietly closed the book.

"What are you doing?" Maggie was back, frowning.

Startled, I sat down, my legs shaking. "Nothing. I had to get another pencil."

"Can you help me with my quiz?" she whispered.

"Girls," Mom said. "I thought I asked you not to talk."

"Maggie's talking," I said loudly, and my sister's eyes widened.

Mom called, "Come in here, please, Margaret Anne."

Face flushed, Maggie hurried into the other room. She'd get demerits for sure. She might even get spanked. I grabbed her test. For crying out loud. I'd never taken Spanish and even I knew that *queso* was *cheese.* Picking up a pencil, I started to fill in her answers.

I GOT GOOD GRADES, but good wasn't enough in homeschool. Anything less than perfection was evidence that I wasn't trying sufficiently hard enough to obey the Lord, that homeschool was a waste of everybody's time and I might as well go to a public school. If I got a 90, my father asked what happened with the other 10 points. Recently, I'd aced an algebra quiz, and as I sat basking in my accomplishment he'd handed me extra credit homework.

"But I got a hundred," I'd said, incredulous.

"Does somebody have an attitude problem?" he snapped.

Across the table, Maggie stared down at her textbook. "No sir," I said. "But—"

"Are you sure about that? Who gave you the ability to learn algebra? And who can take it away quicker than you can say 'pride goeth before destruction'?"

"'And a haughty spirit before a fall,'" Maggie quoted softly. I wanted to slap her.

And so, in a roundabout way, I concluded that the only way to succeed was to excel, to become so good—on paper, anyway— that my parents could find no fault with me. I learned to shut off my brain and fill in the correct answer and tell them what they wanted to hear. I dedicated myself to my studies, holing up at the library for hours, laboring over research papers that only my mother would ever read, helping my father type up prayer lists for Wednesday night church. I ratted out my sisters and kept a close eye on the kids in Junior Church, monitoring the girls to make certain their skirts covered their knees and the boys to be sure their hands weren't dug deep in their pants pockets playing pocket pool. My whole world was studying and self-control and the Bible. Perfection was my obsession. I even cut back to just a few hundred calories a day until I could burn off my stomach pooch. I was living a life of calculation and control: pleasing my parents, obeying the Lord, with a few exceptions, and growing into an obsequious, cringing ball of emptiness, holier-than-thou—especially if you didn't count my nighttime secret.

You'd think I would've had trouble reconciling my double life, my strict belief system, with my cheating, lies, and growing sexual curiosity. This duplicity was arguably un-Christian and required increasingly complex mental gymnastics to justify. But I had role models: my parents, pastor and wife so full of certitude and sanctimony, praising the Lord on Sunday and talking trash about church members on Monday. We prayed for dear Deacon X and his wife that they would give up the sin of cable TV, even as my father stopped by their house when the World Series was on. When Mrs. Z came by our house one day to drop off church linens she'd laundered, my father watched from behind the living room curtains, quipping as she left, "Call the Department of Licensing, there's a boat without a license plate out there." I laughed at this—my father had a wicked wit—but later I thought about fat Mrs. Z and all the times I'd seen her praying up front at church during the weekly altar calls and I felt sad.

Every human interaction my parents had seemed to be an opportunity to establish distance, to sever any connections founded on anything but the Lord, to judge and reject all who didn't meet their harsh standards. We didn't talk to supermarket clerks, because they sold alcohol and cigarettes and as such were instruments of Satan. Police officers we treated with exaggerated courtesy, because law and order were precepts ordained by the Lord, but in the coming End-Times the cops would become tools of the state and hence our obeisance was probably temporary. Not even my grandparents were exempt, receiving harsh comments for skipping Wednesday prayer meetings here and there and for their occasional pinochle game with neighbors.

More and more I feared my parents' ruthless eye, the spotlight gaze examining my flaws, finding my inevitable shortcomings, and casting me out of their hearts. Regardless of all I was doing to prove myself worthy, if they deemed my motives and my heart—me—not spiritual enough, then what? Punishment, damnation, a lonely life without God and my parents? I felt empty most of the time, but I figured that was probably just my excessive dieting.

WE LEFT FOR PROSSER at 5:00 AM Saturday. Dad drove the van, listening to sermon tapes and drinking coffee from a Thermos. The rest of us dozed. I woke up as we turned into a gravel parking lot. "You girls worked hard to get here," Dad said, pulling into a spot. "I'm proud of you for doing well on your tests. The Lord is too."

"We'll see you at lunchtime. You two stick together," my mother instructed.

I climbed out of the van, stiff and yawning. "You think Rob and Aaron are here?"

Maggie shrugged. "I need to go to the bathroom." As we walked away from the van, she added softly, "Thanks for helping me with my test."

"Next time, study," I snapped, and walked ahead of her.

Crossing the parking lot, we eyed the other kids heading toward the church. The girls seemed impossibly cute in jean skirts and flats; the boys were like beings from another planet, laughing and shoving. At the bathroom we joined a long line.

"Hey. That's a pretty crazy jumper," a girl behind us said, cracking her gum.

Pleased, I smoothed my corduroy jumper and said, "It's

vintage. I got it at a thrift store."

"My gramma has one exactly like it," her friend said, and the two giggled. "What're your favorite jeans?"

"We don't wear pants," I said, trading looks with Maggie. The kids here were from pretty liberal schools and churches. These girls wore skirts above their knees and loads of makeup.

"I like Jordache baggies," the girl said.

The line moved. Maggie went into a stall.

I stared at the row of hand dryers on the wall. I'd been so excited to get here and already it was shaping up to be a long day. How did these girls know, just by looking at me, that I was a square, a loser? What would it feel like to be a part of their little clique, invisible but accepted, lovingly kidded, the way it happened in books and in my imagination?

"So my cousin gave me a Judy Blume book to read," the friend was saying quietly.

The Jordache girl gasped, clearly shocked and impressed. "No way."

My breath caught in my chest. I heard a flush and prayed no stall doors opened just yet.

"She's Episcopalian," the friend said, as if that explained something. "I mean, a Judy Blume book. My mom would freak if she found out!"

"I read Judy Blume books," I said ultra casually, I hoped.

The Jordache girl turned to look at me like she'd smelled something offensive. "Those books talk about gross things," she said.

"People who do those things are gross," her friend agreed.

Now everyone in line was looking at me. I tried to shrink within my senior citizen's jumper. I did those things. Those things felt good. When I touched myself, I felt so warm and safe and loved—if only for a few minutes, before the guilt and shame moved in. Could these girls tell by looking at me that I did those things? Oh dear Jesus, why had I opened my mouth?

A stall opened up and I ducked inside. When I came out, Maggie was waiting, looking worried. She'd applied lip gloss. "What's a Judy Blume book?"

"Nothing," I said, hurrying her toward the door, away from the Jordache girl and her friend who were giggling inside the handicap stall. "I haven't read any. I was just kidding."

"You better not be hiding books from Mom and Dad," she said, pushing past me and out into the hall.

AT THE LUNCH BREAK we spied Rob and Aaron at the dessert table. "Let's go say Hi," Maggie said. I glanced around the cafeteria. No sign of our parents but I was sure they were somewhere nearby, watching and omnipresent, like the Lord. I was so nervous as we moved closer to Rob and Aaron that I thought I might faint.

We all said Hi. I added, to Aaron, stammering a little, "How you?"

He grinned and said teasingly, "I fine."

"You guys going to the midnight skate tonight?" Rob was busy piling cherry crisp on his plate.

Maggie said, "No."

"Maybe," I said, even though I was pretty sure we wouldn't be allowed.

In the afternoon, I tied for second in the Sword Drill, a competitive Bible verse lookup contest that rewarded nimble fingers and intimate knowledge of lesser-known books of the Bible, such as Haggai, and Second Thessalonians. As I stood onstage with the other champions, shaking some youth pastor's hand and accepting a shiny satin rosette embroidered with the image of a Bible, I cast an embarrassed, covert glance at the Jordache girl, but she and her friend were busy whispering and giggling.

Next, there was special music played by a band with an electric guitar. The song definitely had too much of a rock-and-roll beat for my parents, but they couldn't very well march us out of our seats up front without causing a ruckus, so Maggie and I sat furtively tapping our feet along to Amy Grant's "Everywhere I Go" while everyone around us sang along and clapped.

After the final sermon, Preacher Todd, from Portland, who was movie-star handsome, stood at the altar and implored everyone to get right with the Lord. All the visiting pastors and pastors' wives, including my parents, stood at the front, waiting to pray with sinful teens. Even with my head bowed, I could feel the weight of Mom and Dad's eyes. Guilt churned my stomach. I thought about The Book, hidden under my mattress, remembered the way I'd bragged about it in the bathroom, trying to make myself look— what? Worldly? Experienced? Cool? Everything my parents—and the Lord—abhorred.

Maggie pushed past me and went forward to confess her sins. I could already see how this would go. She'd pray for forgiveness, get right with the Lord, and later she'd confess about both of us cheating, possibly even mention Judy Blume. If I stayed in my seat, my punishment would just be that much worse. The only thing now was to go forward too, and repent. I'd have to show my parents The Book, have to confess to lying and deceitfulness. Would they have to know about the rest? About *those things?*

I walked slowly to the front. Ten or twelve kids were already kneeling at the altar, many crying, one slender boy sobbing openly into his folded hands. My mother met my eye and smiled slightly. A woman with her hair up in a bun knelt beside me. "Oh Lord, hear our prayer for forgiveness," she prayed, and, yielding to the bubble of sadness swelling inside me, I wept, more from hopelessness than penitence for my sinful mind and hands.

Maggie and I waited around for our parents afterward as they said good-bye to their pastor friends. The auditorium cleared out pretty fast, everyone anxious to get over to the roller rink. "Should we ask if we can go?" she said.

"They saw us go forward, right?" I said. "Maybe they'll let us go skating."

"Maybe," she said hopefully.

In the van, I sat on the edge of the seat, seatbelt unfastened, watching out my window as the Jordache girl and her friend laughed and climbed aboard a school bus that would take them skating. Our father slipped off his suit coat, settled into the driver's seat, and poured lukewarm coffee out of his Thermos. It seemed, from his frown and protracted silence, that something was on his mind.

"Daddy, could we—" Maggie started, and my stomach did a little nervous flip.

He held up a hand, sipped his coffee with a deliberate slurp. "I don't know about the rest of you, but I think the devil must be pretty pleased about now. All that rock music and long hair on a bunch of so-called Christians."

"I can't get over the girls' hemlines," Mom said, equally disappointed. "They all looked so worldly."

"Somebody explain it to me. All right? Is this what the Lord had in mind?" Dad said. "Miniskirts and a sermon weaker than McDonald's coffee?" He started up the engine.

"A lot of kids went forward and got right with the Lord,

though," I said, looking at Maggie. Her eyes were dark smudges against her pale face.

"Well," he said, seeming slightly mollified.

It was a long shot, but I had to try. I added, "Dad, do you think—could we go skating . . . "

His eyes met mine in the rearview mirror. "You mean with those boys you girls were chasing around at lunchtime?"

"We weren't chasing," I said. "We were just talking."

He stepped on the brake so hard that I slid halfway off my seat. "Is that right?" he asked, turning around to look me in the face. "You just got right with the Lord, and now you want to go skate around in pitch darkness to rock-and-roll music with a bunch of boys?"

"No, sir," I said, my voice barely audible, a biblical divide yawning between the truth and my words. I scooted back and let my tears come again. After a while, after I stopped crying, I reached into my bag and pulled out my Sword Drill ribbon. I stroked the pillowy red satin. It glowed in the van's dim lighting. This ribbon meant something. I'd won it. But even still, I felt so guilty: All the Bible verses in the world couldn't hide the fact that I was a colossal fraud. Agatha Christie would have found me a worthy foe.

"You did good, sis," Maggie said to me, softly, consolingly.

"Did well," Mom corrected from the front seat. "And yes, honey, you did well."

Disappointment was welling up so deep inside me that I thought I might drown. "I could have done better," I said.

My father said, nodding, "With more practice, next time you ought to get first place."

So he agreed: No matter how well I did, I would always be failing on some level, could always do better. This realization was my now, my future. We sped on down a dark, two-lane highway. I settled into my seat, cheek pressed against the cool glass. Dark-hearted as I was, confession could wait awhile. If my best would never be good enough, what was the rush? I'd tell my parents about The Book— but in a few days, after I returned it to the library. Maybe I'd reread it first. And those things? They were private, they were for me. They were the one thing in my life that no one could take away. The van rolled on toward home. I closed my eyes and imagined myself in my bed, safe and warm under the covers, exploring my body's geography with my restless fingers.

Body Language

Pamela Helberg

My parents and I had just returned from a long Sunday morning at church and I was starving. During the last half hour of services I had tried in vain to sing and pray loudly so that no one could hear the deep empty sounds coming from my gut. As soon as we got home and I changed out of my church clothes I headed straight for the kitchen to make myself a toasted cheese sandwich and a cup of tomato soup, my favorite Sunday lunch. My thoughts were focused so intently on getting the bread perfectly browned in the frying pan that I didn't see or hear my parents suddenly double-team me. Dad came from the living room while Mom snuck up behind me from the dining room, tears streamed down both of their faces.

"Pam Sue, your mother and I need to talk to you," my father said tightly, his voice modulated to neutral with a hint of loving concern.

Uh oh, I thought, *this cannot be good*. I turned off the stove and scanned the kitchen for a possible escape. They each blocked a doorway, effectively making me their prisoner. I took a deep breath. "Why? What's up?"

"Sit down." My mother stepped away from her post and pulled a chair out for me. I intuited that I should obey.

"Pam Sue, your mother and I love you very much." This loving concern, these tears, felt like a bad omen.

"I love you too," I said with a slight hint of a question. My stomach clenched with dread. I knew what was coming next.

"What is this this this . . . sickness? Are you and Chris lovers?" my mother blurted out.

My heart jumped and my eyes stopped focusing, the kitchen began to spin.

"We are very concerned for you, young lady. We don't want you to go to hell." My father began sobbing. His face bright red. "We don't want to spend eternity without you."

I had never seen my father cry, and his unmasked emotion scared me. I couldn't look at him. My desire to run away grew stronger.

"What kind of game are you two playing?"

"We know you are more than just friends," my mother spit out. "What you girls are doing is a sin. You will go to hell."

This omnipresent threat of hell had dictated most of my choices throughout adolescence, and while I wasn't always a good Christian girl, I did spend much of my time pleading with God for forgiveness, hoping for redemption so I wouldn't spend my hereafter burning and screaming and gnashing my teeth with the unrepentant masses.

"Pam," my dad said, "we can't just sit back and watch you destroy your chance for eternal life."

I could feel my face growing hot with anger and panic. I looked down at my hands to avoid my parents' eyes. I couldn't speak.

"I almost died having you," mom said through her sobs," and I will *not* sit back and watch you go to *hell.*"

I knew the story of my birth, but this was the first time my mother had wielded it as a weapon for Christ. I recoiled, ever more certain that, until I'd met Chris, my whole life had felt awkward and out of sync, and now things were beginning to feel good and right. I finally felt loved and known by someone, and seen, instead of hidden, judged, and condemned. The unfairness of it all angered me. Why did my happiness have to result in losing my parents' love and support? I had just turned eighteen, yes, and I yearned for independence, but I wasn't ready to be without my family, not yet.

"I'm sorry," I whispered, terrified and panicked. I wanted nothing more than for this interrogation to end. "I'll never do it again. I promise we'll stop." I was willing to say anything to make the nightmare end. But my parents weren't ready to leave the ultimate destiny of my eternal soul in my young and incapable hands, and they demanded I go with my father that very night to see Pastor Gary for a laying on of hands. A healing, they called it. If only it could be that simple.

I was grateful for the silence and the air-conditioning in the car as Dad and I drove to the church later that evening. I didn't know what was more oppressive, the stifling August heat or the afternoon's dismal events looping endlessly through my mind. I kept recalling my parents' insistence that my relationship with Chris would lead me directly to the gates of hell where I would spend eternity suffering in fire and brimstone, smoldering away with the rest of the sinners as we writhed in agony forever. Didn't I know, they'd asked me repeatedly, that lying with a woman was the most egregious of sins?

Didn't I know? Of course I knew. I had highlighted 1 Corinthians 6:9 so many times in my Bible that the verse had practically disappeared.

As my father and I left the comfort of the cool car and made our way across the still-steaming tar parking lot and into the stuffy sanctuary, Corinthians thrummed within me along with a multitude of other Bible verses.

Leviticus 20:13: "If a man lies with a man as one lies with a woman, they must be put to death." Romans: "Even their women exchanged natural relations for unnatural ones. Men committed indecent acts with other men, and received the due penalty for their perversion."

I knew them all by heart, had memorized each admonition as well as I had memorized the luscious curves and contours, the sweet and secret depths of Chris's body. How could I not know that what I felt for Chris was a sin? But how could I go forward without her? I couldn't, not in this life. I would worry later about the hereafter.

As I trudged after my father up to Pastor Gary's office, I left my body, remembering the very first time Chris and I had indulged in what I had been taught were perverse and unnatural relations. We had met at summer camp a year before and immediately became inseparable. After camp was over, although we lived about two hundred miles apart, we often spent the weekends at each other's houses, always sharing a bed, snuggling before sleep, a habit that had begun at camp.

That First Night was just another night after a long day of hiking and stealing furtive and passionate kisses on the trails near my house, dinner with the family, a bit of television—yet I felt a new, more powerful longing welling up within me. On That First Night a surge of confidence and courage coursed through me as I moved my hands over Chris's lean athletic body, holding my breath and daring myself to touch her in new and forbidden places: under the waistband of the boxers she wore as pajamas, farther up and under the T-shirt that covered her taut stomach and firm breasts. She did not stop my curious fingers, welcoming my explorations with subtle shifts of her body and small happy sounds. As my fingertips found tender and exquisite flesh, I breathed heavily, and moaned softly. Soon, we were moving together, her hands now on me too, desperately seeking each other's soft spaces. Our bodies pulsed as one as sweet instinct enveloped us. I clung to her, sharing this fierce and lovely ride until rainbows arched from my toes and our breathing slowed, my hands still exploring, caressing her damp and trembling limbs.

"Welcome home," Chris whispered and kissed me softly on the lips. Home indeed. My world immediately felt complete, as my mysterious adolescent yearnings resolved into this new expression, these new ways of speaking to the girl I loved. For a few minutes in the quiet aftermath, I reveled in this fresh intimacy, in the joy of our mutual exploration and discovery.

But later That First Night my euphoria came to an abrupt end when I panicked, suddenly terrified I had just doomed myself to eternity in a pit full of wailing, burning sinners. By finally giving in to temptations I had fought my entire adolescence, had I just succumbed to earthly pleasures and forfeited any heavenly rewards? I leapt from the bed and hastily recovered my abandoned pajamas. I looked briefly at Chris, who slept peacefully already, and ran up the stairs to the living room where I flopped into my father's recliner and prayed. I tried to speak in tongues, but, as usual, the special prayer language eluded me and I settled for plain English.

My church taught that the gift of speaking in tongues is

bestowed upon believers who are baptized in the Holy Spirit. Mere mortals receive this special language, a secret code, in order that they might have a direct and private conversation with the Lord. So far, I was not one of those chosen to have this gift. I'd always feared that God had long ago abandoned me as lost.

"Dear Lord Jesus," I begged, feeling the creeping weirdness I always felt when talking to this Invisible Being I was supposed to be devoted to, for, while I had been raised in the church, its yoke weighed on me, heavy and uncomfortable. "What have I done?" I cried. "What shame have I brought upon your holy name? Forgive me, Father. Forgive me for giving in to Satan's temptations and earthly pleasures. Help me, Lord, help me to resist these terrible urges, to look only upon you and your love for me. I love you, Jesus. Thank you, Jesus," I muttered and rocked in the recliner. "Forgive me, forgive me." As I pleaded for my very soul, still a small part of me was not quite ready for redemption, not ready to dismiss as sinful the completeness Chris and I had just shared. I was so wracked with guilt and righteous anger that I didn't hear Chris come up the stairs. I jumped at her touch and her voice.

"Where'd you go?" she whispered, genuinely puzzled. "Why are you in here?"

Darkness enveloped the living room so I could just make out her silhouette.

"What are you doing?" She moved closer, touched my shoulder.

"Praying," I said, my cheeks flushing with embarrassment.

"Why?"

"Because we shouldn't have." I answered, my conviction waning the moment I saw her. "What we just did, it's a sin."

"Really?"

"Really," I said. "Romans 13:12, 'Don't participate in sexual promiscuity and immorality . . . " my voice trailed off, and when she took my hand and gently pulled me from the recliner and led me back down the stairs, back to bed, I did not resist.

THOUGHTS OF CHRIS, OUR bodies entwined, our fingers and lips seeking each other's pleasures, filled my mind as Dad and I entered Pastor Gary's windowless office where I imagined I could smell the stench of sin: burning human flesh, brimstone, fear. Pastor Gary was a stocky man, balding with wisps of black hair, dressed in a black T-shirt, black jeans, black cowboy boots. He reminded me of Neil Diamond. I hated Neil Diamond.

"Pamela, I am just very pleased that your daddy spoke with me about your afflictions," he drawled in a leftover Texas twang. "I am so excited to pray with you tonight, to cast these demons of homosexuality out, to let our good Lord and Savior in to heal your wounded soul." His feeble attempts to reassure me only scared me more.

He motioned for us to kneel in front of his massive walnut desk, on the plush rose-colored carpet. My father knelt to my left and put his hands on my head and lower back. Pastor Gary knelt in front of me, his hands on each of my shoulders, closed his eyes, and began beseeching God to join us. I closed my eyes compliantly, but the anger I'd felt earlier in the kitchen was still swirling inside me, faster and more furious than before. I wasn't ready for this "demon" to be cast out of me, no matter what the consequences.

"Jesus! Holy Spirit, Heavenly Father, *glooooooorious* Son of God, be here with us now," he commanded. "Touch this young woman, fill her with your love and forgiveness."

"Yes, Jesus," my father said softly. "Touch Pam with your

healing love." Hearing my father's voice calmed me a little. I suddenly remembered to breathe.

For a few beats, the two men waited expectantly, ready for Christ Himself to burst through the door, sword drawn, prepared to do some serious spiritual battle with my homosexual inclinations. I desperately needed a way out of this prison of love and good intention I'd found myself locked in. As the men continued to murmur quietly, my mind drifted back to Chris and what she would think of me in this particular situation. I had given up trying to explain my family's faith to her after that first night. She refused to understand, having been raised Catholic (who are not even real Christians according to our church). Evidently the saints interceded on her behalf and the afterlife was of no serious concern to her. Besides, as our intimacy deepened, I saw absolutely no benefit in pushing my crazy religious beliefs on someone fortunate enough to have escaped them thus far.

I remained trapped between the bliss of our love—this new intimate language we were learning—and an absolute fear of divine retribution. My god was an angry god, an Old Testament god, a god who did not take kindly to any sort of sexual activity unless performed within the confines of a traditional marriage, and, I suspected, only then in the missionary position and for procreative purposes (though to say this out loud would have only revealed the deepening fissure between my parents' faith and my own budding certainties).

Pastor Gary's voice boomed, startling me out of my reverie. "Hahkahlafalafalah. Holy Spirit, be with us now. Hahkawaffleahfalalah. Hahkahwaffle waffle ah."

Those chosen to speak in tongues allegedly all receive different prayer languages, and, like snowflakes, no two are alike. To my ear, they all sounded eerily similar, and Pastor Gary's sounded disturbingly like a Saturday morning breakfast order at IHOP.

"Jee-suzzzzzz, have mercy on this child's soul. In your name we *command* the demons of homosexuality to leave her now! Malakalafalafala makawaffle ah." As Pastor Gary did his best to cast the demons out, I silently begged them to stay.

I sensed my father muttering in his own prayer language next to me; I fixated briefly on his short aspirations and the occasional soft *pop* as he moved his lips. I could hear him fighting back tears, reminding me of the risks I faced if I chose Chris over eternal life.

Could hell be any worse than being trapped on my knees in this office, being prayed for against my will for demonic forces to depart from my body?—forces that gave me both great pleasure and terrible guilt. I could not imagine life without Chris, never touching her again, but I also couldn't imagine going on without the support of my family. Eternal agony of endless burning, endless suffering, loomed all too real for me side-by-side with something I didn't even understand about myself. I knew I had to figure out a way, at least temporarily, to keep both my family and my relationship with Chris. If Judgment Day were to arrive anytime soon, God could see how I was trying to do the right thing, couldn't He? Maybe He would see fit to at least let me past the pearly gates. I didn't need a mansion made of gold, just a small humble cabin far away from hell's furnace—and someone to love. I started to tremble.

As my knees grew achy and my spine stiffened and my feet got numb, I remembered all the other times people had prayed over me, all the times I had answered the altar call and gone forward at the end of the church services to receive my own baptism in the Holy Spirit, my own secret language. So many believers I couldn't count had laid their hands on me or waved their arms in the air over me as they prayed for God to touch me with His grace, prayed that I would be slain in the Spirit and receive His secret code. But each time I went forward, desperate for this spiritual currency, I came away speaking only English and some rudimentary high school Spanish. Now, tired of fighting a confusing internal fight and sad for my parents, who loved both God and me, I continued to tremble on my knees in Pastor Gary's office, knowing that both men would attribute my involuntary shaking to God working within me. Only I knew that I shook with the fear of making an impossible choice. Emotionally exhausted, I just wanted to go home.

I took a deep breath and tried to get myself under control.

A simple solution to my immediate dilemma was within my own power, I just had to use it. I cleared my throat and tried to act confident.

"Barreemabeanabarreemah," I raised my arms slightly, palms up. "Barreemabeanahbean." No demons left my body, and my head didn't spin around while I projectile vomited, but my soul floated above us, hovering over this strange trio trying to make sense of the scene.

"Hakabarreemabeanabarreemah," I gave the *R*'s a trill for authenticity. "Barremabean. Holy Spirit, thank you."

I felt Pastor Gary and my father relax next to me. They continued to murmur in their prayer languages, thanking Jesus over and over:

"Praise you, Jesus."

"Thank you, Lord."

"Thank you, Jesus."

"Praise you, Lord."

"Amen," I interjected, hoping to wrap things up.

"Amen!" Pastor Gary agreed emphatically.

"Praise the Lord," my father said, weeping for the second time that day. "Praise the Lord."

As we walked back to the car, Dad put his arm around my shoulder and gave me a little squeeze. "I love you, kiddo," he said.

"I love you too," I said. I knew I had won an important, if temporary, reprieve from the impossible choice I would someday have to make. I had no idea of the struggles that lay ahead as I learned to speak the new language of my love for Chris while uttering the secret words that kept me bound to my family and friends.

If life begins with the splitting of a cell, my lesbian life began that night in Pastor Gary's study. I was not made free from my burdens, but I split into two selves. My inner and outer being were forced to separate, setting me on a long and arduous path to rediscover what would make me whole again.

A Mother in Israel

Stephanie Durden Edwards

My head presses firmly against the back wall of the Relief Society room. The room is in the back of the local Mormon meetinghouse I attend. I am a Mormon mommy; as a woman and a member of the Church of Jesus Christ of Latter-day Saints, I am trying to make my life fall into step with the things I know I should be doing. So far I have made the right choices. I married like I was taught, "in the right place, and the right time, to the right person." For me, that meant marriage in the Salt Lake Temple to a returned missionary. That was less than three years ago. Now I am twenty-one years old and the mother of a small boy, with another on the way.

My son sits in my lap and plays his favorite game, shaking his head back and forth as quickly as he can. Apple cinnamon cereal flings out of the small blue container in his hand, landing in my lap and on the floor. He is two and loves shaking his head silly. I slide him over to my side so I can bend over my pregnant belly to pick up the cereal from the floor. After I sit upright he begins the game again; more cereal hides in the folds of my skirt until it falls to the floor.

I'm too tired to keep up with this game. The weekly lesson is about to begin, and I don't want to miss any of it. A handful of brightly colored plastic blocks distracts him as I slip the cereal container back inside the diaper bag. I check the floor one more time for any missed cereal, knowing that giving children food in church is technically frowned upon, but three hours of church every Sunday is tough for small children to sit through. Normally my son would go into the nursery—I had waited impatiently for him to be eligible at eighteen months—but he is in a phase where he will not go in without a tantrum. The nursery leader will not keep him if he cries when I try to leave. I wish she would at least try. I want just one hour to sit alone. I wish I didn't feel this way. I hate myself for feeling this way.

Once in a Relief Society lesson the teacher read a poem to the class about having one more baby. I never remember all the words, but the last line sticks in my head: "I'm rocking my baby, because babies don't keep." I look forward to the day that my children are a little older. I look forward to the days that bring more freedom, more time for me. The sanctity of my Sundays in the all-female Relief Society has been interrupted. I don't have long before there will be yet another babe in my arms. I want to want to rock my babies. I want that to be enough.

I try to listen hard, to glean from the lessons the instructions I need to become a better wife and mother. I need help. I need to find contentment in the world of small children and nursery rhymes, aprons and dinner at the same time every night. I have to find peace in my place. David O. McKay said it and we live by it. "No other success can compensate for failure in the home." To succeed, to make sure that my children walk the right path, I have to be a good mother. I struggle daily to humble myself, to be receptive to the teachings of the priesthood leaders and the Holy Spirit. They tell me it is my job to submit. I am a woman. My inner being fights against this role; this struggle comes from a place deep inside me. And though I walk around with this conflict always on my mind, I desperately want to be a good wife and mother.

After the announcements the speaker rises and walks to the front of the room. Today's lesson is about the value of motherhood. I have known since my teenage years that good Mormon women are supposed to become wives and mothers and stay at home. I knew this when I chose to live a devout Mormon lifestyle. The little boy on my lap was born just weeks after I turned nineteen. I'm doing my best to become a Mother in Israel.

The instructor begins by passing out small pieces of white paper, each one containing a quote. I want her to come to me, but I am seated in the circle of chairs as close to the door as I can be in case my son disturbs the class. The papers never make it back my way. The sister seated in front of me holds hers up to the woman next to her—the type is small and she asks for help with the words. Both women are large and wear floral print dresses. I look at them and other women like them and I cringe. I am already more than fifty pounds heavier than I was just three short years ago when I got married. I hate the weight. I am scared to death of looking more like a man than a woman. I am scared, but I have no idea how to even begin to lose it.

The speaker is the mother of six children and as slender as a teenage girl. I look at her curiously; she is easily old enough to be my mother and looks like a shampoo model. Her hair is full and brown and perfectly cut. She tells us how grateful she is to be the mother of her six children—her oldest is a mother herself now and her youngest is only a few months older than my son. She begins by reading a quote from one of our Latter-day prophets, Spencer W. Kimball. "The husband is expected to support his family and only in an emergency should a wife secure outside employment. Her place is in the home, to build the home into a heaven of delight." My heart races; this is exactly the type of lesson I need to hear. I have always appreciated being taught the rules about the role of women and mothers and what is expected of me. Sometimes when the lessons are nebulous I feel disappointed. Today's lesson and these quotes make the picture clearer. I long for simple instructions to help me figure out how to be happy in the role I fill.

The speaker calls on another woman in the class to read the next quote. Again, it is by Kimball, and I feel my chest tingle. Kimball became the president of the church on the day I was born. I have always taken that to mean I have a special connection with him.

"Numerous divorces can be traced directly to the day when the wife left the home and went out into the world into employment. Two incomes raise the standard of living beyond its norm. Two spouses working prevent the complete and proper home life, break into the family prayers, create an independence that is not cooperative, causes distortion, limits the family, and frustrates the children already born." She reads the quote with the stern, quiet voice reserved for Sacrament Meeting talks; her tone rises and falls at the right moments, giving weight to the words. She lowers her voice when she speaks of the day when the wife leaves home to work, and her words have the effect on me she wanted. I listen more attentively. I am grateful to hear these words. Like a wayward child craving the firm hand of guidance and discipline, I need to hear the truth. "Feminism is a great evil," a sister in a pale blue dress whispers to her friend in a slightly Hispanic accent. "Feminism is the great destroyer of families."

I begin to pulse with excitement and revel in the extremity of the discussion. The struggle that exists inside my mind revs up with the intensity of certainty that fills the room. Every day when I wake up I feel a sense of sadness, as if I am trapped in this life with no escape. I know how badly I want to do more than stay home and have babies. I want to go back to college. I want to learn and grow and expand my mind. I think of this daily. Then I spend the rest of the day in anguish over my guilt. I am not good enough. I am disobedient, prideful, and unworthy because I want more. I need this lesson.

While the discussion turns lively, a small group of women sits silent. Some of them work outside the home. One is staring at the instructor and I can see the corners of her lipstick-colored mouth twitch. These lessons are always controversial. I would not be surprised if one of the quieter women doesn't get up suddenly and leave the room. I see the eyes of the woman in lipstick dart across the room, over the sea of hands eagerly raised to get their chance to weigh in.

I stare at this silent group. I look at their faces and search for their secrets. I envy the freedom they enjoy each day breathing the air outside the home. I imagine lunch dates and paychecks and their challenges at work—not mornings spent mopping the kitchen floor or afternoons hauling groceries. As I look at them I begin to pick them apart. Surely if it wasn't for their salon nails, designer pumps, and fashionable clothes they could afford to stay home too. I live in sweats and T-shirts, part of the burden of living on my husband's single income.

Meanwhile, the discussion has continued, and the instructor veers from her tightly scripted notes to drink in the comments from the class. Women who work give up their children for a few more shoes in the closet, they say. Working women support feminism, and feminism is Satan's tool to destroy the home and family. One woman recalls the command in the 1970s to travel to the state capital to protest the Equal Rights Movement. The instructor seems energized by the flow of condemnation for working mothers, as if she is finally free to publicly vocalize her own deeply held beliefs that working women are the worst evil in the world. Her slender hands grip the book she's used as a source for the lesson as she clasps it against her chest. She steps forward and lowers her eyes. Several of the arms raised high fall slowly back down. "Sisters," the instructor begins. "I read another quote here that I was not going to share, but the spirit is prompting me to go ahead." I sit closer to the edge of my seat, wishing that my son was tucked away in his nursery class and that I had chosen a seat in the front row.

"Staying home with our children is so very important." The cadence of her words slows and her voice softens. "A study was done and it showed that a child would rather be home with his own mother than in day care," here she swallows and sighs, "even if the mother is in the next room committing suicide."

The two large, floral women sitting in front of me gasp audibly. Their heads turn toward each other and appear frozen in shock. Within seconds their shock melts, and each individual head slowly bobs in agreement. "Amen" they repeat in unison. I just stare straight ahead. I don't nod my head.

My throat burns, indignation wells up from deep in my chest. A faded picture flashes across my mind. I see a familiar dingy couch; a slight blonde woman lies on it scowling at a young girl. The woman on the couch clutches a bottle of pills in her hand. Her mouth moves. She spits threats over the small girl, who cowers on the floor. She is going to take the bottle of pills and kill herself, because no man will ever want a woman with three kids. The girl tells her mother she is sorry, she will try harder to be good. The girl feels her stomach cramp up; she is afraid of what will happen if her mother swallows the pills this time. Her world will break into pieces. Her mother seems to know this. The girl holds down her bitter hatred and begs her mother to stop. She strains to say the right words and holds her breath until her mother is appeased. The girl wonders if her words will work one more time, or if this will be the day she has feared so many times would come. The girl watches in horror as she wrestles the pills from her mother's hand.

Hot tears sting my eyes and my hand shoots up in the air. I don't think about what I am going to say. It comes spilling out.

"I'm sorry. I have to disagree with that. I can't believe that a child would be better off with a mother committing suicide than she would be in day care."

The shock and horror on a dozen faces slowly begins to reflect my outburst. The instructor breathes in sharply. "Are you saying you would put your child in day care?" the instructor asks me. I feel hot in my seat. My son fusses and I shift him in my lap trying to quiet him.

"I am saying," my voice quivers, "that no child would prefer to be with a mother who is going to commit suicide over simply going to a day care center. And I think it is ridiculous to compare the two. Of course he would be better, and safer, in day care than with a mother in the home with severe mental illness!" I say it louder than I mean to. Every eye in the room is on me.

The teacher squares her shoulders. Her eyes narrow and harden. "You are wrong. Listen to the words of the prophets. A mother's place is in the home," she draws in a deep breath. "Period." The last word is firm and final. The room is silent. My son slides down my lap onto the floor. I stand. I reach for the diaper bag, my purse, and my son's small hand. I open the door and walk out of the Relief Society room.

I walk the few short steps to the set of doors at the back of the church. I open the first set of double glass doors to the vestibule in the back of the meetinghouse; my son lets go of my hand and immediately finds a place on the rug to sit. He is gleeful to find such a fantastic place to play. The small vestibule is the perfect playpen; two sets of glass doors gives an excellent vantage point between the familiarity inside and the freedom of the world beyond the glass. He feels safe and he feels free.

I wish I could feel the same safety and freedom. Instead I stand with my hand resting on the handle of the outside door. I stare out at the parking lot. I could leave. I am angry and confused, the words still cutting through me. My heart and mind tell me she is wrong, they are wrong. But I have always been told that when the prophet speaks, the thinking is done.

I close my eyes. I remember my mother on the couch clutching the pill bottle, her thin fingers wrapped tightly around it as I try to pry them free. I think, could that be better for my son than a room full of toys and children his age? But then shame floods over me and I think: How could I have left the meeting?

I could leave more than just the meeting. Right now I could walk out of this church, for good. I picture myself carrying a stack of books, strolling across the lawn of a small college campus. Exhilaration pulses though my arms and legs. For a moment, I think, I can have it. I could do it. I could walk out the door and take a stand. I have seen other Mormon women do it. Why not me?

I could leave my family sitting in their classes inside the church. What would happen to me then? What would that mean for my children? I look out the doors into the brightness and think of the day I got married. If I left now, that day could become a bitter memory. I don't know if I would have a marriage if I left my faith behind. Everything is tied up in my faith.

Nausea passes over me. I hold my breath to stop myself from throwing up. Morning sickness lasted for the entire pregnancy the first time around and shows no signs of stopping this time. I don't know if I want another baby after this one. If I stay, will that be okay? Can I decide that for myself, or will the pressure from family and church leaders be too great? I have no idea how much power I am going to have over my own life.

But outside these doors, I have no idea how much safety I will have. I have no idea what is out there for me or my children. I have no education. What could I do to support my children if my marriage did not survive?

I see my husband's face and think of the others, our family and friends and all the people who taught me in church classes when I was a child. I think of the way they look at me when they see me holding my adorable son. If I walk through those doors, or even if I go to school after the baby is born, will they still look at me with affection? Or will their looks harden, will their arms withdraw?

My eyes open. I look down at my smiling little boy. I know what I have to do.

I turn back, back to the warm blanket of rigidity and rules and order. I humble myself and head back into the fold. I can't walk through that outside door. Not yet anyway.

Poisonous Promises

Grace Peterson

I'm a nervous wreck. While Steve handles the twists and turns on this stretch of highway, I take in the April landscape, swallowing the rising urge to jump out of the car. It's rare to have alone time with my husband, and if I could mute the steady oration of death-and-doom scenarios clogging my gray matter, this drive might actually be enjoyable. Anxiety has been a faithful companion since childhood, but now, at thirty-three, with the birth of baby number four, the volume has been seriously upped. After several futile rounds of bargaining with God, we're taking a leap of faith, and traversing the unfamiliar countryside to seek help from a stranger.

The seed for today's trip was planted years ago, when Steve and I agreed to visit the church of a friend. From all appearances, it was a harmless, even docile congregation, calling themselves

Bible Believers. The sign by the road read CHRISTIAN CHURCH, and beneath it was an open invitation to all who wanted to learn more about the Bible. From the pulpit, I remember, the pastor declared that bad thoughts were "the work of the devil." He said to rebuke those thoughts "in the name of the Lord." I remember I had to look up *rebuke* in the dictionary. Steve was twenty-one then; I was seventeen, ignorant and impressionable. And I felt helpless over that persistent finger strumming the panic wire in my brain.

The journey from believing my *thoughts* were demonic to believing I was completely demon-possessed took several more twists and turns down the road of indoctrination. Choosing Christianity seemed like a credible solution to a life of ambiguity, where questions piled upon themselves and formed a convoluted tangle of disillusionment—the kind of life that results when parents have more pressing matters than their children to attend to. Embracing the ready-made answers for the obscurities of life, the afterlife, and the end of the world, coupled with regular church attendance, gave two lonely souls a sense of belonging—and a sense of purpose. Unfortunately faith did nothing for my anxiety, forcing me to up the ante in search of the so-called rest for the weary the book of Matthew promises.

Although I was much more determined than Steve, we continued our search for pieces to a nebulous life-puzzle, eventually crossing the threshold from mainstream Christianity into fringe extremism. There was something innately gratifying about being radical, as it played on my longing to be intellectual with the best of them. Looking back, I know I was deluded into believing I had finally achieved enlightenment, and the more I immersed myself in the language of my new, edgy spirituality, the more deluded I became. In our little circle, we discussed what was wrong with the world and how our version of things was so much better—if only people would stop being so self-absorbed!

IT'S LATE MORNING WHEN Steve parks under a large weeping willow. As I watch its lower branches dangle and dance in the slight breeze, I suddenly minimize my troubles and feel extremely foolish for coming here to ask a total stranger for a cure. I'm always so impetuous, jumping without calculating the distance, diving in with little respect for the undercurrents and where they might take me. And here I go again.

A fiftysomething man opens the door to Steve's reticent knock. Our eyes meet briefly and a rush of icy air grips me as I confirm that this is the man I've seen from a distance at church, Brock, the man with haunting blue eyes and a slightly self-aggrandizing stance. He's even more intimidating up close.

Brock ushers Steve and me to his modest living room. As we situate ourselves on the generous sofa, I'm immediately drawn to the huge picture window on the opposite side of the room. It provides a repeat of the view I memorized from the car window and helps me get my bearings.

As Brock claims the chair beside us, I get a sense that this is his preferred seating arrangement and that Steve and I have unwittingly conquered our first assignment. Although he seems genuinely glad we're here, I can't help feeling like we're intruding.

Brock leans back in his chair, crosses one leg over the other, and with full inflection reveals his gritty frustration with the modern-day church. This immediately appeals to my fringe thinking. Later I'll learn that this is his way, charging ahead with his opinions in an effort to either influence people or get them to object and force a debate.

Steve is not a debater. He fidgets a bit with his hands and nods, looking for points of agreement while I study the landscape outside the picture window.

Eventually, either satisfied that he's gotten everything off his chest or detecting my impatience, Brock leans forward, looks directly at me, and asks, "So, what are you afraid of?"

Stifling a burst of resentment over his brash intrusion, I swallow, take a deep breath, and begin my confession. "Um, well, I'm afraid of everything," I mumble, looking down at my sweaty hands. "I feel like something bad is going to happen all the time. And sometimes I can actually see it happening in my mind, like the car going off the road or the house crumbling on top of me. Plus I have these really grotesque images of cutting and torturing people." With that, I quickly glance at him, feeling an infinitesimal sense of release. Like this small admission of a breach in my sanity has in some obscure way begun to heal it.

Another sigh. He shifts, gives me a half smile, and asks about my family history.

"My parents got divorced when I was nine," I say. "My dad was angry and physically abusive. My mom was distant and uncaring. My parents didn't like kids. We were all basically ignored."

"What do you remember about your grandparents?"

"My grandpa died when I was nine, so I don't remember much about him, just riding in his car. I don't remember where we went though."

Unlike professional therapists who, I'll later learn, often find it imperative to keep their assumptions to themselves, Brock nods, smiles, and states emphatically, "Your grandfather took you places and molested you. Was he a Mason?"

Took me places? Molested me? His statement is alarming and highly implausible, but I've heard about people blocking out memories. I just never felt like I had done that. Then again, how would I know? I feel shaky. With little time to process this bombshell, I feel compelled to say something. "Um, I think so . . . " I struggle to recall images of my grandparents' home of so long ago. Then I see it. "I remember his red hat," I blurt. "I wasn't supposed to touch it." It's the first memory I've had of my grandfather in years.

"A fez. All the Shriners wear them. This means he was a probably a thirty-third-degree Mason."

Brock is in his element now. With an earnest gleam in his eye, he educates Steve and me on the underpinnings of Freemasonry—a Luciferic secret society veiled as a humanitarian organization based on the teachings of a man whose name quickly escapes me when a flock of birds lands in the field outside. I watch as they peck at some unseen morsels until something frightens them and they fly away.

Outside—the only place I feel safe. Those vast, open spaces are where I'm free and nothing can fall on me and no one can sneak up on me.

Brock's essence pulls me back into the room. For hours he continues his history lesson. Sometimes he pauses to ask me more questions. I tell him about my family, and he actually believes me and wants to help me. I've never been to any kind of counseling and now I can see the appeal. Being believed and heard means *everything*.

As Steve sits rapt, I feel something I've never felt before: understood. And I feel hope. Never has anyone offered to free me from the torture of my almost-constant inner visions of peril—my never-ending panic. The hope of healing is all I need for this total stranger to quickly, almost magically, become more to me than I can wrap my mind around. A protector? A rescuer? A lover? He frightens me but he appeals to me too. Like a budding heroin addict is drawn to a needle for the first time, my confidence in Brock becomes a visceral force coursing through my veins.

STEVE AND I SPEND the entire day and evening here on the sofa with Brock in his tidy living room. He's offered us snacks, but I haven't had an appetite. He continues to interrogate me and instruct us in the ways of deliverance.

Finally, when he's satisfied that my anxiety and intrusive images come from the Masonic demon of my grandfather, he leans forward in his chair and extends his hand.

"Take my hand," Brock demands. "Healing requires complete submission to Jesus Christ."

I'm too reserved and fatigued to ask what this entails and, besides, it's getting late and I'm sure he'd like us to leave. I've got to hurry things along by showing that I'm cooperative. Obeying, I reach over and grip his hand.

"Now, look in my eyes."

This is much more difficult. I've never been good with eye contact, especially with men.

"Spirit of her grandfather," Brock implores, looking directly into my soul, "I command you by the authority of Jesus Christ to tell me your name." Then he says to me, "Now, tell me the first thing that comes to you."

I nod, my eyes burning with what must be the demon in me.

"I hear the name of my grandfather," I say, hoping this is the right answer.

"Did you enter her through sex abuse when she was a baby?"

"Yes." I don't know where this voice is coming from but ignore my uncertainty and comply.

"Are you defeated?"

"Yes."

"Then I command you to take all your underlings and go to the pit of hell."

Brock pauses for a second, lets go of my hand, and asks, "Did it leave?"

"I think so," I say, trying to sound confident, even though I don't know what sensations one is supposed to feel when a demon leaves.

The clock peals out a series of chimes. Brock ignores it, sits back in his chair, and says nothing. His penetrating eyes observe my movements. I can't look at him for more than a few seconds at a time. Exhausted by everything that has transpired today, I finally summon the wherewithal to offer a meek "Thank you."

Brock smiles at me briefly, then looks at Steve and says, "I'm amazed at how many people are coming to me who've been abused by the Masons."

Steve nods.

ON THE DRIVE HOME, I'm in a fatigued daze. Brock's account of my history is definitely farfetched; but it has this twisted appeal too, like, as horrible as sex abuse is, at least someone noticed me when I was a child.

By the next day, my mind has slid back to doom territory. It's April and still cold, but I can't close my front door for fear I'll be trapped. I cry. I pray, trying to wrap my mind around this new history Brock has dredged up. "God, if Brock is right and I really was abused by my grandpa, please show me a sign," I beg. "I need to hear Your clear direction that I'm doing the right thing by trusting this man."

Shortly after making my plea I feel myself mysteriously drawn to the boxes I keep in storage in the basement. I hate going into this confined space, where the walls would crush me if we had an earthquake, but at the moment I cannot resist the urge to follow this new voice in my head. As I thumb through an old family album, the tiniest corner of a photo tucked behind another peeks out at me like a beacon. I grab it and bring it under a light. My grandfather, circa 1960, is lazing in a chair. A Masonic newspaper is in his lap.

Ah ha. My grandfather really was a Mason! This photo confirms it. It's the *sign* I've been asking for—God's confirmation that Brock is on the right track. I'm sure of it.

Back in the house, I contemplate whether the photo is a good-enough reason to call Brock. I want—need—to hear his voice, but I also don't want to intrude.

I decide to call. "Hi. Brock? This is Grace. I, um, wanted to let you know that I found a picture of my grandfather and he *really was* a Mason."

Brock is in a good mood and seems genuinely pleased to hear from me. He listens and then reminds me that as a Christian I am guaranteed victory over the dark forces if I just *believe*.

We talk for a half hour. As the conversation winds down, a needle releases its complicated elixir and Brock's essence flows freely through my bloodstream. I feel relief after the long day's ruminations and supplications.

"By the way," he says. "I want you to have nothing to do with your relatives. They might try to lure you back into their version of the facts."

"Okay," I say, having eliminated most of them from my life over the years anyway. Then, wrapping up our phone call, I confess, "I'm still really anxious and I keep seeing images flash through my head of my hand cutting my kids with something sharp."

"We didn't get to the bottom of it," Brock states without hesitation.

There's more? The exhilaration of picturing myself back in Brock's living room for another session of being the center of someone's attention is reason enough to have any demon. Soon, when Brock has time, he assures me, I'll resume my rightful place at the feet of the one anointed by God. While my incentive for our first meeting was clear, any reasonable rationale for a second meeting is swallowed up in my murky pool of unmet needs.

OVER THE NEXT SEVERAL months, my relationship with Brock grows deeper and more intense, with frequent phone conversations and face-to-face sessions, sometimes with Steve, but mostly alone. The bulk of that time is spent with him trying to get me to adopt his fearless mindset. He believes that the demon is holding on to my erroneous, fear-based belief system.

"You need to get your thinking in line with the scriptures," Brock insists, more than a little annoyed with my current desperation. "Read your Bible. Kick that demon in the teeth."

As encouraging as he is, however, Brock is also temperamental. Interpreting his moods becomes my raison d'être, and I live my life accordingly. Riding the coattails of a forty-five-minute call, I'll spend the rest of the day writing him a letter, either praise for his infinite kindness or a scathing rant written with the blood pooling on my arm after I've cut myself in another round of self-punishment.

Brock vacillates between being compassionate and affirming or terse and snappy. I never know which mood he'll be in when we talk, and I alter my moods accordingly. "Sarcasm," he calls his meanness in a half-assed attempt to soften the verbal blows he regularly delivers.

Steve is intimidated by Brock's strong personality. And maybe he's jealous too, I'm not sure, but I can feel Steve slowly slipping away as Brock becomes more central in my life.

"People don't understand me," Brock grumbles one day during a particularly animated rant. "I put hundreds of hours into helping you people and all I get is criticism. And, what's worse, I get more flack from church members than from any Masons."

Whether he does this intentionally or not, our relationship becomes an us-against-them scenario, and the air of exclusivity is a palpable, hungry monster. Brock's candid frustrations swallow up our phone time; I'm the willing listener, honored to oblige this man who has entrusted me with his secrets. It's a privilege to be so close to Brock, but at the same time I hate myself for allowing this weird role reversal to take hold. I'm sure it's based on my need for his approval but, while I'm meeting his need, I'm unable to verbalize how desperate I am to have him take my anxiety away.

God appointed Brock to help me, I remind myself. The photo of my grandfather confirmed it. I've got to have faith.

MONTHS TURN INTO A year, then two, then three. Brock's ministry is a part-time endeavor, and when he's jaunting through his other obligations, my boiling desperation and resentment make me a bitch to live with. *How dare he get to live his life while I'm hanging on the edge, waiting for him to make time to help me like he promised!*

I'm not quite sure whether it's guilt that spurs my indebtedness or my subtle manipulation to get attention, but I tell Steve, "I feel like we need to pay Brock something."

Steve disagrees and suggests seeing a psychologist instead, but I spew venom back at him. God appointed *Brock* to help me. I asked for a sign and He gave me one. Steve gives in.

Sometimes I see myself as an urchin who's missed the school bus. As it drives off into the distance, I'm overtaken by a sickening, debilitating feeling of being left here alone—abandoned.

IT'S A SATURDAY, FOUR years into my relationship with Brock. I keep my eyes glued to the clock. It's been *two days* since I've heard from him, and I can feel my withdrawal symptoms getting dangerously close to exploding. After an entire morning spent internally debating over whether I should call Brock or not, I've decided to pick up the phone and go for it. Still, I'm not sure whether he'll be in a good mood or not, and this makes me extremely nervous. I don't want a verbal attack. I want reassurance that I haven't been forgotten. But worse than a bad mood is if he answers and informs me he's meeting with one of the other women seeking his help. It's mostly women he works with. When jealousy and abandonment collide, it gets really ugly!

No answer.

I feel sweat forming at the nape of my neck. My hands begin to shake. If I don't get outside, the feelings of abandonment will strangle me and I'll explode. Quickly donning my running shoes, I wipe tears and mascara-smear from my puffy face and avoid eye contact with my kids. It's bad enough that Steve has to live with a pathetic excuse for a wife, but my kids . . . *oh my precious kids . . .*

Forget stretching. If I pull a muscle or get shin splints it will just prove that I'm a hopeless excuse for a human being and that I deserve every bad thing I get. I begin circling the gravel loop in our rural driveway. It's only an eighth of a mile, so I complete the circuit quickly. Again and again, I circle.

As I run, words pour out of me. "Why did You bring Brock into my life? To torture me? I thought You were supposed to be a loving God," I scream toward the clouds, stumbling over the occasional rock jutting out of the earth. *Brock's probably meeting with one of the other women,* my obsessed mind muses. *They all live closer to him than I do. They're better at doing what he says. I'm a loser, left to suffer.*

A slight breeze cools my burning body. The motion of the clouds above me alternately blocks and lets in sunlight as I continue to propel my body forward, seeking the relief that dangles just ahead but then disappears once I get within reaching distance.

My mind obsesses about my most recent visit with Brock. I asked him if I could schedule appointments with him, "so when the abandonment feelings get intense," I told him, "I can focus on, and comfort myself with, the prearranged date of our next session."

"I don't cower to demons," he scowled.

Rehearing this in my head cuts deep in my soul. I keep picturing a giant zipper running the length of my body. No matter how much I will myself to do so, I just can't seem to open the zipper and crawl out.

The agony of this gargantuan weight in my gut begins to make running impossible. I slow to a walk, heaving, crying hysterically and loathing myself.

The demon isn't in me. The demon is me. I'm a demon. No wonder it won't leave. It's not a separate entity. It's me and I am it.

Tears stream down my face as the full impact of this

realization takes hold. *I don't exist. There is no me. I'm a demon, posing as a human, existing in a human body.*

I sit down, take off my shoes, find a sharp rock, and use it to scratch my feet until I see blood. Bleeding is the only thing that makes sense to me—letting all the bad blood pour out.

STEVE, SILENT AND TENTATIVE, parks the car and we disembark once again. Brock has agreed to see me, but not alone. He has something important planned for all of his devotees.

I push aside the turbulence in my gut at having to share this experience with all of Brock's "others" and hold Steve's hand as he knocks on the door. I ignore Steve's worried expression and remind myself that, if I refuse tonight's moonlight baptism, I could miss my healing.

" . . . These people are *programmed*. They *split* at three years of age and grow up fragmented and susceptible to the forces of darkness . . . " Brock ignores Steve and me as we enter. He's already addressing the crowd of twenty or so unfamiliar faces in his living room, and he doesn't look up to acknowledge me. I feel my heart cinch at the rebuff.

He reads a few Bible passages, then launches into the evening's agenda—his latest idea about how to heal us all. "When we get to the creek, it will be dark. The moon will be straight over us. Each woman will take communion. This is when we'll begin the baptism, keeping each one under the water until she begins to panic and flail around. Then we'll hold her under a little longer until she stops. This will reverse the internal split and heal her."

While Steve stands with the rest of the group, I hover in the back. All these people make me nervous.

I suppose I should be "readying myself" through prayer, but I'm tired. Brock's experimental healing methods haven't helped me so far. I don't have the energy to pray. It would be easier to just go home, and yet I also feel that if I don't comply, I might miss my healing and be cursed with a legion of demons for the rest of my sorry life.

As the crowd heads out to their cars for the drive to the creek, I walk over to Brock and ask him if he'll ride with Steve and me since I haven't seen him in a while.

"I'm riding with Gena," he tells me, then looks at Steve. "Gena's worried that someone is going to kill her."

Once we get to the creek, I can see Brock and a few other men who have already arrived. They're standing in the current, looking at me, waiting for me. As I slog through the waist-high water toward them, I can't help but feel like this is just so freaking stupid. I'm mad that Brock won't pay any attention to me and that Gena, obviously a drama queen, is a higher priority to him.

The moonlight shimmers on the surface of the water and the smell of algae takes me back to my childhood and my father's terrifying swimming lessons. But I'm not a child any longer, and the feelings of anger and rebellion nix the required contriteness I know I should muster for this sacred event.

Brock is saying something, praying maybe, I'm not sure. I'm hovering above myself, deafened by my own insubordination as I ruminate on how pissed off I am.

Without warning and with the communion bread still in my mouth, a bevy of hands plunges my body into the icy water. Instantly, I'm a little girl again, learning to swim, frightened by my father's violent methods. Fueled entirely by involuntary reflexes, I flail and fight, my panic causing a torrent of splashes and bubbles, magnified a hundredfold under the water. And then the adult me finally realizes I was totally unprepared for the distress that Brock's latest procedure is intended to cause.

Finally my panic wins, or the men figure I'm hopeless. They let go and I reemerge, filling my lungs with precious night air. I cough. Water drips off my nose and I rub my eyes as I trudge my leaden body toward the shore. I've got to get away.

But with only a few more steps to dry land I stop myself. No, I can't leave. I can't miss my healing. I turn and wade back to Brock and the other men. I'm prepared now, I tell myself. I'll do it right this time. I don't even look at Steve, who stands at the edge of the crowd.

"Just let me . . . catch my . . . breath . . ." I beg.

But the second time is no different than the first. I fail once again. We might as well go home.

BACK AT THE CAR, I shiver in the backseat, completely undone, humiliated. Steve starts the engine. I can't look at him, but I'm sure he's exhausted from years of watching my devotion to Brock destroy me.

As Steve drives, saying nothing, I have time to evaluate the night.

I'm sure Gena performed flawlessly, but I just don't have what it takes. God is disappointed with me. I lack the faith I need to get healed. And I'm too rebellious. Brock has told me this many times. Now he's got proof.

I try to make sense of my fucked-up life. I'm addicted to Brock in the worst way, but I'm also a free spirit. And the two don't mix. I'm ashamed of my flawless ability to sabotage myself, and I'm helpless over this crazy, forbidden draw toward Brock. I don't have the slightest idea how to escape my conundrum. *Are there twelve-step programs for people-addicts?* I wonder. I can see that the person I'm asking to help me get well is the person who's making me sicker. But I asked God for a confirmation and I thought I'd received it. I've tried to stay within God's will.

I think of what the Bible says about God being a jealous God. Am I being punished? Is God withholding a victorious healing because I'm placing too much importance on Brock and not enough on Him?

YOU COULD CALL IT an epiphany or the final straw or the wake-up call or even the seven-year itch, but the end finally comes months later. In a moment of frustration during yet another unsuccessful healing session, Brock blurts, "You irritate me!"

I wonder if I just heard what I think I heard. *I irritate him? Seriously?* Strangely, this is what it takes to break the spell.

I irritate him.

I don't cry. I don't come undone and write him another scathing letter with my blood. I guess I'm numb with the realization that I finally succeeded in destroying my relationship with Brock.

I can only hope there's another path to healing out there somewhere.

Tilapia Mikveh

Susan Tive

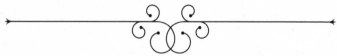

I'm standing barefoot in the darkness. The light from the summertime stars flickers like crystals in the infinitely sloping sky. The gravel under my feet is cold and sharp. Somewhere out in the blind vastness small rivulets of water lap against stones. I can't tell where the dark night above meets the equally black water below. The air smells fishy and alkaline, odd for the high mountain desert of southern Colorado's San Luis Valley.

Just a few moments ago I was inside the overheated double-wide of the pond's owner, Eileen. Her trailer smelled like Lysol and meatloaf and she was excited about having visitors. I sat quietly, embarrassed, as my husband, Geoffrey, explained to her that we would visit only a few times during the summer, after dark, and wouldn't need to stay more than half an hour. She didn't ask questions. "I 'spect all religions," she said, and without hesitation granted me permission to take my monthly soak in her artesian pond full of tilapia fish.

Eileen doesn't care that her pond, filled by water that flows freely and naturally into it, meets all the stringencies of Jewish law to create a perfect mikveh, or ritual bath. For centuries Jewish women have gone to great lengths to immerse each month in *mayyim hayyim,* the living water that makes us clean after our menstrual cycles have finished.

Eileen also doesn't care about the battery of personal hygiene chores I have completed in order to dunk myself in her tilapia breeding pond and emerge from it "purified." I've trimmed my nails, scrubbed my soles, and cleaned my belly button. I've combed and untangled all the hair on my body including my pubic hair, run Q-tips around my earlobes, and determined with one last internal check that I am no longer menstruating and haven't shed blood for seven consecutive days. I do all this because I am obligated to make sure my body is completely unobstructed: When I immerse, the water will reach every part of me.

Eileen doesn't care about any of this, and I don't blame her. I don't care much myself. As I sit on the faded orange sofa in her fake-wood-paneled living room I teeter between anger and exhaustion. *Let's get this thing over with already.* That's what I wanted to say to Geoffrey as we drove away from our summer farmhouse hours ago, leaving the kids with a sitter. On and on into the night, we passed one obscure valley town after another until finally Geoffrey took a left at the ALLIGATOR FARM FIVE MILES AHEAD sign. Apparently, Eileen's pond wasn't the only commercial or tourist enterprise taking advantage of this artesian-rich part of the valley.

Geoffrey was proud of himself for having found the tilapia pond so that we could keep the laws of mikveh during our summer in Colorado, and he instantly declared it kosher. Five years after his Orthodox conversion in our hometown in northern New Mexico and our overnight adoption of the entire Orthodox rule book, our practice had devolved into a desperate mash-up of book learning, creative guesswork, and convenience.

The fledgling Orthodox community that initiated Geoffrey had sputtered and then dissolved, one family at a time moving away to a larger, established city with a school, a butcher, a fancy mikveh. With the recent departure of the last in a succession of failed rabbis, our newly religious family was left alone to make do with the few stragglers that remained. In the summertime, living on our small farm in the San Luis Valley, we became even more exiled. There were no other observant Jews for hundreds of miles. Denver, the nearest viable Orthodox community and thus kosher mikveh was, at best, four hours away.

In this vacuum of community Geoffrey quickly grew confident in his role as the final arbiter of our family's Jewish practice. Even the occasional phone calls he used to make when he found himself over his head and needing to check in with a knowledgeable rabbi were no longer deemed necessary. But I was ill prepared to go it on my own, armed with only my good intentions, my Art Scroll prayer book filled with copious notes and helpful transliterations of all the important blessings, and a few years of observant life on training wheels. Without a sisterhood to teach and support me, the beauty and meaning of my practice was slowly being choked out by Geoffrey's unilateral interpretation of the law.

My job seemed simple—follow the rules: Care for the children, cook the proper food, keep the holy Sabbath, and go to the mikveh— but it turned out to be enormously complicated, with many details to abide by. A pot used for meat could not be used for dairy; the

Sabbath began strictly at sundown, preferably eighteen minutes before the final rays disappeared beyond the horizon. Keeping the laws of mikveh required an entire week's worth of daily inspections of the discharge on my underwear. It was mandatory to keep pinpoint, accurate track of any blight that might derail my "seven clean days" before immersion. Mired in the details and mildly obsessed about doing everything to the letter of the law, I posed no challenge to Geoffrey's hours of Mishnah study, long sessions praying behind closed doors, and self-assured supreme confidence. I was dedicated, preoccupied, and worried Geoffrey would find fault with my inevitable slipups. His decrees stood unopposed.

I SEE THE FAINT outline of the pond as my eyes adjust to the darkness. It's about one hundred yards to the other end. I dip my feet into the warm, smelly water and hear the faint sound of a pump pushing water around the pond. Soft mud squishes up between my toes as I slide my legs through the water, testing its depth and the slope of the shore. *Just how big are tilapia fish, anyway? Do they bite?* I wonder as I walk out of the water and stand nearby.

Geoffrey flashes on the headlights of the Ford Econoline. "Need some light?" he asks, jutting his head out of the van, where he sits smoking his pipe and listening to an Everly Brothers tape. The faint drone of harmony escapes out the open window, and I am angry. Even in this dislocated moment, Geoffrey, with his large black velvet yarmulke, droopy eyes, and well-worn cowboy boots, manages to look serious, pious, as if there were nothing ridiculous about being out here in the middle of nowhere in the middle of the night.

"No, it's better without headlights," I shout, trying to hide the irritation in my voice. "Maybe after."

The lights abruptly cut out, and once again I'm blinded to the nuances of the landscape. I stand in total darkness until my eyes readjust, more quickly this time. I have to stop thinking about going into the pond, submerging myself, and giving in to this ritual that I don't believe can help me any longer or we'll be here all night. "You shall do and then you shall know" (*na'aseh v'nishma*): These words from Exodus rant in my head, reminding me that it is not important whether I like mikveh, or even believe in it. What's important is that I do it: follow the rules, and fulfill the commandments. The answers will come later, if they come at all.

Five years earlier the rabbi's wife had handed me a slim hard-cover book and a black velvet pouch with a stack of small white cloths inside it. For months I studied the details of mikveh immersion, memorizing the minutiae of *taharas mishpacha*, or "family purity." Weekly meetings with the rebbetzin were filled with the dos and don'ts of mikveh preparation and practice. At the end of each lesson, the rebbetzin always recited a few magical tales about the rekindled romances and marital harmony this ancient practice had spun for our ancestors.

I learned the laws. While bleeding, I was *tumeh*, "unclean," "closed," and not permitted to pass the ketchup at the dinner table or remove a stray hair from Geoffrey's shirt. Until bleeding ceased and an additional seven "clean" days passed, there were to be no words of endearment, no compliments, no goodnight kisses or hugs.

Which was much like the rest of the month. At first, mikveh was my hope of reigniting the physical and emotional passion of a cooling marriage I no longer knew how to warm. This ancient set of rules promised to hold my family together as it had held the Jewish people together for centuries. It seemed worth a try. However, it didn't take much studying to realize that the whole practice was mainly orchestrated to maximize the possibility of conception. My days of bleeding plus seven clean days conveniently added up to ovulation. At the moment when Geoffrey and I could reunite, I would be at my most fertile. And if, like a good Orthodox Jew, I used little or no birth control, the possibility of our union falling into the "be fruitful and multiply" category was not left to chance. Those crafty rabbis promised marital bliss and a "honeymoon every month." What they were really after was double-digit offspring.

I PULL DOWN MY skirt until it lies in a ring around my feet, lift up my shirt and bra, and toss them away from the water. Stepping out of my skirt, I roll my underwear down my legs and add them to the pile. In an ordinary mikveh, there is a set of stairs or a small ladder, not to mention a matronly mikveh lady who interrogates you before you are allowed to enter the water. Her job is to look you over for loose skin and recite the final checklist of tasks to make sure you've prepared your body properly. I walk to the pond and once again step lightly onto the sharp gravel that quickly gives way to soft mud laced with fish debris. There's no one there but me. I wade out up to my calves.

The pond is bathwater warm, and I can see steam rising up from the surface. I move deeper, shivering. The water, now past my knees, feels inviting as it envelops my legs. This plunge will change my spiritual status and purify me. I will become *tahor*, opened and cleaned and once again available to my husband's touch. A touch I can no longer feel. Even though it's July, the thin air of this massive basin, trapped on all sides by the Rocky Mountains, feels unwelcoming. There are no clouds to keep in the heat of a full day's blazing sun. No fresh-cut hay, honeybee, or flowering clover lingers in this thin air. The only sign of the season is the constellations, magnificent Leo at its zenith and Cancer arching forward. A zillion more stars make the sky a solid dome cupping the sunken valley. The mountains circle, their snowcapped peaks reach toward the incomprehensible, toward those twinkling lights, the whole world wrapped in the ribbon of the Milky Way. I see only three lights, the shining faces of my children: Ben and Joel and my baby daughter, Tova. Stretching my arms over my head, I hold my breath and dive farther out until the water reaches my shoulders.

I immerse myself three times, as is the custom. Between each dunk, I stand up and wipe the hair away from my face. After the first dunk, I pause for a moment and recite the proper blessing. I thank God for commanding me to immerse. I ask Him to purify me, to wash away all my sins and sorrows, all my transgressions. I ask this even as I question what these are.

Each time I sink down, holding my breath for as long as I can, I enter the silent and timeless world of the matriarchs, my mothers. In ponds halfway across the globe, in centuries long before I was born, Jewish women bared themselves in water much colder than this. These nameless, faceless women immersed, let themselves be surrounded, let themselves be opened up despite risks, poverty, bad marriages, too many children, famine, pogroms, persecution. Immersing with the strength of women to renew and repurpose again and again. The female body spins itself around in phases like the moon, sometimes full and giving like a ripened fruit, other times meager and hidden like a seed buried underground. I am a Jewish female body performing the commandment a Jewish female body is obligated to perform. This is the moment of purity. This is the moment in which I linger, floating in the darkness. The warm water lifts the weight of my body and the heaviness of my doubts off my bones.

After I finish the third immersion, I swim to where the water is shallow and walk out to the edge of the pond. The air is even colder now as I grab my towel, shuddering. I huddle inside it. Faint wafts of steam come off my body and float out into the night. I scrub my legs and torso with the towel. A fishy odor oils my skin.

In the starlight, I find my clothes lying in a heap on the dirt. My body feels warm and relaxed as I dress quickly and head toward the van. Inside, the air is stifling and thick with sweet pipe smoke. The Everly Brothers croon as I toss my towel onto the floor. "Ooh, la la . . . wake up . . . " Before I climb inside, I take one last look at the water and the reflection of the stars, one last glimpse at the women watching over me.

Geoffrey turns to me and, coming closer than he has in weeks, gives me a peck on the cheek and squeezes my hand. "All clean?" he asks. And we rattle our way back down the lonely stretch of highway under stars that I hope will guide me, or at least illuminate the long road home.

Witness

Melanie Hoffert

So this is how it happens, I thought. My brother is lying in my claw-foot tub, naked except for a washcloth over his penis. His olive skin is turning purple and his hands are starting to curl like the leaves of a plant wilting in a time-lapse video. "Dave," I whisper, hoarse. It is early morning, the room a sea-green hue; light is just starting to bleed through the windows. I grab the plug near Dave's feet to drain the water, then whip a towel down from the rack so I can cover the rest of his body. *This is how it happens,* my mind repeats. *The moment when everything gets fucked, when a life-altering event changes a family.* All these years we had been spared, my parents and us four kids: all of us relatively healthy, no horrible accidents, my siblings all married now and having meaty, ripe babies. But this was it, I assumed, the moment so many people face, when something goes terribly wrong.

Dave's eyes, ink-jet blue, piercing, are both the eyes of the person I know today—the quiet, stubborn, creative man who focuses on new hobbies, obsessively, until he masters them—and the eyes of the kid I knew so well, my companion, my little brother, two years younger, who would eat only hot dogs and kicked at the front door, inconsolable, when our parents left us with sitters.

I am the oldest of four. David was number two, and when he arrived I was ready for an ally. At night, when the house was still, I would talk to him through the bars of his crib, telling him we would always be best friends or crying to him if I had been scolded. "At least you still love me," I would say. In the mornings, I stood in front of a long skinny kitchen cupboard that held the cereal boxes. Dave watched me with curiosity from his windup swing. Before I sat down to eat I always kissed his head, pushed the orange vinyl seat that cupped his warm diaper, and asked, "What should I have, Davey?" He could not talk back, but always looked at me with trusting eyes.

DAVE'S FACE STARTS TO lose form; his lip veers down on the left side. He looks at me like he did as a child from that swing, with eyes asking about life, trying to make meaning of the world. "I cawn't tawlk. Loowk awt my hawnds. Wha is wrong wif me? I cawn't strwaiten my hawnds," he says.

"Oh God," I whisper to myself. My heart is pounding, creating a dull thud I can feel in my ears; blood is surging through my body, like it would at the first deadfall of a roller coaster. "Dave, I'm going to get help." I grab his tangled hands, hold them in mine, and try to reassure him. "Just breathe." I run to my bedroom, find my phone, dial 911, run back to Dave. I tell the dispatcher to send someone, quickly, something is wrong with my brother—he might be having a stroke, or something, I don't know. I hang up. Dave is slumped over the side of the tub now, still changing color, turning a darker purple, and trying to uncurl his hands. He can't. He tries to talk again, now with a pause between each word. "Tell. The. Kids—" My chest aches as he starts to relay a message for my precious niece and nephew, one a baby and the other two years old. *He thinks he's dying.*

"Dave," I look into his eyes. "Dave," I say, calling whatever part of him that can hear me to absorb my words—to believe what I am about to say. "Dave," I say, again, cupping his face and stroking his head, "You are going to be okay. Do you hear me?" I feel these words rush through me from a primordial source within my cells. I know, with conviction, what I'm saying is true: "Dave, I promise, you are absolutely going to be okay."

I am not referring to his body—I have no idea what is happening or what is to come. I am talking about his soul. And this is important because, thirty minutes before, he told me he doesn't think there is a God.

I WAS TAUGHT TO be a witness in tenth grade, when the repetitive, sleepy church my family attended in our hometown of five hundred could no longer feed my growing spiritual hunger.

As a child I felt particularly close to God when I played in the trees that framed our farm. There, with sticks breaking under my feet and the moody prairie sky overhead, I knew God could hear me. Evidence abounded. When I was eight I found a wounded robin. Terrified our dog would eat her, I put on yellow rubber gloves, scooped the bird into my hands, and gently lobbed it into the air. Instead of taking flight she tumbled to the ground. I tried again and again, desperate to save her. Finally, not knowing what else to do, I knelt in the soft grass and prayed. When I opened my eyes the robin took a few steady steps and flew away.

In the church I attended as a child, though, God felt far away. Every Sunday I repeated prayers out of the green Lutheran Book of Worship, listened to the sermon, and then feasted from a spread of potluck dishes that glistened like an acre of bubbling, volcanic earth at Yellowstone. Afterward my family returned to our farm, where we shed our church clothes and napped like a pride of lions on our parents' waterbed until our next feeding. For most of my early life this was how I understood religion: as a routine, and separate from the God I felt in nature.

As a teenager, influenced by my best friend, Jessica, I started to listen to Christian music—swoony, dreamy, enchanting music. The voices stirred a yearning in me for the sweet feeling of God that eluded me in church but that I felt in the trees. The voices in this music called to me from the world beyond my small Lutheran church. Jessica and I started to exchange Bible verses in notes too. Looking up the verse she handed me each day was like finding a secret code, leading me deeper into a relationship with God. Within months of our transformation we decided to attend a Christian youth gathering in a larger town.

The gathering was unlike anything I had ever experienced. At first I thought people acted rather strangely, walking around in an otherworldly coma, asking if I had been saved. But then I started to get into the flow of the event. Christian rock bands performed, we danced and sang, speakers preached to us about turning our lives over to God, and at breaks we gathered in small groups to talk. In these groups people wept, moved by the Holy Spirit.

This new way of experiencing God, with riveting emotion—led by leaders who identified as "saved" or "born-again" and not by a denomination—appealed to my spiritually disposed young mind. At the retreat I was awash in a love so palpable I felt as if I was being drenched in holy oil. The air I breathed was electrified, perfumed by lilacs, budding apple trees, and ripe cherries—even though I was inside. The universe seemed charged, alive, and connected to the divine. So when one of the speakers asked us to raise our hands if we were ready to recommit our lives to God, I stretched mine into the air.

That weekend I learned that what was going on at my church wasn't enough; that the fire of the Holy Spirit needed to catch ahold of everyone I came into contact with; that I needed to be—was *called* to be—a witness. And witnessing was critical because, if I didn't convince people to follow Christ, to shut off the secular world and dedicate their entire lives to God, they would be doomed, their souls destined for hell.

"DAVE, JUST TRY TO breathe slowly, okay?" I am shaking but focused. "I'm going to unlock the door. I'll be right back." I run down the stairs to where my other brother, Donny, the youngest, is sprawled on an air mattress in my living room. My brothers are staying with me in Minneapolis for the weekend to go to a Twins' game.

"Donny, get up!" I kick the mattress, but he doesn't move. I run to unlock the door. Next I squat and with all my force shake the bed, all the while wondering if Dave is still breathing. "Donny, get up, something is wrong with Dave. An ambulance is on the way."

Donny groans and rolls, "Huh? Whatever. I don't believe him. I'm so sick of his crap," he says, disoriented.

I have no time to explain. "Donny, this is not a joke. Get up. Hurry! And open the door when they come," I yell as I run back up the stairs.

I am thankful to find Dave breathing, but he is still in the same position, hands curled like he's crippled, face hanging like he has Bell's palsy, eyes looking at me for answers.

AFTER THE YOUTH RETREAT I grew frustrated with everyone back home. Sitting idly in church, repeating prayers, and singing hymns wasn't enough—people needed to embrace the Holy Spirit. And it was my job to show my family, my church, and my classmates the *real* way to God. Jessica and I organized the first ever "See you at the pole" morning at our school, where we'd gather at a designated time with others all across the country to say prayers. I also started to wear Jesus T-shirts and pin a tiny cross on my collar. At home I listened to Christian music and read my Bible. I felt like a righteous rebel for God.

During this time Dave had just entered high school. I told him how important it was to develop a relationship with the Lord. I bought him tapes of Christian hard rock groups that mimicked the music he liked. I expected him to follow my lead, as he had always done.

The boys in my class found it thrilling to target my brother with alcohol and parties as a way to taunt me, the Bible-banger. I'd hear, secondhand, about Dave getting drunk. Furious and panicked about his salvation, I asked him to consider what God thought of his behavior, reminding him of the love and peace he'd find if he lived his life for the Lord. Dave was quiet, his eyes angry.

All the while I was experiencing my spiritual transformation, I was also in love with Jessica, an inconvenience that would cause me to look at things differently in a few short years. In my mind, the love I felt wasn't wrong because it was founded on our connection to God. I had known from age four that I was gay. And when I ran in the trees, wild and young, full of wonder and believing in miracles, I never felt like a sinner. The God I knew was the giver of this love, in fact. But the more involved I got with fundamentalist Christianity, the greater the tension grew between my feelings and what I heard from spiritual leaders. I kept my struggle hidden. As the years passed my inner world became locked in a painful struggle between the voice of the zealous leaders, who told me what God thought about same-sex couples, and my own inner voice that whispered something entirely different.

AN HOUR BEFORE DAVE got into the tub, he'd been lying next to me in my bed, and I'd been annoyed. We could have been kids again, under the covers, with a flashlight. Back then we'd be giggling and drawing pictures on each other's arms. Or, if I felt evil, I'd be telling a scary story to bring my little brother—who believed anything I said—to tears. But we were not kids and I was tired. My brothers had come home, late, after a night out on the town.

At four in the morning they had tumbled into my house like wild buffalo. I'd stood in my robe, watching as they ravaged my fridge and—squeezing my arms, flashing their big grins—told me not to be mad. They are as close as two brothers can be and in many ways almost clones of one another: Both are handsome, with kind faces, easy smiles, big eyes, shaved heads; and they share the same hiccuping laugh. But Donny is almost a foot taller than Dave, and emotive, a big hugger, a talker; Dave is reserved, tentative about affection, usually quiet, conveying his feelings mostly via a furrowed brow.

After they had taken their fill, Donny hit the air mattress. Dave bypassed the couch I'd made up for him, followed me upstairs, and dove into my bed. I ignored him, crawled to the other side of the bed, and pulled the covers up to my nose. Whether he slept on the couch or next to me, I was intent on getting a couple more hours of sleep.

"Mel, Donny is mad at me," Dave said.

"Go to sleep, Dave," I said.

"But he's mad at me," Dave repeated. "We had a fight tonight."

"Dave, Donny isn't mad at you. Donny loves you. Now go to sleep."

"No, he doesn't. He thinks I'm a bad person."

"He doesn't. And you are a not a bad person. Go to sleep," I said, hoping he would grow bored and drift off.

"Does too! What do you know? You weren't there," he said, whining. I realized right then that I *was* in bed with my four-year-old brother—the alcohol-induced version.

I sighed and decided to indulge him, "Why, Dave? Why does Donny think you're a bad person?"

He turned onto his side, away from me. "Because I told him I don't think there is a God. And he is mad at me. And April thinks I'm a bad person too. She's always reciting Bible verses, asking me what God would think when I don't want to go to church."

With this admission I realized I was in for more than a drunken ramble. I opened my eyes and braced myself. April is Dave's wife, a beautiful woman with an open and loving disposition. She, like Dave, can be strongheaded and stubborn. And she is a devout, faithful, deeply convicted Catholic. I have no idea what she would make of this news.

"I'm sure April doesn't think you're a bad person. What did she say?" I asked.

"I haven't told her. I'm terrified. She's sooo religious."

"Dave, April is religious, yes—but she's also understanding and open and a thinker. You should just tell her what you're feeling," I said. "It's better than not talking. She'd probably appreciate it."

"I don't know how to talk about it," he said.

"Well," I thought for a second. "You know, Dave, just start with this: April, I need to talk to you, and I need to feel safe. I want you to hear what I'm about to say with an open heart and not judge me." I imagined this was too soft, too mushy for Dave. I imagined he would burst into laughter—instead he burst into tears.

I tumbled inside to hear my brother crying next to me, especially since he rarely exposed his inner thoughts, much less his raw emotion. Part of me wanted to turn away, plug my ears, and not see, like I would have had he cut his finger as a child and run to Mom. Simultaneously I felt the weight of this conversation—the importance to get it right this time.

"Mel, do you think there is a God?" he asked, sobbing.

This was such a complex, tricky, loaded question. My family and I don't often talk about God or faith. They are as devout in their routine today as we were early on. But for years they thought of me as the religious one, the one who went to a Christian college, the one who worked as a camp counselor, the one who studied each tissue-like page of the Bible, demonstrating to everyone what active faith looked like. I was, after all, on a mission to save their souls. But over the years my perspectives had transitioned; I had changed. And I had no idea what they thought about my beliefs today.

"Dave, I sort of think there is this creative energy that made us. And we are all a part of it. We *are* it. And I think there are many paths to understanding it, or God, or source. And all those paths, all beliefs, just lead to the same impulse. But religion has distorted a lot. I think the human translation of the divine has become harmful."

"But you think there is *something*. I don't even believe there is something. I thought when I'd have kids it would change my mind. But I don't feel it." He was still sobbing, pent-up contemplation leaving his body. And I was feeling sick with care for him.

"Dave, I think that's okay. You may feel differently some day or you may not. But you are not a bad person." I put my hand on his back, wishing the moment would pass, that the air would shift and he'd be okay. But a deeper part of me knew this release was years in the making, and that somehow I had contributed to his pain. I also realized how much I had changed from that young witness who'd clung to dogma, on a mission to save souls.

"But everyone thinks I'm going to hell."

"Well. Everyone thinks I'm going to hell too, because I'm gay. So we'll be there together," I said, hoping to make him laugh. Then I felt something—an old anger, a stirring. "Judgment, Dave, is the greatest sin in my mind. No one has a right to judge you. This is your life and your way of making sense of it."

We talked for several more minutes until Dave calmed down. "Davey, you just need to relax. Let it go. You don't have to figure out everything now, or ever." I waited for his response.

"I think I'm going to take a bath," he said.

"Ah, great idea," I said, surprised but encouraged by the thought of him relaxing. "I'll get it ready for you."

I drew his bath, sprinkled salts in the water, and got out a clean towel. I thought about baptism, and communion, and Jesus washing people's feet. At one time I'd been drawn to these rituals, these miracles, enchanted by their mystery. I remembered how when Dave and I were kids I'd smash white bread, pour grape juice, and give him communion. He watched me. He listened to me. Then more memories surfaced: the years I scorned him about his parties, and the times I told him his music was evil. I remembered how silent he'd become, and, for a time, how distant we'd been. Now, no longer trying to convert him, drawing a bath for my brother somehow seemed holy, a different kind of baptism. I wanted the water to soothe him, to wash away his fear.

After he settled into the bath I listened for the movement of water and then crawled back into bed. A few minutes later I heard his voice.

"Dave, did you say something?" I said quietly.

"Mel, come here," I heard Dave call again.

This was odd. My brother would never call me into the bathroom with him. I cracked the door and stuck in my head. "Dave?"

"Mel, I just don't want to drown," Dave whispered. His face was flush. I went in and knelt by the side of the tub. He was sweating. He looked terrified. "Mel," he said, not sounding like himself. "I don't want to drown," he repeated. I was still trying to make sense of his words and the panicked look in his eyes when he started to breathe heavily, like a dog in a desert. Within seconds, he was gasping for air. This was when things started to go bad.

A DOZEN PEOPLE HAVE filled my small bathroom. A policewoman bends down, shining a light in my brother's eyes; behind her paramedics cram into the area. I retreat into my bedroom to give them space. I can see, through the crowd, someone strap a plastic mask over Dave's mouth. After several long minutes of commotion, people start to back out. A paramedic tells me that my brother will be okay. He has probably experienced a panic attack, the paramedic says, which induced hyperventilation and then extreme hyperoxia. With too much oxygen, Dave's body had started to shut down. I sit on the edge of my bed and only now start to shake.

THE NEXT DAY, WHEN it is all over, after my brothers leave, the house is quiet. We had said few words to each other as they'd gathered their things. I think each of us felt exposed—the moment too blinding.

I go into the bathroom to collect the wet towel I had used to cover my brother's body. Standing near the tub, the place where I thought Dave was dying, I sink to the floor and cry the purest sort of cry—like at a death, like at a birth. Sadness fills me for what the world, people in the world, like me, had pounded into my brother, had planted in him, had established in him—a sense of unworthiness, a fear to explore his own inner world for answers, a silencing of any words of searching, seeking, questioning. And this oppression, I was certain, had just played out in concentrated, physical form—choking him, suffocating him, drowning him. I cry for myself, too: for the young girl who lost her own version of God, a God that lived in the trees, performed miracles, and granted all forms of abundant love. The cry flushes me. It is a cry of relief, a cry of rage, a cry of love—but mostly a cry of thankfulness that I had, I hoped, finally been able to be, after all these years, the right sort of witness.

Eva

Leila Khan

"Look, I think we should ask your mom to come up," my husband, David, says.

I sit on the floor next to the turquoise-and-green Fisher-Price bouncy chair. Looking down at our newborn, Eva, I stroke her forehead. Water comes to my eyes.

"God, I thought I could do this on my own," I say, looking up at David. "But it's just not possible." My shoulders sag as I fold the edge of Eva's pink fuzzy blanket.

Nothing in my life, not the marathons I have run or the one-hundred-mile rides I've cycled, nothing has prepared me for the intensity of the physical pain between my legs after the delivery. This pain takes my breath away each time I sit up to nurse Eva or stand to change her diaper. Everyone warned me about the pain during labor, but nobody told me about the burning and throbbing that lasts for days after giving birth. Nobody told me about all the leaking, bleeding, and crying. No one told me that staying home with a newborn all day would be so lonely.

By the time Eva hits her two-week growth spurt, I am deliriously exhausted by the endless cycle of nursing, burping, changing diapers, and carrying her around all day while David is at work. In my sleep-deprived, beleaguered state, my inexperience and worry overwhelm me. But it's her cries that get me by the throat each time.

During her delivery, Eva's umbilical cord got wrapped around her neck, compromising her heartbeat and causing her distress. She had to be extracted quickly by forceps. Now, each time she wails waves of guilt and fear wash over me. I imagine the crushing pressure of the forceps on her temples, and her traumatic entry into the world. I remember the indentations on either side of her head when the nurse first placed her at my breast. I blame myself, and find myself praying silently to Allah. *Allah, please help me. Please give me the strength to make it through this.*

I agree to ask my mother to come and help. When I call her to discuss the details, she says, "I told David you would need me after your delivery, but you never listen to me. You can't do this alone. You need family, and you need Allah."

I GREW UP IN a conservative Pakistani Muslim home. Although we never lived in Pakistan or any other Muslim country, our home visibly reflected our roots. Regardless of whatever country to which my father's work took us, a clock from Mecca was programmed to play the call for prayer five times a day. Walls were covered with framed Koranic verses, rolled-up prayer mats sat in the corners throughout our home, and rosary-like beads hung from doorknobs.

Incense sticks glowed, teabags boiled for hours in water with cardamon and cloves, and our houses perpetually smelled of fried onions and cumin.

My siblings and I slept in a *shalwar kameez*, not cute pajamas with Disney motifs. We thanked Allah when we began meals and when we finished. We thanked Allah when we sneezed. We prayed five times every day, read the Koran each evening, fasted each year during the month of Ramadaan, and celebrated Eid with sweetmeats, new outfits tailored in Pakistan, and gifts of crisp new dollar bills when the month of fasting ended.

My mother constantly told us that Allah knew everything about us, even the dirty, naughty thoughts at the bottom of our hearts. "He is watching. He knows when we sin," she said. She warned us that punishment for our sins was always around the corner.

One Sunday, my mother decided to implement an idea proposed by the local youth group coordinators at our mosque. "Do you have a spare notebook?" she asked. I nodded. "Good, every day you will make a list of all your *sawwabs* and all your sins. At night, we can count up your sins and your good deeds. Then you can pray to Allah for forgiveness before sleeping." She clapped her hands to stir us to action. "Let's start now!"

Each evening after the completion of my prayers, I dutifully recorded the various Allah-pleasing activities I had performed that day, such as bringing my mother a glass of water or folding the entire family's laundry. But I often lay in bed at night weighted with guilt and fear. I worried about having daydreamed about a boy during prayer, for letting a few drops of water drip down my throat as I brushed my teeth while fasting, or for hating my mother when she slapped me for making mistakes while reading the Koran. I worried because I hadn't included these sins on my list and Allah knew it.

During high school, I became aware of how differently my non-Muslim classmates lived. My classmates wore shorts and bathing suits, had boyfriends, and weren't worried about sin. I had to wear long-sleeved shirts and ankle-length leggings under my P.E. T-shirt and shorts. They talked about camping trips, bonfire parties at the beach, and going off to college. I wasn't allowed to talk with boys on the phone or attend any of the formal dances. Even my classmates who went to church enjoyed their youth groups, overnight retreats, and Christian rock music. Their lives seemed light and carefree. Mine felt like a never-ending list of good deeds and sins, and the unwritten lies that went along with this daily reckoning.

BY THE TIME I went to university, I yearned to break free. I was so tired of worrying about Allah all the time, and having my curiosity muzzled. Although my parents initially insisted that I commute each day the 120 miles from our home to college and back, they eventually decided to let me stay in the dorms in light of my three speeding tickets. Their decision came with a list of admonishments about sinning and Allah's punishment if I misbehaved.

"Remember, Leila, Allah knows and sees everything. Be good and you will do well at university," my mother said as she signed the check for my housing deposit. I always nodded my head in agreement.

AT UNIVERSITY, I DID what every good Pakistani Muslim girl does not do. I smoked Marlboro Lights and drank, tried recreational drugs, danced on countertops in dive bars, and lost my virginity to my white, art-major boyfriend who looked like Flea of the Red Hot Chili Peppers. I desperately wanted to enjoy life, so I followed the example of those around me who seemed to be having such a good time. I wanted to stop being that girl with her arms folded tightly across her chest, a worried frown on her forehead.

My rebellion grew into an enduring rejection of the fear and guilt with which I had been raised. I soon rinsed my life clear of all religious practice and dogma. I stopped praying, reading the Koran, and fasting. The frequency with which I called out to Allah slowly diminished. I even pushed back against the marriage my mother was trying to arrange for me. I wanted a joyful, self-determined way of life.

My parents were horrified and distressed. They thought that, once I graduated from college, marrying me off to a Pakistani doctor or engineer would set me straight. "Leila, you'll be turning twenty-one next year. We must start thinking about marriage seriously now, or you will get too old. I was eighteen when I married your father," my mother said. "Rouksana, Auntie's daughter, just got engaged to a doctor and she's eighteen," she added. Each time we spoke, she updated me on all the engagements and marriage proposals of the other girls in our community.

My mother's efforts intensified as my graduation date neared. She called me one afternoon, breathless with excitement, "Leila, the Ahmed family is interested in you for their oldest son. He's an *engineer* with a degree from *Stanford*. Oh, thank you, Allah, for your kindness. Leila, this is a perfect match for you. The Ahmeds are a *very good family.*"

I shrugged and agreed to meet him to appease my parents and to buy myself some time. A few weeks later Amir and I met for a coffee without parental supervision. This was his way of letting me know he was somewhat progressive and modern. I listened to him tell me about his studies, his job in Silicon Valley, and what he wanted in marriage: "stability, security, and support."

HE WAS NICE AND kind, and ready to settle down. But I had just started my personal journey. Several days after our coffee date, his parents came forward with a proposal. My mother was ecstatic. "Oh Leila, this is Allah's reward for all your good deeds! Such a good boy. Such a good family. You're a very lucky girl!" she gushed. I hesitated, arguing that I wanted to go to law school first. My mother tried to persuade me that I could do both, marriage and law school, *if my husband agreed.*

"Ma, please. I don't want some man deciding whether I can go to law school or work as a lawyer. Please, try to understand." I blinked back tears of frustration. For years I had watched my mother struggle with her financial dependence on my father. When his business blunders had cost our family all our savings and jeopardized our financial security, my mother's feelings of powerlessness left a lasting impression on me.

"But it's your duty to do as we say. It's written in the Koran. You must obey your parents." She glared at me as she tucked her ivory headscarf behind her ear.

"I don't want to marry him. You can't force me. That's also written in the Koran." I lowered my eyes, trying to soften my defiance.

"You listen to me, Leila. I know all about the things you have done at UCLA. You have disappointed us so much. If you refuse to marry Amir, I will curse you so that you never succeed in life. You will fail and fail, and when you come crawling back to me, begging for forgiveness, you know what I will do to you that day?"

She stared at me with unblinking eyes. "I will kick you so hard in your face, you will never be able to get up."

"Ma!" I gasped, inhaling sharply. She stormed out of my room. I sat down on my bed, trembling with anger and fear. A mother's curse is very heavy, and I was terrified of how it would affect my future. I was sickened by how she wielded our religion to force me to submit to her will. In my head and heart I wondered, *How can you have Allah in your heart and say such things?*

I never recovered from the violence of her words. Although growing up I had gotten used to her harsh physical and verbal outbursts in response to my disobedience, the promise of this curse was irreparable.

HER WORDS HAUNTED ME for over a decade. Rejection letters from my top law school choices, a broken engagement with an Italian Catholic man, living alone for five years during my thirties, and being laid off from my law firm job of eight years. As I went from one struggle to the next I would hear her, however faintly, repeat in my ear: "You will fail and fail."

I turned back to Allah in these moments of despair, unfolding a prayer rug that I kept in the back of my closet or carrying *tasbih* beads in my coat pocket that I thumbed surreptitiously while sitting on a train or on a flight. I needed comfort but I also felt angry. *Ya Allah, would you really uphold such a curse? Am I such an awful person for wanting to live my own life? Have my sins been so great to deserve such heartbreak?* Even as I went through the motions, I punished Allah by questioning or denying his existence. My attempts to return to Allah were halfhearted and short-lived.

My relationship with my mother was similarly tempestuous. Reconciliations occurred every now and then because each of us wanted harmony in our lives, but our differences always tore us apart. Long periods of estrangement followed, ranging from a few months to a couple of years. We often didn't call each other on birthdays or Eid, and I rarely called her on Mother's Day. No congratulations were forthcoming after I informed her that I was accepted to my dream graduate school in London, or when I ultimately succeeded in transferring to my law school of choice.

During a two-year stint for my law firm in Brussels, my mother and I did not see each other at all. But even if my life often seemed incomplete because I had such a barren relationship with my mother, was not married, did not have a child, and, for a while there, did not have a job, even if my headscarf-wearing cousins seemed to have abundant lives with their arranged marriages, proud parents, and several children, I wouldn't submit. I didn't want to return to Allah and my culture simply because I had been beaten down by life outside. I wanted to do life on my own terms.

WITHIN HOURS OF HER arrival, my mother has spread out the religious paraphernalia that had adorned the houses in which I grew up. A prayer mat lies open in the corner of our living room, a small, thick Koran sits on our long oak dining table, and recitations of Koranic verses my mother finds on YouTube play on my MacBook. A few days into her stay, she resumes her campaign to convert David to Islam. Although she is relieved that I finally met someone, she still has trouble accepting a non-Muslim for her son-in-law.

"David, did you have a chance to look at the Koran I gave you? The English translation is very good," she says, eyeing our tall, wooden bookcase stuffed with novels and old textbooks.

"Yes, yes, it reads a lot like the Old Testament," he mumbles.

FOR THE MOST PART, David takes my mother and her religious accessories in stride. Other than celebrating a bar mitzvah to please his paternal grandfather, David grew up in a secular household. His father was Jewish and his late mother was Christian. David is unfazed by the Koranic verses my mom coos in Eva's ears to soothe her, or the way she rhythmically pats Eva on her back to "*Allah-hoo, Allah-hoo.*" When my mother panics after seeing the pits of "holy" dates from Mecca in our compost bin, David apologizes, explaining he didn't know they were holy or that she saved them. The only thing that visibly irks him about my mom's stay is her headscarf.

"Does she have to wear it in the house?" he asks, while peeling a grapefruit. I mean, it makes her seem so alien to me. I can kinda understand why Sarkozy banned it in France."

I raise one eyebrow. The ban on the headscarf angers me and, usually, I am quick to argue about how utterly undemocratic such a prohibition is. But now, with a newborn to care for, I feel void of any fire, and I don't want my husband to feel uncomfortable in his own home. "I can ask her to not wear it," I offer.

David shrugs. "I just prefer it when she doesn't," he says, referring to the times my mother forgets to wrap her head in David's presence. I agree. It seems silly that an elderly woman has to cover her hair to remain modest in front of her much younger son-in-law.

One night when Eva is crying inconsolably my mother comes flying into our bedroom with one hand on her head, holding down a piece of cloth that barely covers her skull, the other hand reaching for Eva.

"Ma, come on, David doesn't care if your hair shows. Plus, it's four in the morning. Really. Is it necessary for you to wear the *dopatta* in our home?"

The following morning, my bare-headed mother comes into the family room with a triumphant smile.

"I just spoke to the mullah at our mosque. He said I don't need to cover my hair in front of David. A son-in-law is like a son, so there's no problem."

"Great, Ma, thanks." I smile back at her, relieved and grateful. In that moment my heart softens to my mother and her conciliatory gesture.

Even though I was skeptical of my mother's intentions when she first arrived—I assumed her true intention was to make sure that Eva was exposed to Islam—she has been surprising me during her stay. Each morning she prepares breakfast for us. She fries eggs, butters toast, and makes milky, spicy chai. She feeds me an assortment of nuts to improve my lactation and recovery. She holds Eva while I shower, and readily changes her soiled diapers. She waters our wilting plants. In the evenings, she cooks curry and rice before David gets home. She tells me how happy she is to finally be a grandmother and how perfect Eva is.

Her helpfulness eases the strain of my worries. And these days I worry about everything. Has Eva recovered from the delivery? Is she getting enough to eat? Is it okay for her to sleep with us at night? Why does she always cry in the car? Why can't I make her stop crying? Why is David unable to soothe her? When will this get better? When will I enjoy this? Why can't I stop worrying? Why do I feel joyless in motherhood?

I am bewildered by the depths of my joylessness. I am bewildered because I waited so long to find the right person with whom to have a child, and because I thought that I would happily manage all the life changes ushered in by a child. David and I both were thirty-eight when Eva was born. According to the medical world, I was of "advanced maternal age," but, in my world, I was only now financially, professionally, and emotionally ready for a child. David and I were thrilled when I got pregnant and couldn't wait to be parents. We enlarged the pictures from our ultrasounds and taped them to our refrigerator. We chose Eva as our baby's name in my second trimester because her name belonged to all three faiths in our heritage and because it means "life."

But her complicated delivery traumatized me, and the grief keeps surfacing. One morning after breakfast, Eva starts fussing and my mother tries to placate her with no success. She tickles Eva under her chin and, laughing, says, "Oh, Eva only wants her mummy, right Eva *jaan*? Okay, okay, I understand. Mummy is your favorite." She straightens Eva's onesie and hands her to me. Taking Eva into my arms, I hum "Twinkle Twinkle Little Star," which quickly settles her down. I smile as she gazes up at me with her large, brown eyes, and I feel such tenderness toward both my child and my mother.

W HEN MY MOTHER HAS been with us for two weeks, I decide to tell her the story of Eva's delivery. I am hopeful that we can embark on a new relationship based on our shared desire to give Eva a happy family life. I sit cross-legged on the dark blue sectional sofa with Eva at my breast. I take off my glasses.

"Ma, you know, my delivery really shook me. My water bag broke, but I was not having contractions." I pause, recalling the morning I woke up with my underwear soaking wet. "The doctor said that if I didn't go into labor within twenty-four hours, I would need to be induced. I tried all day but nothing worked.

"They put me on Pitocin, which gives you artificial contractions," I explain to my mother, who delivered all three of her children naturally. "These contractions were so horrible and intense, I didn't think I could make it. But after eight hours of these crazy contractions, I was only dilated by half a centimeter."

I picture David's face, his brown eyes ringed with dark circles, his forehead creased with worry. He held my hand through the contractions and kept me confident we were barreling down the path of labor.

"They said I had to be given an epidural." A golf ball rises in my throat. "That got me dilated, but she was still very high up. I guess she just wasn't ready to come out," I say ruefully. "But each time I pushed, her heart rate decelerated. The doctor told me he would use forceps to get her out, and well, that's how she came out. The doctor said we barely missed an emergency C-section."

My mother sits stony and silent while I continue.

"After Eva came out and they placed her on me, I started having bad convulsions, so they sedated me. David held her for the first three hours of her life." I decide to skip the part about how the convulsions started after the pediatrician examined Eva and told us the forceps had caused mild nerve damage on the right side of her face.

I pinch my lips together to stop trembling. I want to cry and scream at my mother that it wasn't fair. After a blissful and uncomplicated pregnancy, this was not the glorious, natural delivery I had imagined for Eva and me. I want to tell her I was shocked by how little control I'd had over the situation. Through the tears coming to my eyes, I look at my mother's face, seeking softness or warmth. I want her to hold me the same way I am holding Eva, cradled in my arms.

My mother remains motionless except for her head, which she shakes back and forth slowly. "I don't know what to say, Leila. Next time, pray to Allah during your pregnancy. I can give you some verses that you should recite."

I stare at her. *That's it?* I scream in my head. But exhaustion and sleep deprivation numb me to the lack of sympathy in her response. I am too tired to get worked up, too drained to explain what I need from her. All I keep thinking is how I don't ever want to be like her. I suddenly realize that, as I embark on my journey of motherhood, I will have to break these cycles of hope and disappointment, reconciliation and estrangement with my mother, because this is not the example I want to set for Eva. It won't be easy, but if I am going to be the accepting parent I hope to be, I must start practicing now.

I look down at my tiny baby, her lips puckered around my nipple, steadily drawing milk, her head full of straight black hair. I stroke her right temple. *I will give you so much love. I will always offer you warmth and affection. I will always be your safe spot.*

I WISH I COULD offer her a religion as well, but my experience has robbed me of one that I would want to pass on. I don't know a version of Islam or any other religion that is kind, gentle, and compassionate enough to give to my child. But these are the values I will pass on as a parent. And perhaps, one day, Eva will find the religion I always wanted but never had.

The White Lie

Nikki Smith

Fundamental Doctrine #20: Sabbath
The beneficent Creator, after the six days of Creation, rested on the seventh day and instituted the Sabbath for all people as a memorial of Creation. . . . The Sabbath is a day of delightful communion with God and one another. . . . Joyful observance of this holy time from evening to evening, sunset to sunset, is a celebration of God's creative and redemptive acts.

F riday night dinner, especially with guests, was always hectic. At times I wondered why I continued to put myself and my family through this gauntlet of housecleaning, cooking, bathing, and hair washing—all before that golden orb disappeared below the horizon.

Of course it was easier for me than for many of my friends since I taught at a Seventh-day Adventist University, which closed on Fridays at 2:00 PM to allow us believers to go home and get ready. But regardless of this extra time, I always felt like I was running the fifty-yard dash and barely making it to the finish line.

I was nine when my mother came back to the Seventh-day Adventist Church. From fifth grade through graduate school, I was immersed in the Adventist way of life. Between the classroom, my church attendance, and my mother's strict tutelage, the moral certainty of my church was instilled in me. I believed fervently in the church's theology, followed all its precepts given through the Bible and Ellen G. White, our prophet, and, most assuredly, asked for forgiveness of every sin, big or small, so that I could claim my Christian salvation. This was why I continued to prepare for the Sabbath, to eat no meat and wear no jewelry, to avoid drinking and dancing. This was why I'd spent four years in the mission field—one on my own in South Korea and three with my husband, Lee, in Guam—and why I now spent my days educating the next generation of believers. I engaged in this weekly Friday night chaos because I had been raised to believe in the Truth: the capital-T Truth of the Bible and the claim that Seventh-day Adventists were the only church that followed God's laws explicitly.

The Adventists' emphasis on perfection was the reason I pushed myself to be the ideal mother, wife, university professor, Sabbath School teacher, homemaker, and hostess. In return for my faithfulness, God promised me eternal salvation in the afterlife and assurance and peace in this one. The only problem was I had not attained the promised serenity of this life. I studied, prayed, attended services, gave my tithes and offerings, donated my time, and followed all my church's teachings, but still I couldn't see God's "well done, my servant" smile. All I could visualize was His fiery eyes burning through my soul and saying, "You can do more. You're not good enough."

Where was this abiding happiness the preachers kept promising? Why couldn't I attain that surety of God's forgiveness?

MY HUSBAND, LEE, WELCOMED in Barb, newly separated from her recently announced gay husband, and her two sons. She headed toward me with a tossed salad just as I finished putting the dishes on the table. "You boys can sit with the other kids at this table," I pointed to the small card table I'd set up in the corner of the dining room.

Next, Doug, a fellow university colleague, and his school-teacher wife arrived, as did Bill, who had once been a minister but now sold Adventist books door to door. Bill stepped into our foyer with his new wife and their little girl. Soon all twelve of us (including the five children) sat down. We said grace and plunged right in to both our vegetarian potluck meal and our weekly religious debate. It was Sabbath, so our talk would be centered around biblical matters, and with this varied group I anticipated a lively theological discussion. But I wasn't ready for the topic to be the one that troubled me most often in my private thoughts.

Barb, who was usually soft-spoken, started us off with a question. "Who do you think will be saved? Just us Adventists? Other Christians? What about non-Christians, or heathens?"

I sighed. *Here we go, again.* It had been a hard day and I wasn't up for this one. Doug, our card-carrying Mensa member, cleared his throat and intoned, "Well, Dr. Maxwell, who teaches my Sabbath School class, believes that anyone whom God accepts as 'safe to save' will go to heaven. This means people who will be able to 'fit' into our heavenly paradise will be there. Those who would just be too unhappy won't get in. The question is, will a person want things that are not available in heaven, like alcohol, cigarettes, or meat? Will they want to keep the Sabbath? He may not be an Adventist, but if his character is in keeping with God's requirements, he may well want to fit in . . . to please God."

Grace, Bill's wife—probably one of the most conservative in the group—shook her head in disagreement. "No. I believe our prophet when she said that there are many people who will be as if they never were. They will go to neither heaven nor hell because they never had the chance to know the Truth," she said with finality.

I glanced around the group. Heads nodded in concurrence.

Bill took it from there. "Well, that's why we have to spread the Gospel. It's our church's responsibility to bring as many as possible into the fold. Everyone should have a chance to make a decision. Who will they choose? God or the devil? As a church we need to give more money and send more missionaries into foreign lands. The world needs to know the Truth."

This question of who would get into heaven had been secretly tearing at me ever since I'd returned from my own missionary work five years earlier. And my dinner companions' answers were the same old litany of arguments that had never felt satisfactory. I felt a flutter in my chest as anxiety (or was it anger?) clawed at me. How could we think our church of a few million people could proselytize to the billions of people in the world? I believed in spreading God's word, but I also knew it was impossible to reach everyone. And why would God want to annihilate most of the world simply because they hadn't heard the Gospel? More importantly, if He did, was this a God I wanted to believe in and follow so fastidiously?

I could feel the anger build, like a slow heat, starting in my

heart and moving up to my throat until I could taste words forming in my mouth. Too suddenly, I blurted out, "I just can *not* imagine a God who wouldn't admit to heaven a Laotian, a Tibetan, an
African who'd never even heard the word *Christian*. How can an
all-loving, just God deny eternal life to someone just because he was
unlucky enough to be born in a pagan country? I can't see God that
way . . . it's just . . . too mean."

I looked around the table. Lee's mouth gaped open. Bill was
shaking his head, obviously formulating a theological response,
while Barb wiped her mouth and hid behind her napkin. Even the
children's table went quiet.

At first their response to my outburst made me even angrier.
Then I was just embarrassed by my own admission of doubt. A long
heavy moment of stunned silence hung in the air.

"Well, who's up for dessert?" I said finally, pushing my chair
back to retrieve my apple crumble from the oven.

Fundamental Doctrine #18: The Gift of Prophecy
*One of the gifts of the Holy Spirit is prophecy. This gift is an identifying
mark of the remnant church and was manifested in the ministry of Ellen
G. White. As the Lord's messenger, her writings are a continuing and
authoritative source of truth that provide for the church comfort, guidance,
instruction, and correction.*

FOR MONTHS THE DISCOMFORT I'd felt during that Sabbath
dinner conversation kept cropping up in my consciousness. Our
brief debate had freed up the dissonance within me, and I now grappled with a cascade of doubts on a daily basis. I prayed and studied
for clarity, but my uneasiness remained.

Several months later one of my teaching colleagues walked into my office and closed the door. Howard came across as a conservative, play-by-the-rules type of guy, but under his buttoned-up exterior he was a free spirit who was always questioning. I had feared he had stopped going to church altogether lately, but I couldn't ask. I didn't want to know if he had actually fallen that far.

It's funny I was concerned about his churchgoing during my own crisis of faith, but I still couldn't picture myself abandoning the Sabbath by not attending church. Questioning and criticizing the church I could handle; leaving the community was a Mount Everest. I didn't want him to expose me to the same slippery slope I suspected he was sliding down.

Howard sat down and leaned forward, holding up a book, and even though we were alone whispered, "Nikki, you must read this. You're not going to believe it, but Ellen G. White was a fraud!"

I jerked away from him, irritated, my mind screaming at me to get him out of my office. I was already feeling exhausted and guilty for questioning the Truth. I had gone through college courses evaluating my prophet's spiritual gifts; my professors—smart people, all—had accepted her prophetic abilities and piety, though some less vigorously than others. Belief in Ellen White and her writings were central to my life. Without her, other church doctrines would be thrown into disarray. Could I even entertain the possibility that she was a fraud? Could I spend the time and energy it would take to evaluate such a heresy? I took a deep breath.

"Oh come on. It's probably just a disgruntled member who wants to blame the church for everything," I sighed, signaling my desire to get back to work.

"No," Howard shook his head vigorously. "In fact this author has been an SDA minister for many years. He's done extensive research with a ton of examples showing where Ellen White copied complete passages from other authors and claimed them to be hers. Read it for yourself and then tell me what you think."

He placed the book on my desk, turned, and left.

I looked down at the title, *The White Lie*. Was this some sort of joke, calling our prophet a liar? I hurriedly threw the book into my bottom desk drawer. I didn't want to read it, let alone risk anyone seeing it on my desk.

For the rest of the day the book's title kept intruding into my thoughts . . . *white lie, white lie*. By five o'clock I opened my drawer and stared at it, turned it over, and read the fly leaf. Finally I reasoned I at least needed to know this pastor's claims so that I could rebut his arguments.

That night, after the kids were in bed and Lee had left for a church deacons' meeting, I slipped the book out of my handbag.

Settling in on my side of the bed where I normally sat for evening devotions, I took a deep breath and opened the book. I realized that the author, Walter Rea, was the same minister my brother (also a minister) had recently praised for his ministerial gifts. I leafed through the chapters and saw that it was heavily annotated. Extensive footnotes gave proof of copious references and corroborating material. As an academic, I knew this meant I could verify (or refute) whatever this book might say. It certainly looked as if Elder Rea had done his due diligence.

I quickly read through the introduction to get the gist of the book. Then I stopped and stared at my quiet bedroom.

What the author was proposing was absolutely earthshaking to any Adventist who fully believed in Ellen White as a prophet— especially to someone like me who had been protected from outsiders' views of my church for my entire adult life. Elder Rea was suggesting—no, absolutely stating—that Mrs. White was a complete fraud and that the church, down through the years, had not only hidden this fact but had embellished her "gifts" to make her words seem to have come directly from God. I was breathless. Could this possibly be true? I wouldn't even entertain these ideas if they came from a nonmember—but Pastor Rea was one of us.

"The *true believers*," the text read, "will be the unwary, the fearful, the guilt-ridden, the overzealous, the well-intentioned, the unquestioning. Lacking personal confidence in God, they seek him through their chosen saint, who they think has an unfailing pipeline to the heavenly places."

Was I an unwary "true believer" taking Ellen White's words as gospel because the church exalted her as a messenger from God? Was it possible I'd been naive in accepting what I had been told for decades?

My heart beat faster. As my eyes raced through this incendiary publication, Mr. Rea laid out his treatise fact by methodical fact about the beginnings and growth of this church . . . my church. He recounted how Ellen White had suffered from a traumatic brain injury before she began hearing God's voice and prophesying to her followers. He explained how she and the other church pioneers had come up with the Sanctuary Doctrine after Jesus had failed to return in 1844 as many had believed He would.

Sadness and confusion settled over me. If even part of what I was reading was true, I knew I'd have to respond to this new information somehow. Although I'd felt the need to hide my own slowly growing crisis of faith, I do not advocate intellectual dishonesty.

I badly wanted to ignore the possibility that my whole inner schema was about to crumble, but I knew I couldn't. I got out of bed and snuck down the hall to our family room. Kneeling in front of my bookshelf, I pulled out several Ellen White books to check Elder Rea's references, hoping he'd misquoted or misunderstood. But I quickly ascertained that, at the very least, Walter Rea had gotten his E.G.W. quotes right. Cross-legged on my cold, drafty floor, I stared into space again, barely breathing. My head reeled with the possibility that my church—that I—had been taken in by a brain-injured woman with a penchant for plagiarism.

But this book of accusation I'd spent my evening with was saying even more than that. It was claiming that the church itself was complicit in this fraud and had, in fact, been both enhancing and perpetuating her claim of prophetic abilities.

I unfolded my aching legs, shoved the books back onto the shelf, and slammed shut *The White Lie* firmly and decidedly. Before I tossed out the foundation of my entire life, I needed more information.

Fundamental Doctrine #22: Christian Behavior
We are called to be a godly people who think, feel, and act in harmony with the principles of heaven. This means that our amusement and entertainment should meet the highest standards of Christian taste and beauty. While recognizing cultural differences, our dress is to be simple, modest, and neat, befitting those whose true beauty does not consist of outward adornment but in the imperishable ornament of a gentle and quiet spirit.

It took years to come to terms with *The White Lie*, and during that time I lived my own version of deceit. I maintained my good-Adventist behaviors—wearing no jewelry except my wedding band, keeping the Sabbath faithfully, paying my tithe on time and to the penny, drinking no caffeine—but inside I became a seething, questioning skeptic. The more I came to the painful but inevitable realizations, the more I knew this double life could not be maintained, that at some point something would have to give. I dreaded that impending moment. My entire life had been dedicated to the Adventist church; my job depended on it and my whole family revolved around it. There was so much to lose.

Lee was having his own crisis during this time, also questioning his rigid beliefs, but we each respected that we had to make our own decisions. Short of walking away from the church, I looked at several options for myself. I could stay and pretend I still believed in Ellen White. Or I could ignore the lie the church had been founded on and focus only on Jesus—at least I still believed in that part. In a desperate attempt to work out my dissonance I attended several meetings with Pastor Desmond Ford, a brilliant defrocked SDA minister from Australia who challenged the Adventist emphasis on works rather than on righteousness by faith. His teachings made sense. Could I stay—but with some reformed understanding of my faith?

In that vein, Lee and I had joined a more liberal SDA church where we had many friends. But the end for me was at hand, partly precipitated by grief. Three horrific events brought my faith to its proverbial knees.

First, a drunk driver hit our friend's car as she was driving her children to school. Her eight-year-old daughter sustained a severe spinal injury and was left in a coma. Next, a newly married couple from our Sabbath School class was camping in Yosemite when a fellow camper picked a fight and slugged the man in the chest. Due to a genetic anomaly, our young parishioner became instantly paralyzed on impact. Then another young member was implicated in a drug deal and faced imprisonment.

These tragedies happened in quick succession. Everyone in our congregation fasted and prayed fervently for positive outcomes, but in each case our prayers were not answered: the little girl died, the groom never walked again, and the young man went to jail.

I was devastated. I'd been taught to believe in miracles. Even though I was coming to terms with the falseness of my prophet, I still longed to have faith in a loving God who listened to prayers and doled out real justice.

As our community grappled with grief, our liberal Sabbath School class uncharacteristically decided to study a non-SDA book written by a Jewish rabbi, *When Bad Things Happen to Good People*, trying to reconcile what we wanted to be true about God with the unfairness of these three terrible situations. Some in our congregation reasoned that since God knows the end from the beginning, He knows the best time when someone should die. Since we didn't know what would have happened in the life of the little child who died, for example, maybe God took her while she was still saved. Maybe later she would have left the church or done something to bar her from heaven.

This and similar arguments were supposed to give comfort, but I couldn't buy in. I found myself coming away from every Sabbath School discussion thinking that God was acting more like a deadbeat dad than a loving Father who watches out for us.

The final straw came near the end of fall quarter. Dr. Hopp, the dean of our school, came into my office and cheerfully told me she had an anecdote to share. She had never chatted with me before, so I welcomed her and listened intently as she launched into a story about a former master's student.

"Remember, in graduate school, the South African minister in class with you?" she started.

I nodded. I remembered Hugh. I'd liked him.

"You realize he didn't graduate, don't you? Do you know why?"
I shook my head.

"Back then Dr. Mervyn Hardinge [the dean of Public Health] came to me and said he'd received a tip that Hugh, who was married and was doing his field work in Arizona, was carrying on with one of the other students. The dean planned to ask a friend of his to visit the campground where Hugh was staying and befriend him. This way the dean could find out what was going on. The dean's friend reported back that he'd met Hugh and the student he was allegedly having the affair with, and that he had in fact seen the woman at Hugh's campsite the next morning."

"Oh," I said, looking down at my hands. I was shocked to hear this story coming from my dean, who had usually been quite professional. She was now stooping dangerously low, not only for an academic head but also for an Adventist. Though it was actually quite prevalent, gossip was frowned upon in the church, and her self-righteous tone made me anxious.

"So the dean caught him red-handed," Dr. Hopp said gleefully.

"I guess so," I responded, uncomfortable. "Listen, I just realized I have an appointment," I said, gesticulating that I needed to wrap up our exchange.

"Sure. Almost done," she said. "Anyhow, we all agreed that Hugh had to be dismissed. He and his girlfriend were both kicked out of the graduate program. Then of course this led to him being removed from the ministry." With delighted finality, she ended her tale with the punch line she'd come in to deliver: "And, would you believe it, a few years later, Hugh got cancer and died."

I flinched and felt my throat go tight.

She popped out of her chair and suddenly left my office with no explanation as to why she felt she needed to tell me this story, giving me only a judgmental look of "see what happens when you mess with God and the church."

My blood ran cold. Why had she told me this? Did she actually think I'd be glad to hear about this man's demise? Or had she sensed my less-than-fervent commitment of late—was this a warning of some kind?

In the end, it didn't matter. Her narration was enough to put to rest my own emotional struggle and deliver me to a decision. I no longer wanted to work under or be part of a church that had such vindictive and heartless leaders. Like the volume knob on a radio, my faith in the the Truth had been slowly decreasing; with this one final twist, it switched off.

I went home early that day, stunned. And yet, at the same time I also felt relieved that my years of questioning had found resolution. I no longer questioned walking away from the church, the only employer or faith I had ever known.

Fundamental Doctrine #11: Growing in Christ.
As we give ourselves in loving service to those around us . . . His constant presence with us through the Spirit transforms every moment and every task into a spiritual experience.

THAT SUMMER, JUST A few months after the dean's revelatory story, my family went to Lake Mead for a houseboat vacation. One Saturday morning found me sitting atop the houseboat sunning and reading a *National Geographic* magazine (condoned for Sabbath consumption). The cover story was about the age of the Earth and the early formation of its continents. Usually I'd bypassed these types of articles since I had been taught that God made the world in six literal days only six thousand years ago. Now, however, sitting within the majesty of towering cliffs, I plunged into the article with an open mind. I read breathlessly as I acknowledged for the first time the irrefutable evidence of nature and geology. There was so much I didn't know, so much I'd never exposed myself to.

I leaned back into the warmth of the sun hitting my face. In that moment, I didn't need to search for the elusive impossibility of the Truth. I didn't need to constantly beseech God for forgiveness, a practice that had only made me feel anxious and discontent. I no longer needed to ignore my cognitive dissonance or keep myself pure from the evil influences of the world.

In the stillness of that Sabbath moment, I realized that the most important thing for me was to have love in my heart and to be kind, to follow Christ's words of being merciful, to be a peacemaker and to do good for other people. That was it. It didn't matter what I believed about the State of the Dead or if I held that Ellen White was a prophet or if I wore jewelry.

In the months to come, I would continue my gradual and painful separation from the Adventist ways and community. I'd find other work and grieve my losses one by one. Lee and I would find new ways of thinking about faith and love. All of that would come. But for now, I closed my eyes, and as I did so, years of fear and anger gave way to a precious moment of peace.

EXODUS

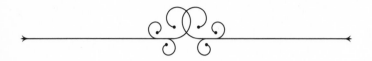

Always Leaving

Donna M. Johnson

I guess I was always leaving. Even when it was my mother who drove away, waving through the dusty rear window of someone else's car, while my brother and I went to live in someone else's house. Even then. Especially then. She always promised not to leave again, then God and Brother Terrell came calling, relentless in their need.

For almost as far back as my memory stretches, my mother traveled with Brother David Terrell and his rolling revival show. She played the Hammond organ for the morning, afternoon, and evening services he held under his big gospel tent. When she wasn't in the services, she was praying or reading her Bible or homeschooling the Terrell kids, all while trying to feed, bathe, and keep my brother, Gary. and me relatively safe. Everyone said it was hard to raise kids traveling with the tent. So when my mother began to leave us behind, I didn't blame her. She said she was doing God's will, that he had chosen her to help spread the gospel. I wondered why God, who everyone called good, was so greedy. Why couldn't he leave our mother alone? Why was he so utterly without pity? I tip-toed to the edge of these questions throughout my early childhood, then, seeing no place to go, backed away.

My mother had been a different sort of girl, gifted and full of faith instead of questions. The stories her father, an Assemblies of God preacher, related from the Bible took root in her imagina-tion and shaped who she was in the most literal way. Like the boy Samuel in the Old Testament, she heard God call her by name, a sign he had chosen her as his own. She could play any instrument she picked up, and this too, she believed, was a sign of God's favor. My mother believed God had something important for her to do, something bigger than marriage and kids, something that would use her musical talent and take her all over the world. Like most women who came of age in the fifties, she married anyway. When it didn't work out, she returned home, pregnant and towing a toddler. She had almost given up on a bigger life when the whirlwind that was Brother Terrell blew through her father's Assemblies of God church. She sold all our belongings and signed on as organist for his traveling tent revivals. I was three and Gary was one. This was the beginning of our time with the tent, a time that lasted for almost three years, before our mother began leaving us behind. So brief a time, and yet its memory flashes through the years, a welcome and a warning.

The tent was little more than a pile of rough moldy cloth until a team of men with names like Red and Dockery pulled it from the belly of the eighteen-wheeler, sewed it together, and cranked the winches on the center poles. By opening night they had transformed a dirty brown canvas into a nomadic cathedral that billowed thirty feet in the air.

It was the dawn of the 1960s. Thousands of people came from hundreds of miles to hear Brother Terrell preach. People too poor, too black, too white trash, too uneducated to matter to most of society. I remember the slow, apologetic way they moved down the sawdust-covered aisles and between the long rows of wooden folding chairs. "Excuse me, excuse me." Their eyes sliding toward the ground, as though their existence were an affront. The way their thin, nervous kids trailed behind. They came for hope, healing, salvation. They came to see the show. Brother Terrell ranted and paced and riffed on scripture for hours at decibels that exceeded legal limits.

"Bles-sed, I say bles-sed, are the poor. You are the ones, the only ones, the ones ordained before time, the ones whose names are written in the book."

He is bent over, running up and down the aisles; the veins on his neck pop up. Hundreds of hands wave in the air. A murmur rises from the audience and builds. Yes, Lord. Yes, Lord. Thank you, Jesus.

"The kingdom of heaven is yours. I said it's yours! But you got to get up and claim it. I said get uuuuuup."

People jump to their feet across the tent, arms outstretched, palms up, reaching for something none of us can see. From my seat in the audience I watch my mother on the platform, high above me, a gapped-toothed smile on her face. Her hands begin to pound out a backbeat on the Hammond and the music takes over. Feet shuffle and stomp. Bodies flail. Faces register utter forgetfulness, bliss. Mothers, fathers, and children churn the sawdust and dirt into a heavy haze that hangs in the air. I stand on my chair and watch, hoping that whatever has possessed them will take me as well, and praying, always praying, that it won't. I watch people stumble through the haze and fall against each other. I watch them wilt or slam backward like felled trees, slain in the spirit. I watch Brother Terrell on the platform, eyes closed, dancing with his hand on his hip. The microphone bounces on his chest.

I watch the crowd begin to move toward him. Everyone breathes the same breath, prays the same prayer. Here there is no separation. I want to belong in this tent, with these people. I close my eyes, but I cannot summon their delirium. What would it feel like to give myself to God, if I just stopped thinking? Would I see angels, speak in tongues; hear God's voice like my mother does? Would I twirl in front of the altar until I too dropped in the sawdust? I open my eyes.

Brother Terrell stands at the edge of the platform above the prayer ramp and waits, his right hand outstretched, red and hot. Everyone wants to be touched by that hand. They carry stretchers to the front. Frail, knobby hands reach up for him. People say they are healed. A tumor vanishes. A woman with a huge stomach. Then, *whoosh*. Nothing. We tell the story again and again. The memory and the story distill over time into a mythology of belief, but no one says this. We say we believe.

We move the tent every two to four weeks. Brother Terrell preaches a gospel of sacrifice. He and my mother put all their money back into what they call the Lord's work. We eat baloney and pork and beans. Brother Terrell's wife doesn't like it. She says her kids need better food, better clothes, a real home. My mother says Betty Ann doesn't understand. Something in Brother Terrell reaches out for my mother. I can feel it, and then one night I watch his hand travel to her knee while we are driving. Betty Ann doesn't want my mother to be alone with her husband.

The adults have dark circles around their eyes from praying all the time. God will meet our needs if we pray harder. We pray day and night. Someone donates a house for us to stay in for a few weeks. Everyone says it's a miracle. There is no electricity or indoor plumbing. Believers bring bags of squash from their garden. We eat squash every day for weeks until finally the squash plants give up and stop bearing.

I watch Brother Terrell perform miracles under the tent and notice that they are whole and perfect. I watch the lame beat their crutches into splinters and walk. The blind see. The deaf hear. I wonder why the miracles in our regular life are always half finished, as though God loses interest and wanders off. Once I start to think this way, I can't stop. The realization dawns on me that not everyone is healed. It's a test of faith, my mother says. Randall, Brother Terrell's son, hemorrhages blood, a river of blood. I watch it pour from his mouth and stain the sawdust while his daddy preaches on and on about faith. Blood splatters the windows of the car we travel in, flows across state lines and rises like the tide in the rooms of the motor courts we pull into when we're too tired to go on. Randall is always dying. The doctors say he will not live to grow up. His daddy prays and he gets better. The doctors say he can't last much longer.

This went on for forty years. When Randall finally died everyone said, I thought he was going to get a miracle.

I was five and Gary was three the first time my mother left us behind. One day we looked up and she was gone. A few months later she was back. She came and went like this for three years. She always cried when she told us she was going back on the road. I didn't cry, but my brother Gary did. Once I pulled him off the chain-link fence that separated us from the car that drove her away. I watched the blood run down the scratches on his skinny kid legs. I watched his mouth stretch into a wide, red *O*, like the entrance to a carnival fun house. I was always watching.

I prayed my mother would return for good, and eventually she did. She made a home for Gary and me, a home Brother Terrell visited between revivals. I watched him emerge from my mother's bedroom, sleepy-eyed and sheepish. I asked my mother if this was adultery, and she said no, because they were married in God's eyes.

The focus of Brother Terrell's preaching switched from divine healing to giving everything to God. He told believers they must sacrifice everything for the gospel. They sold their homes and cars and gave the proceeds to him. Brother Terrell bought the World's Largest Gospel Tent, a red, white, and blue canvas that ran the length of two football fields and seated between five and ten thousand, depending on how close together the chairs were placed and who tells the story. There didn't seem to be enough wattage to light that tent. From a distance, the faces of the crowd appeared as bright little ovals against a sea of shadow. Brother Terrell's followers were so united in their love and support of him the press called them Terrellites. When they ran out of money to give, they brought family heirlooms, china, silver, and wedding rings. When they ran out of valuables, they took off their shoes and gave those to him too. I watched the wealth accumulate; fleets of Mercedes, airplanes, movie-star horses, and house after house.

My mother said God had blessed Brother Terrell for all of his years of hard work and sacrifice. She became his ghostwriter, and her monthly articles always appeared in his magazine under his byline. It was in one of these articles that Brother Terrell, through my mother's words, laid claim to the prophetic mantle. He dressed all in black for tent services and fasted for months at a time. Jesus, God, and the devil spoke to him. He prophesied earthquakes, bombings, plagues of locusts, famine, war in the streets, the numbers 666 stamped across foreheads as well as hearts and minds. I watched people scribble his every word into spiral notebooks. The turbulence of the sixties and seventies lent credibility to his prophesies.

No one questioned Brother Terrell for fear of divine retribution. They believed he was God's anointed, a pure and holy man. They did not know about his relationship with my mother or the three daughters he had fathered with her. I was twelve when my first sister was born and fifteen when the twins came. I asked my mother how she would keep these girls a secret and what she would tell them as they grew up. She gave me the same answer Brother Terrell had given her: Jesus will come before then.

We left the babies with a neighbor when we attended Brother Terrell's revivals. Over time the atmosphere under the tent shifted from celebratory to ominous. Brother Terrell stripped off his shirt onstage and ordered the men who worked for him to beat him with a belt. There is a price to be paid, he said. I watched the audience wail and cry and rock in their seats, arms folded across their chests and stomachs. I cried too, for him, my family, myself, for all of us.

Oddly enough, during the prophetic period our home life was the most normal it had ever been. We lived in the same house and I went to the same school for three years. Brother Terrell ranted against the evil of the World, but, compared to the tent revivals and our personal lives, the world seemed like a tame and friendly place. The families of the kids I went to school with seemed like good people. I liked the way their parents knew things, the names of trees and birds and past presidents. I liked the way their knowledge infused the world and the things in it with a sense of importance and permanence. My family valued the invisible over the material, dreams and visions over reality, the spiritual over flesh and blood.

In my early teens I spent hours walking the land around my mother's home. I watched morning break over the pasture and scatter light this way and that. I watched the sun withdraw in the evening, its long golden light caressing the grasses as it went. I watched the birds rise and wheel above me in a single sweep of motion. If I looked at something long enough, the veil that separated me from it fell away. There was no *I*. There was no *it*. There was only connection. This experience first came to me in early childhood when one of the caretakers my mother left me with locked me out of the house for hours each day. I found in that solitude what evaded me under the tent and in church—the ability to slip the bounds of my own self-consciousness. And yet, it was not so much an annihilation of the self as an affirmation of belonging. I began, without realizing, to think of these experiences as sacred.

I still believed Brother Terrell knew the Will of God and that his ministry was divinely ordained. But the questions that had always been with me grew louder as I got older. Questions about the nature of God and his will and the nature of Brother Terrell and his relationship with my mother. Why did God demand everything dear to us? Why was it okay for Brother Terrell to accumulate wealth when he told his followers to give up their possessions? Why was it okay for my mother and Brother Terrell to live as they did? No matter how hard I prayed, the questions and the doubts they brought would not go away.

Meanwhile the Terrellites were preparing for the end-times. Thousands of them moved to backwaters across Texas and the South, designated by Brother Terrell as Blessed Areas. These places would provide the only safety during the apocalypse, which was imminent. My mother announced that we too would soon move closer to one of the Blessed Areas. I didn't know much about who

I was or who I would become, but I knew I couldn't move to the middle of nowhere to wait for the world to end. Especially since everything in me was still waiting for it to begin.

I took the only way out. I married. My husband was twenty-three and the second-smartest student in his law school class. I was fifteen. After the wedding, my mother and family moved away. I did not know their whereabouts for a time. My mother said the secrecy helped ensure their safety during the apocalypse. For me, there was isolation. There was grief. There was a longing for my own kind. God, my family, Brother Terrell, the tents, the Terrellites, and everything I knew were tangled in a single knotty reality that felt like home. I could not leave one without leaving the other.

I attempted on occasion to rejoin the Terrellites. My husband and I attended a revival where we met a woman with a young son who seemed genuinely deaf. Brother Terrell prayed for the boy and he heard. This miracle turned us into believers for a time. Then all the old questions returned. The constant internal interrogation of everything I had been taught was true caused a rift in my soul that would not heal. I experienced my lack of faith as a character flaw, and I hated myself for it. I turned that hatred on my husband, and we divorced. Life became one long alcohol- and cocaine-fueled party. I contracted an illness doctors could not identify, and, after months of fevers and aches and unexplained weight loss, I went back to the tent. Brother Terrell prayed for me, and I woke up well the next morning.

Jesus tells a story in the New Testament about the deaths of the rich man and Lazarus. The rich man goes to hell and begs God to send Lazarus from heaven to warn his brothers to change their ways so that they too will not end up in torment. God replies that the testimony of the dead is not enough to convince an unbeliever. And so it was that the magic of miracles could not compel me to stay.

It would be easy to say I left the Terrellites because of my mother's abandonment, the deceit and money grubbing, the harsh and uncompromising view of God. These are reasons people understand, and no doubt they played a part. But in the end these reasons are simply pieces of the story. I have come to understand that a large part of why I left, why I was always leaving, was not because of anything my mother or Brother Terrell did, but because of who I was. Or rather who I wasn't. What I am talking about here is a vision, a vision that haunted, inspired, and remained with me through years of agnosticism that nonetheless found me kneeling in an Episcopal church from time to time and sitting zazen in a corner of my room. It is a vision of the tent, stretched out along the outskirts of town where the trash and outcasts congregate. She opens her grimy canvas wings and pulls them under, old and young, black and white, poor and poorer. They clap and dance and wave their arms. They jabber like idiots and smile like angels. The differences that drive them apart fall away. They are, for a few hours, one people. It is always them, never me. I am on the outside watching. This is where I will make my home. This is where I belong.

Separation

Colleen Haggerty

Mom reads me the acceptance letter to Western Washington University. The relief in her voice is palpable. This was what we both hoped for when I mailed in my application two months ago. But now, in my medicated daze, I can only mimic her smile, and wonder if college is even possible anymore.

A few days later, my drama teacher, Miss Tarr, visits me in the hospital with my script for *Funny Girl*. On the last day before Christmas vacation, I'd quickly scanned the casting list in the hallway near the drama department. Next to Mrs. Strakosh my name was penciled in! I spent winter break thrilled with the thought of a singing role in a musical. But now I know I can't be in the play. Still, here is Miss Tarr, smiling, eyes determined, like she is doing me a favor. How can they expect so much from me? College? Acting? Everything has changed.

The car accident has ripped more from me than half my leg; it has torn my picture-perfect future into shreds. This accident is worse than when my father suddenly drowned four years ago. Even though that hurt more than anything I'd ever felt, my Catholic faith taught me to believe that death was simply "God's will." God wanted Dad with him. It was his time. But why would God do *this* to *me*? The stirrings of deep anger roil in my gut.

I turn my gaze down to my stump. Yes, this is the name that doctors, nurses, and now I call the remainder of my leg. Only those of us with appendages that have been whacked off, like a fallen tree, get the honor of using this ugly term to describe a part of our own bodies. The small stump under the white blanket ends too quickly. Enclosed in rolls and rolls of casting material it is too wide. This lump makes me sick, and I'm sure it'll make everyone else sick. I turn my eyes away.

The word *stump* reminds me of a tree outside our kitchen window at home. Native Americans once cleared the land and left a stump, which serves as a prized reminder of their existence before our arrival. I feel a kinship with that lost tree. I wonder if it was as painful for the tree to be whacked by an axe as it was for me to be hit by a car. The tree stump is buried, camouflaged by salal, and it's actually pretty now. My stump will never be that pretty. I will never be that pretty.

WHEN MY FRIENDS VISIT me three days later, I notice how they force themselves to look at my face. I sense their morbid curiosity, their desire to gaze at the remainder of my leg, the small bump hidden under the bed covers.

"Did you hear about David and Sandy?" Karen asks. Karen and I have been friends since sophomore year, when we met in our first play together. "They broke up!" Leslie, another friend from the drama department, chimes in, "I heard David is really bummed about it, but Sandy acts like she doesn't care." David and Sandy are the golden couple of the senior class. I listen as my friends report on the couple's latest crisis, but it seems trivial and meaningless. Their words sound like the schoolteacher in the Charlie Brown comics: "*Wah-WAH, wah-WAH, wah-WAH.*" I smile, nod my head, and laugh when they laugh, but I feel as disconnected from them as my leg is from my body.

I am grateful that Glen hasn't visited me and I hope he doesn't. I've had a crush on him since my first play sophomore year. We've had fun together hanging out backstage with the cast, but we've never spent time alone. I'll be mortified if he sees me in the hospital looking like this. Nobody mentions him, and I don't ask. But secretly I'm curious to know if he's heard about my accident. Does he care? I've spent hours fantasizing about him, but . . . If he didn't think I was cute before, he certainly won't now.

As I lie in my hospital bed later that night, frustrated and forlorn, I weep, feeling separate and alone. Gail, a kind nurse, hears me whimpering and comes into my room. "I'll listen," she says softly.

"They all feel so far away and in another world. They don't understand what I'm going through." She explains that my friends are too immature for me now and that they can't understand. This doesn't help me. I don't want to be the mature one. I don't want my friends to have to "understand" me. That is for grown-ups. I just want to be a senior in high school. I want to turn back the clock a week and replay the whole scene. Take two. In this scene I don't get hit by the car. I go back to school the next day and I gossip about my classmates, take my tests on time, and show up for rehearsal.

MY EYES POP OPEN and it is dark. The hospital is cold and quiet save for the distant hum of this huge edifice working around the clock. Flowers pack my room, masking the antiseptic odor. I don't need to look at the clock; I know what time it is. I've been here for a week, waking up every morning at 3:00 AM to stabbing pain and an incessant deep ache that begs for another dose of medication. I still insist it be given to me by injection instead of orally. The act of taking a pill, putting it in my mouth, holding a cup of water, and swallowing requires too much effort.

I lie with my arms bent at the elbow, hands resting palm-up beside my ears, as if in surrender. I can't sleep any other way. The cast digs painfully into my crotch, and any attempt to readjust my position serves as a nauseating reminder of my missing leg. It is unnatural and disturbing how nearly weightless the absence of my leg feels now. The doctors tell me I lost about twelve pounds of leg. I am reminded of how it feels after a long hike carrying a fifty-pound backpack. When you reach camp and take off the pack the sudden lightness of your body is a relief, but now that weightlessness does not feel like relief, it just reminds me that part of me is missing.

I look out the window at the Space Needle decorated with Christmas lights. For the first time in my life, a twinge of uncertainty and doubt about my faith surfaces. All of my life, the story of Christ's salvation has sustained and comforted me—especially since my dad's death. Now I feel Jesus has betrayed me.

It isn't fair. I've been the "good girl"—reliable, responsible. And, for the past six months, I've dutifully gone to Mass every day before school with my mom. I praise God every morning; I love Jesus and try to emulate him. I adore Mary's quiet strength and want to be as pure and chaste as she was. I'm proud of my Catholic upbringing and my Good Girl status. To my high school friends, I've gallantly referred to myself as Colleen Wait-Until-Wedding-Night Haggerty. Everyone laughed when I said this, but we all knew that I meant it.

The reward of a good life will come, I've been promised—it will come. But this is no reward.

These new feelings of uncertainty and doubt leave me with a tight panic in my chest. *Maybe there's no reward for me because I'm actually being punished!* There's a boy in my choir class with a deformed hand. The first time I noticed it, my stomach lurched, and I had to keep the bile from exploding from my mouth. I can't bring myself to sit next to him, let alone talk with him. Whenever I find myself near him, I am certain that his deformed hand smells like a garbage dump on a summer's day.

Then there was the time when I was in fifth grade and I volunteered at a home for the physically disabled. The first time I went there I was assaulted with the stale, disgusting odor that permeated the house. With a mixture of awe and disgust I watched a man with shortened arms play the piano. Another resident, a young woman with a huge, warm smile, had arms and legs that were so deformed she scooted around on a gurney. Like most of my recent visitors have done, I focused on her face so I didn't have to see how distorted her body was. It was the only way I could keep myself from throwing up. Just before I was scheduled to return there, I got appendicitis, and that ended my volunteer job. I was racked with guilt at the relief I felt that I didn't have to go back. Yes, God is probably punishing me for my sin of being disgusted by other people's deformities.

My faith assured me that my relationship with my dad was not over when he died, it had merely changed. Although I missed him terribly, my faith in his altered existence allowed my life to carry on without him. But this tragedy is different. How can my life possibly go on now with a part of *myself* missing?

If I learned anything from Dad's death, it is that God is calling the shots. What happens to us here on Earth is determined, not by fate or by chance, but by God's will. God makes the decisions and I'm supposed to accept them.

Right now, this isn't good enough for me. I feel buried by anger, crushed by doubt, and overwhelmed by panic. God's decisions don't make any sense. I stifle the desperate need to yell, at the top of my lungs, "FUCK YOU, GOD!" This is what going to Mass every day gets me? This is what saying *no* to the wrong crowd means? As long as I obey you, stay a virgin, go to confession, don't swear, obey my mom . . . Well, it's a long list, but as long as I do it all, I'll be rewarded. Right? If this is my reward, no thanks! And why me? God doesn't ruin the lives of other people who keep fewer rules than I do. *I bet David and Sandy have had sex and it doesn't look like God has punished them*, I almost say out loud. *This isn't fair and it isn't right!*

I don't even care that I might be committing a sin just by thinking these blasphemous thoughts.

I LIE AWAKE A long time fretting. I worry about acting in the play, I worry about walking around a college campus and I worry about how my relationships will change. One fear about my future in particular nags at me: What man will ever want me now? I don't know a lot about sex; I have only kissed a few boys and still consider that icky. But I know that during sex I will be naked. I know that legs wrap around bodies in moments of passion, and I'll have only one leg to do the wrapping. *Who will ever want to make love to me now?* I imagine a disgusted husband on our wedding night, seeing my ugly body for the first time. I imagine myself in his shoes. If I were him, I would want to know what I was saying yes to for a lifetime.

In the dark on my seventh night in the hospital I come to an agonizing but practical decision, and I decide to tell my mom about it. My stomach tightens as I remember a conversation a few years ago when Mom assured my sister and me that she and Dad were virgins on their wedding night. I know she'll be disappointed by my decision. All I've ever wanted is for her to be proud of me.

In the morning, Mom comes in for breakfast. With me in my wheelchair, we sit near the window of my hospital room, which overlooks the steeples of the nearby Catholic church. The gray January light streams through the window, filling the room with the same heaviness that rests in my heart. Her eyes look at me with a mixture of sorrow, strength, and pain. They let me know I can share my thoughts and, at least right now, I won't be admonished. She sits next to me, holding my hand.

"Mom, I need to tell you something," I start, taking a deep breath, "I think you should know that I've decided to have sex before I get married."

She looks over at me and raises her eyebrows.

"My future husband needs to know what he's getting into," I quickly add. "It's only fair to let him see all of me and know what it's like to have sex with me so he'll know if he'll be grossed out." I wait and watch her face.

She looks away from me out into the gray Seattle day. Then she quietly nods her head, pats my hand with hers, and says, "Okay."

Her quick agreement surprises me. Does it mean I am right? She knows about sex. She knows how ugly my disfigured body is. She agrees that I *will* gross out my future husband. I am filled with deep disappointment. I wanted my mom to argue with me and reassure me that I'm still beautiful just the way I am. I wanted her to get indignant and guarantee me that no man would ever be grossed out by my body. The last thing I expected was her approval.

My heart feels hard from betrayal and anger. The kind of hardness that protects from cruelty what is vulnerable.

THAT NIGHT, ALONE AGAIN at 3:00 AM, I pray what will be my last prayer for a long time. "God, you shouldn't have done this to me. I have worked so hard to be good. Don't expect adoration and blind faith any longer. I'll deal with what you've done the best I can with or without your help. But I won't hold my breath." This isn't a threat or an ultimatum. It is my last stand against this unfair, sinister prank.

The reliable rules of reaping what you sow, of being rewarded for good behavior, have changed. God changed them midgame, and so I will too. Though I still need God's help, I'm not going to ask for it. He doesn't deserve that respect.

I turn my head away from the colored Christmas lights glimmering outside my window and gaze toward the warm yellow glow of my call button. I push it and lie back to wait for the nurse to arrive with the next injection.

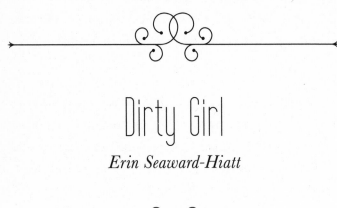

Dirty Girl

Erin Seaward-Hiatt

My mom kept an arsenal of romance novels that lined the higher shelves of our home library. Judging by the pristine quality of the dust jackets and the tightness of the bindings, I suspect she never got around to reading any of them. She was a lab technician who spent her second shift cleaning up after four kids and occupying a double-wide rocker with her high school sweetheart. After all that, who has time for rippling muscles splashed across a page?

As a little girl, I often stood en pointe atop a wobbly skyscraper of never-consulted encyclopedias and dropped my mother's pink-and-purple romance novels—one by one—into a neat stack at my feet. I was playing author. In my mind I was a dashing copper-haired beauty, clad in a flowing dress and laced into a corset that barely contained my heaving breasts. I was a serious grown-up just like the women gazing up from the jackets of these grown-up books.

One day I held a reading before a corps of taffeta-clad Barbie dolls and cracked open a volume at its midpoint to a randomly selected paragraph. I was new to reading but the best in my class, so I wavered only a little as my tentative, little-girl voice visited the subjects of thrusting manhood, supple breasts, and coming together as one. My face grew flush, and I gently closed the book, blushing into my appliquéd teddy bear sweatshirt.

I've often felt at a loss to describe the singular moment when sex clicked for me but, looking back, I could have done worse than what I found in my mother's library. Apart from the lurid and naked-sounding mechanics of it all, I discovered in the romance novels a humanity that whispered to my little-girl spirit. This mysterious force called sex was responsible for about 80 percent of the world's happiness and always occurred by page ninety. It sounded beautiful and alluring, so why did the topic make me—and everyone, really—uneasy and eager to change the subject?

IF MY MOTHER'S LIBRARY was my first primer to sex, religion was a close second. One spring, the gospel waited for me in a dollar-store Easter basket, tucked indiscreetly between a chocolate rabbit and the new pop album I'd been begging for. In that spot, the Bible was a bridge between my life before and the road ahead—an indelicate message to put away childish things and join the ranks of the God-fearing. As I lifted my bounty off the table, the plastic wicker cried out beneath the weight of eternity. I withdrew the leatherette volume and cracked open the cover to read the inscription: *"With all my love and the Lord's, I hope we lead you in the right direction. Mom."* I was fourteen.

When the Easter egg hunts were over and the Resurrection long forgotten, I ate my way through a basket of waxy chocolates and read Genesis. The opening pages were familiar to my young, middle-American mind, but soon the story took a hard turn. God had a striking abundance of sexual advice and admonition. Incest was forbidden and then commanded almost in the same breath, and there was an unsettling preoccupation with rules for pairing up—who can sleep with whom, when, and for what reason. The guidelines of this arbitrary but lofty canon landed a crushing weight upon my shoulders. Why was God so vengeful? If I tumbled into bed with the right person at the wrong time, would I always stay unclean? How could a loving deity damn anyone who simply hadn't heard all the hair-splitting rules?

"God never meant for us to follow every little rule to the letter," my mother said one evening while wiping down the dinner table. "You're just supposed to sit down and read a few passages here and there. For *inspiration*. As long as you believe, you're saved." But how could that be true? Why write the book if you didn't expect people to follow the rules? My Bible landed softly in a drawer and stayed there until high school.

I STARTED GOING TO the Mormon church because I was dating Paul, a Mormon boy, and in the way of high school romance we assumed we would be together until one of us died in a tragic pie-eating contest. Our dates culminated in lulled whispers about undying love, eternity, marriage—which always led to the impossibility of a future together unless I was a Mormon too. I put aside my fear of Christianity's weight long enough to get me to his church on Easter Sunday. I wanted, at the very least, to say I'd tried.

At my first conversion meeting, a twenty-year-old missionary handed me a navy-blue Book of Mormon, standard church issue. Beneath the title, foil stamped in gold, were the words ANOTHER TESTAMENT OF JESUS CHRIST. The Mormons are nothing if not bold; from their pulpits untrained ministers preach the glory of the Bible and sprinkle in the church's singular narrative about Christ's ministry to the ancient Americas. Put away doubt, and even a skeptic will cheer at the church's description of a humble farm boy praying for truth and receiving the wisdom of a prophet.

The God of Mormonism had a fatherly touch. He was less willing to fly off the handle over a botched burnt offering or fumbled prayer than the God I'd read about in Genesis. Mormon dogma was forgiving and offered modern prophets, a wealth of scripture, and temples that would provide salvation for even those who never got around to it in life. It was beautiful and thorough, so when my boyfriend asked if he could baptize me, I willingly threw on an unflattering, white jumpsuit and reclined in a shallow font at the foot of an overcrowded reception room. My mother sat in the front row, and I saw complicated joy from behind her Mona Lisa mien as the afternoon sun shone through an opalescent pane.

AS TIME PASSED, I became enraptured by the majesty of Christ's ministry and the Resurrection—the cornerstone of Mormon faith. When I converted, I converted to Christ, and all the other little add-ons seemed incidental. No tea or coffee? No problem. Weekly seminary? No one said you could become enlightened without doing a little homework. Always wear a skirt to church? Lucy Stone would turn in her grave, but who wouldn't throw on a pencil skirt to impress a major deity? I embraced the minor Mormonisms with pride, attending three-hour church services and offering up epic prayers before nodding off to sleep each night. After all, what were these slight peculiarities compared to the reward of eternal salvation?

As I grew closer to the gospel, the rules were harder to follow, and my relationship with Paul became rocky. He wanted sex. I knew by now we shouldn't. The pressure compounded with every night that he stormed from my parents' house, fuming that I had once again blocked the kick that would have landed us on God's vengeful side. Each night that Paul slammed the door in my face, I returned to my quiet room fighting back the bitter confusion that comes with being young and trying to do the right thing. On a really good day, Paul would take my hand and insist that Joseph Smith had brought the world God's lost truths, that obedience to his revealed laws would bring us to Celestial glory. On an average day though, he would get me alone, fondle me through half of *Pulp Fiction*, and leave in a huff when I refused to take my pants off. I was paralyzed, knowing that sex was a given in teenage life for most of my friends, but also that my newly adopted church asked its youth to maintain chastity with all the maturity and discipline of a Jedi. In moments when sex seemed like a savvy move, I played back the magnified evils of wanting to feel sexy and desired—evils covered at length at my young women's meetings at church. And while I never felt wicked for acknowledging my sexuality, rules were rules. And I'd agreed to follow every one of them in exchange for something much more important than the twenty-eight-second experience of sleeping with a high school boy.

Besides, if I crossed the line, I'd have to repent to both God and the local bishop. This meant I could not partake of the weekly sacrament, I could not attend the temple, where soul-saving ordinances take place, and I could not lead a church meeting in prayer. If I gave in, I'd be denied the things that I now felt kept me strong.

ONE SUNDAY, SISTER JOHNSON clapped her hands together to settle the chattering throng and gestured toward a plate she had brought to class of oatmeal-raisins dusted generously with dirt and small bits of yard clippings. "I brought cookies for everyone to share! Go ahead . . . everybody take one." We recoiled, and I glared into her sunny face, irritated.

"You girls wouldn't want to eat a dirty cookie, now would you? If you lose your virtue before marriage, you're just like this plate of cookies here," she intoned, a sly, accomplished smile edging across her dimpled face. "And *nobody* wants to eat a filthy cookie."

Her clever prelude out of the way, Sister Johnson launched into a lesson covering such godly topics as abstinence and modesty, and how good boys won't be knocking down the door for girls who dress in shorts and form-fitting tops—practically walking pornography. The message was clear: If we wanted good husbands—the ultimate aspiration for a committed Mormon girl—we had to enter marriage as flawless as the glittering diamonds that would someday grace our fingers. If I gave in to my boyfriend, I would be tainted forever. Christ himself couldn't fix me. Even after earnest repentance, a stain would show on my countenance, and all the good boys would see right through to my sullied core. And because boys are just more sexual than girls, I could be sure that the guilt would fall squarely on me as the only party lucid enough to cry out and stop a sin.

I was confused, though. Atonement was supposed to take care of everything, wasn't it? It was a comprehensive benefits package that absolved you of liability as long as you pursued forgiveness sincerely. If you cheated on a calculus test, you could pray on your own and be forgiven. But with sex, the message was blurry. If you had sex, you'd now be dirty, and this was not a sin you could work out just between you and God. You needed the help of the bishop to be reinstated with God and the church, you had to tell a mortal man every juicy detail. And even though you'd technically be forgiven, all the cautionary tales screamed that you'd never be the same again.

A FEW MONTHS LATER I became a dirty cookie. Paul said he loved me, and that I must not love him if I didn't put out. Why was I being such a frigid bitch? It wasn't like anyone else followed the rules, so we really didn't need to tell the bishop until we were ready to get married. It was my job as his girlfriend, and I needed to either put out or get lost.

I told myself I slept with him because I wanted to, but really what I wanted was to feel sexy and worth discovering. He wasn't a good guy, but he was my boyfriend—maybe the only one I would ever find. I couldn't conceive of my future beyond track practice and half-dissected frogs. So, I began having sex at sixteen, and I wore the guilt like a mask until my sophomore year of college.

THE REALITY OF OUR intimacy lingered on through my first few semesters of college, placing a shameful gulf between who I was and who God wanted me to be. I felt my sexuality negated my positive spirituality, but still I tried hard to be a good Mormon girl. One night my roommate bounced into our apartment and announced that she'd told the bishop about her high school boyfriend and was finally ready to return to the temple. She'd been a wreck for months, going about her college life without really enjoying it because of her sin-burdened heart. Tonight, the glow had returned to her face, and her eyes glimmered as she told me how much better I would feel once I got my own confession off my chest.

"It's no big deal!" she promised.

Maybe she was right. Fear was paralyzing me; without taking this next step I would remain stagnant, always falling short of the transcendence I so desperately sought.

Two days passed before I could get up my courage. Then I met with my bishop in a hot, little room in the basement of my dorm complex at the Christian university I attended. The bishop had silvery hair that offset a kind, suntanned face. He had the look of a seasoned grandfather, the kind of guy who wears Tommy Bahama to a picnic and knows the names of all his grandchildren's pets. His sparkling eyes calmed my nerves, and I eased into one of the uncomfortable folding chairs that flanked a small table.

It was the first time I'd ever been alone with him, so we started with some perfunctory getting-to-know-you questions. He let fly an arsenal as if he were reading the questions off an index card: "How are you? Where are you from? What is your major? What do you want to do with that?" The cinderblock walls were Spartan, the headachy beige offset by only one embellishment: a printed reproduction of Christ tacked onto a thin strip of cork. The Savior's eyes blazed as the bishop and I shared our trifling pas de deux. The familiar eyes urged, *Tell him why you're really here.*

The overhead light began to buzz when my confession spilled

indelicately into the open air between us. The bishop's grandfatherly demeanor retreated now, leaving just a tired, old man, poised to hear about my erotic life. His stewardship as a church official required him to pry, to know the full story. I struggled to meet his eyes as he pressed me for details. Had I had intercourse, or just heavy-petted? How often? Was it still going on, or had I stopped the behavior? Had it been just the one partner?

I snuck a glance at him with this last question. Deep creases formed on the bishop's leathery forehead. I sighed and relayed the most personal parts of my life, unsure of which details were need-to-know and which would only make him blush. When I was through, the bishop did not scold my disobedience or pen a brief letter recommending my expulsion from the church's university. Instead, wearing the same wooden expression he'd adopted earlier, he told me that, thanks to Christ's atoning sacrifice, I could repent, be forgiven, and return to the temple when I was ready.

"That usually takes six months to a year," he said with a slight smile, and I wondered why temporal months meant so much to an eternal God. Still, I allowed myself to breathe again, and my heaving sigh expelled the guilt that had chained up my soul. When the meeting ended, I walked out of the office by way of a dank stairwell and into what I hoped would be a new and brighter life.

Only it wasn't brighter after my confession. After four years together, Paul and I still lived half a country apart. At the university I had friends, a schedule that would never quite fit on my tiny white board. Back home, Paul had little else but paranoia and free time. More than once a week he'd pick a fight at forty cents a minute and then admit he'd done it to keep me on the phone. Insecurity consumed him. I thought that hormones had made him forceful in high school and that the distance was doing it now. When I returned home later that year I married him, hoping it would all go away so that I could enjoy the man I wanted so badly to see in him.

At least legally wed we wouldn't clash with the church, and I would be fulfilling my duty to commit my life to my only sexual partner. Soon after the wedding, however, Paul abandoned all remaining pretense of emotional stability and grew violent. I finally had to leave him to protect myself. By my junior year, I was a divorcée peering out at my whole life from the horizon, with nothing but a box of clothes and a blender. I'd repented for what I'd done, but if church had taught me anything, it was that searching for a new boyfriend would mean explaining why I was a dirty cookie, and why I hadn't waited. Life would be more complicated than ever.

ON A SUNNY AFTERNOON just before my last semester of senior year, I made my way through an ostentatious conference center built by the CEO of a successful multilevel marketing company. *Here I go again,* I thought. In my haste, my stiletto heels clacked hard against the high-polished marble in the foyer, sending ghostly echoes dancing through the open space. I shuffled past a small bistro where two youngish businessmen chatted over lunch. Across the hall stood a wide bank of elevators that would carry me upstairs for an audience with the CEO, who moonlighted as my area's bishop.

I stepped into the spacious lift and pushed the FOUR button. When the elevator glided to a halt, the doors parted to reveal a small reception desk. I gave my name to the man seated behind the counter and had barely sat down myself when the CEO swung open his door, revealing a cavernous maw of an office.

"Thank you for meeting me here. Erin, right?" he said as we

shook hands and bellied up to a sprawling conference table in a room affording a view of snowcapped mountains.

"No problem, Bishop. I appreciate your flexibility on such short notice."

I hadn't been under this bishop's watch for long, so he opened with a smattering of vague and easy questions, just as my first confessor had. Nervous and wanting to get to the point, I spat out details about my hometown in Illinois, how I was the only Mormon in the family, and yes, that is hard sometimes. Halfway into explaining what my major was, I paused. I was going to have a panic attack if I didn't come out with it.

"Actually, Bishop, I wanted to talk to you because I've done something I want to repent of." He wore a grave expression now and waited for me to elaborate. "So I've been dating this new guy for a few months now. Spencer. And we really care about each other. I actually think he might be the one. And after my divorce I never expected I'd meet someone as good or kind or exciting as he is. We've been getting much closer lately, and, well . . . "

"You went too far?" The bishop was kind but severe. I nodded, my shame washing over me. He pressed for further details. Just how far was too far? Were we talking about intercourse or something else? Did I realize that oral sex and intercourse were equally severe in God's eyes? Did I remember what the Book of Mormon says about premarital sex?

Of course I had read many times what the Book of Mormon says. That dog-eared page in my scriptures was scarred with underlining. The message stood indelible on the flimsy page: Sexual sin is second only to murder. This meant that, despite my exhusband's abuse over the years—all the quiet manipulation culminating with the physical danger that led up to our divorce—because it hadn't killed me, under Mormon ideology he was far more righteous than Spencer was, though Spencer only committed the sin of covering my body in an arrangement of sweet and well-intentioned kisses. As a devout Mormon, I was asked to take this doctrine seriously, and I did. But for one brief instant, it occurred to me how shortsighted it was to regard those tender and beautiful moments with Spencer as pure lust, comparable to murder, a grievous sin to be constantly lamented. It was illogical—and *wrong*.

Suddenly I didn't want to confess. Instead, I wanted to explain that this had happened because I was twenty-one and for the first time felt deeply in love with a beautiful person, that this was *normal*, but that I cared enough about God that I was going to try to make it right.

Penitent for the second time in my life, I sat before another old man I'd just met and mustered all the faith I had to pour forth my intimate secrets in an attempt to reconcile my secular joy with the laws of heaven. Once again, I was told not to worry, that although the sin was severe, it could be erased. When Christ was through with the situation, it would be like it never happened.

"Of course," he said after a moment's arrest, "I don't think you should ever see that boy again."

I shuddered. No, that couldn't be right.

Spencer himself was the bridge between my growing doubts about faith and my desire to pour myself back into the gospel. On the night we met I had been ready to give up my religion for good, to drop out of college, quit my first real job, and head back East a failure. Religion wasn't worth it if solitude, divorce, and decimated self-worth were the fruits of trying so hard to do the right thing. But Spencer had looked deep into my spirit and beckoned my most valuable qualities to surface. It was like he had crashed through the ceiling of my rickety life, an emissary from my better self. Without meaning to, he drew me back from the edge and convinced me to take a second shot at being something more than a wreck. And he did it all without being anyone other than the one-and-only Spencer.

How could Spencer, of all people, not be worthy of my future? Without him I'd surely meet other guys and wind up with great friends, a satisfying career—a beautiful life. But you meet only one Spencer. I abandoned submission with the shake of my head. Not see Spencer? The person whom I was sure God had sent to help me?

"Yeah, that's not going to happen," I spat back. The bishop shifted in his seat, uneasy, as if I'd shot him hard in the face with a rubber band. "We broke the rules, and I accept that. But this was only a sin because we aren't married, not because the act itself was ugly or wrong."

He admitted I had a point, and he met me halfway by suggesting I stay away from Spencer until it had been decided that I'd fully repented.

With forced restraint, I ignored the pounding in my temples and the protest stuck in my throat. God was surely worth at least some compromise, so I agreed. The bishop and God took a few months to decide that Spencer and I could be together again. It felt like forever.

A FEW YEARS LATER Spencer and I sat before one more bishop for our premarital consultation. I'd obtained my legal divorce years before, but because I had been married in the temple, I had to get special permission to remarry. I could be married again outside the Mormon temple, but if I wanted my marriage to be eternal, I would need a temple divorce—a sort of *get* for Mormons.

"We'll need to get your ex-husband's approval, of course, and I will need you to write down any sexual indiscretion that happened since you two separated." My new, white-haired bishop had taken the day off from his job as a financial analyst to help us with a mountain of premarital paperwork.

"Well, there was something—but I took care of that with my bishop a long time ago."

"The brethren in Salt Lake still need to know, even if you've repented."

I sighed, my patience beginning to unravel. Would I have to go through the whole story again? Was it really necessary to defend myself before a stranger and repeat the weighty business of admitting fault and reliving guilt? "But doesn't repentance erase the sin?" I tried. "Didn't the Savior suffer so that my sins would be forgiven? Why do I have to keep dragging them out in meetings and writing them down for strange men to read any time I want something from the church?" I watched as the bishop searched for just the right way to soothe me into compliance.

"They just need all the facts so they can make the right choice about letting you be sealed to someone else."

All that repentance, all those nights spent in tear-streaked supplication, and the Mormon Church still wanted a book somewhere with all my sexual sins scribbled in indelible ink. Why was sleeping with someone I loved a sin worthy of a lifetime of red tape? God forgave me, but one old man after another lined up to punish me for believing that sex wasn't the worst way to spit in the face of religion. I didn't believe God lost too much sleep over whom I coupled with, but his Church couldn't get my erotic life off its mind.

The brethren wanted to keep me chaste, demure, and teachable. Women were to be passive nurturers while men became patriarchs and eventual gods. I wasn't a disciple of Christ if I was free-loving, outspoken, and logical. The fate of my eternal life was directly tied to my gender and to my willingness to fill my role and obey these older men. But I could no longer do this without betraying myself.

Sex was complicated and beautiful, an enormous weight and the greatest joy. It was time to turn my back on guilt and embrace a life of joy. My mother's romance novels had long ago showed me the secret joys of living, but religion forced me to separate myself from that joy in favor of submission. I wouldn't do it. *As long as you believe* . . . My mother's advice rang from someplace within me as I walked away from the bishop's office, my hand entwined with Spencer's, and the sun shone over a brand-new God and a guiltless future. The wedding was set for late March, without the temple, and without another fruitless moment devoted to the past. I was free, with nothing before me but faith, love, and eternal possibility.

Can I Get a Witness?

Elizabeth Taylor-Mead

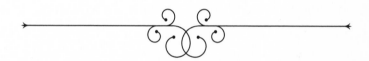

There were only three kinds of books in our house: Bibles, cookbooks, and diet books. None of them offered the kind of nourishment I craved. "The wisdom of this world is foolishness to God" was a common refrain at home, but like Eve, seduced by the tree of knowledge, I knew there were apples in the neighborhood and I was hungry.

I loved school and managed to maintain top grades without any encouragement or even interest from my parents. My parents had no academic sights set for me; we were Jehovah's Witnesses, and, as such, higher education was deemed "unwholesome." Throughout my elementary and junior high school years my family moved often. It wasn't that my stepfather was in the military or diplomatic service. Quite the contrary: He didn't get along with anyone, especially customers. He could not keep a job.

By the time I entered high school we'd settled in a Long Island town with high educational standards and a great library. I made friends with classmates who took part in Vietnam War protests, boycotted grapes in solidarity with César Chávez, and debated the superiority of Stones vs. Beatles. At home, my stepfather, who'd only dipped his toes into the tributary of "the Truth" early on at my mother's prodding, now refused to participate, preferring to call himself a "lapsed Catholic." He took umbrage at being abandoned by his family when we went to five weekly meetings at the Kingdom Hall or out in service, knocking on doors, on the weekend. He fumed, he slammed doors, he issued ultimatums. My mother, like all Jehovah's Witnesses, saw "persecution" as proof that we were special and beloved by "the One True Master." She stuck to her scriptural guns and soon every dinnertime turned into World War III.

I was forbidden to date boys from school. Instead, I was expected to accept invitations from young men in the congregation or those I'd meet at regional conventions with themes like "Fruitage of the Spirit" or "God's Blessings Near at Hand." The boys that set my heart aflutter, however—in other words, those condemned to perish imminently in the global annihilation that would be Armageddon, a.k.a. God's Judgment Day—were smart, funny, artistic, and slightly aloof. Two were particularly magnetic.

Peter, with amber cat eyes and chestnut hair falling over his collar, was a musician. He collected rare recordings by blues singers from the Mississippi Delta. He sometimes walked the school halls with me between classes, teasing me, the missionary in training, by leaning in close, rasping lyrics from a current favorite, like Robert Johnson's "Kind-Hearted Woman Blues."

"I'm gonna get deep down in this connection, keep on tanglin' with

these wires / And when I mash down on your little starter, then your spark plug will give me fire."

Blushing tomato red, the furthest thing from my mind was parsing scripture.

Peter took my breath away when he was close by, but it was George who kept me tossing and turning at night, plotting how I might spend more time with him without incurring Jehovah's wrath. George was an effortless honor student. I was amazed by his intricate knowledge not only of Shakespeare and Cervantes but also of television and movie trivia. He developed the latter skill in order to keep his alcoholic single mother happy. When her regular three-day benders gave way to seesaw periods of self-flagellation and self-pity, George distracted her by providing a running commentary on reruns of *Petticoat Junction* and *The Beverly Hillbillies*. On the after-noons I wrangled permission for us to study together, slightly fudging the optional/required status of the activity for my mother's benefit, we'd sit in his kitchen, chatting and sipping Constant Comment tea, which felt at the time like the epitome of sophistication. More than once I had to leave in a rush, pursued by George's mother wildly batting at me with a broom, screeching, "You'd better get the hell out of here, girl! I'm gonna kick your ass back to Texas!" As she was from Tennessee and we were in New York, I chose to see her boozy threats as surrealistic *happenings* rather than acts of malice, and returned as often as possible.

The boys my mother pushed me to date, the "young broth-ers in God's organization," were awkward and dull, predictable and dismissive of anything that captured my imagination. It was clear to them, and they made little effort to be polite about it, that I was tempting Satan's army by suggesting a trip to the Museum of Modern Art or the Guggenheim on a Saturday afternoon (after service, of course). Instead, they'd treat me to an insipid lunch at a chain restaurant followed by a chaste walk around the park. With increasing dread, I found that most of these dates ended with a repressed daddy's boy trying to plunge his tongue down my throat or stick his hand up my skirt, clumsily groping for a premature peek at paradise.

At first I complained to my mother in the hope that she'd stop prodding me to accept these invitations, but I quickly learned she wasn't going to see things my way.

"Reexamine your behavior. What did you do to provoke him?" she would ask, or "How many times have I told you to wear longer skirts? Men are made of flesh and blood, honey. The sooner you get married, the better."

I DID NOT GET married but instead graduated from high school. Though I wanted to go to college, and my teachers tried to intervene, making appeals on my behalf, my parents wouldn't let me. So I watched all my "worldly" friends take off for college—though some of the boys went to Canada or Israeli kibbutzim to avoid the draft—while I stayed at home and barricaded myself from the constant room-shaking parental battles that raged on.

I was in limbo—neither able to satisfy my mother's plan for me to get with the Witness Protection Program, as I'd begun to see it, for offering believers the only insurance policy against Armageddon, nor able to defy her outright and apply to college. Since childhood I'd been groomed to enter Bethel, the residential facility for JW missionaries in Brooklyn Heights. I had to admit Brooklyn was appealing, but I knew my attraction was more because of its proximity to Manhattan than to my eternal salvation.

My desire to leave kept bubbling up inside me, growing more insistent, a pushy patient in my internal waiting room. But still I didn't go. My obstinate ways, however, became an increasing source of friction at home. Though my mother would take my side against my stepfather when he railed against my dreaminess and lack of common sense, in private she rebuked me constantly, swearing that my stubbornness would be the ruin of us both.

I tried. I continued to go to all the meetings and out in service every weekend. I conducted Bible studies with "people of good faith" who were "hungry for the Truth." Yet I knew in my heart I was starving. I was living an inauthentic life, taking no pride at all in separating "the sheep from the goats." Like a racehorse at the starting gate, I felt pumped to run, snorting at the sight of the track, waiting for the bell to ring and the gate to open to a much wider world.

That gate would open when I turned eighteen. This would be the perfect opportunity to test my mother's commitment to "Render therefore to Caesar the things that are Caesar's; and to God the things that are God's" (Mark 22:21). As she saw it, Caesar, in the form of the U.S. legal system, decreed that I became an adult at age eighteen and would thus no longer be her responsibility. Till then, I was pretty much her property, requiring constant guidance and surveillance. I saw my emotional, if not spiritual, salvation in this argument. We didn't celebrate birthdays, but now my eighteenth would be gift enough.

As soon as I could I secured an inexpensive room in a Queens apartment share and announced to my parents my plans to move out. My stepfather seemed relieved; my mother immediately checked to see if I'd be living close to a Kingdom Hall. I would and so she agreed, perhaps looking forward to a break from the tension between us.

MOVING DAY WASN'T WHAT I hoped for. My mother had a last-minute change of heart. Perhaps she imagined I'd be whisked off to my new living quarters in a chariot sent by Jesus, but to her disgust my equipage was three school friends, home on a college break, honking from a waiting VW Camper. Not able to keep it together, she panicked, burst into tears, and commanded me not to leave. She blocked the door.

"Please, Mom!" I cried. "It will be fine. I'll call you later, I promise."

As I picked up the carrying case of LPs with one hand and my suitcase with the other, she began pulling at my clothes with frenzied force, tearing my collar, and ripping my pants, screaming. "You came into my life naked and you'll leave naked! You think you know anything at all? You'll leave when I tell you to leave!!"

Terrified but determined, I yanked her off me, grabbed my belongings, and ran out of the house and into my scary, necessary new life.

WITH THE HELP OF an employment agency I found a job that felt like I'd won the lottery: secretary to the international sales manager at a major paperback publishing house. My boss, Mr. Alwyn, was an elegant Welshman. One of the first tasks he assigned me was choosing books to be packed in shipments to U.S. military outposts in Southeast Asia—gifts of literary ammunition for fighting the Vietcong. We both pretended he didn't know I was slipping in copies of Dalton Trumbo's antiwar novel *Johnny Got His Gun*.

I did not report this part of my job to my mother, as I'd been taught from an early age that Witnesses must remain neutral. To identify as a pacifist meant I was taking a political stand—at about the same level of "wrong thinking" as pledging allegiance to the flag. I seemed incapable of anything *but* wrong thinking in more and more areas of my life, but I was equally incapable of going back. I should have been reading Watchtower Society publications such as *Make Sure of All Things; Hold Fast to What Is Fine* on my daily subway commute. I tried, but I forgot the words as soon as I read them. I learned that my publishing job not only paid a decent wage, it also offered a complimentary copy of every new title. What I actually wanted to hold fast to was the literary alchemy of these fiction writers. I was thunderstruck by sentences from Donald Barthelme: "There was a sort of muck running in the gutters, yellowish, filthy stream that suggested excrement, or nervousness, a city that does not know what it has done to deserve baldness, errors, infidelity." As I took in these words, my nerve endings donned pom-poms; my eyes became pied pipers, leading me over the edge of a cliff. I was unable to save myself.

In order to pass muster in my adopted environment, in my new life I was an undercover agent disguised as a sophisticated young woman of the world. I didn't want to reveal how small and proscribed my background was. There was so much I didn't know, and social minefields to be avoided everywhere. Invited to join my young coworkers after hours, the conversation often turned to gossip about who was "banging" whom or who was bragging about "going down" on a certain member of a famous band. I nodded, clucked my tongue, and laughed in all the places I hoped were appropriate, trying desperately to evade detection as an alien interloper.

Sex was something never discussed at home. Once or twice my mother had alluded to a passionate relationship with my real father, but I wondered whether when she found "the Truth" by becoming a Witness she simultaneously lost her mojo. I didn't really know anything about how sex worked but I had two images in my mind, both gleaned from movies. One was the moment of recognition, a magnetic, unstoppable falling into each other, and the other was the Tin Man in *The Wizard of Oz*—he needed an oil can to keep him happy and moving.

I was a lonely fledgling, just starting to see myself reflected in the response of others. I allowed myself to believe that I *would* be recognized, met, by an interesting man, and I wanted to have the oil can ready. The familiar *When? When? When?* pulsing through me was developing a lustier tone.

One morning he arrived, pushing the office mail cart. He was dressed in a nubby silk shirt, leather pants, and Frye boots. I was immediately attracted to his delicate face, jutting cheekbones, dark pointy mustache and long black curly hair. He was d'Artagnan, Richelieu, Bonnie Prince Charlie.

He was also tripping on acid, and the rolling cart of alphabetized hanging files he pushed near my desk was not cooperating.

"Well, hello Miss," he whispered conspiratorially. "I can't seem to find your mail. What's your boss's name again?"

"Alwyn. David Alwyn"

His eyes spun like roulette wheels. He was genuinely confused. "So what letter would that begin with?"

"'A' . . . uh, the first one."

Instead of responding to that information he sat down on the corner of my desk and shook his head, sighing, "Nevermore. Nevermore."

"Why are you quoting Edgar Allan Poe?"

"Nah. It's Verlaine. Can't you hear it?"

Le ver est dans le fruit, le réveil dans le rêve,
Et le remords est dans l'amour: telle est la loi.
Le Bonheur a marché côte à côte avec moi.
Ain't it the truth?!
The worm is in the fruit; in dreaming, waking;
In loving, mourning. And so must it be.
Happiness once walked side by side with me.

"Mon Dieu!" I murmured, shocking myself that I managed to swoon and blaspheme simultaneously.

He reached into the top basket, grabbed all the mail that was in the file marked *G*, kissed it, handed it to me, and then sauntered round the corner, out of sight.

Over the next weeks Lee asked me out a few times, usually dinner in Chinatown at Hong Fat, where the steamed dumplings made up for the notoriously rude waiters. We saw the midnight show of *El Topo* at the Elgin, our movie tickets guaranteeing a contact high from all the pot smoke wafting through the aisles; we heard Richie Havens's driving guitar at the Fillmore East. The more time I spent with Lee, the more I felt the arrow of my self sharpening, becoming bolder, more confident.

When I learned my roommates would both be away for the weekend, I worked up the nerve to invite him over to my place. Blocking out my mother's voice intoning dire warnings against the sins of the flesh, I took some cash out of my savings account, went to the lingerie department of Bonwit Teller, and purchased a floor-length, forest green negligee with a plunging neckline. Lee had introduced me to Henry Miller, Anaïs Nin, and *The Story of O,* tomes definitely missing from the Kingdom Hall reading list. I wanted to read everything and then do everything, with him. All of my programming began to unravel.

He was living in the Chelsea Hotel with a California heiress, a situation that presented a conundrum for me. He made no bones about his disdain for monogamy, declaring it "a patriarchal construct that cuts people off from what gives them the greatest pleasure—the freedom to love without restraint." I wanted him to guide me in freeing myself from all restraints. I just plain wanted him.

Despite my best efforts to avoid it, the apostle Paul's pep talk to the Colossians flashed across the screen of my mind the day of our date like a PSA from heaven: *"Keep your minds fixed on the things above, not on the things upon the earth . . . deaden, therefore, your body members that are upon the earth as respects fornication, uncleanness, sexual appetite, hurtful desire, and covetousness, which is idolatry. On account of those things the wrath of God is coming."* Slipping into the green negligee, I canceled my spiritual insurance policy, the throbbing "When, When, When?" replaced by "Now, Now, Now!"

THE SHOCK OF NO longer being a virgin was immediate and dizzying. The "no-backsies" permanence of my fall from grace produced a terrifying and stomach-churning sensation, like the held-breath anxiety of being pushed on a swing from a colossal height. Feeling completely exposed to Jehovah's (and probably, in her own omniscient way, my mother's) scrutiny and judgment, I took shelter in denial. When Lee left the next day, I told myself that what had happened between us, the whole long night of conjoined naked choreography, was only a prelude to "the real thing" but was not actual sex. It had been so easy, so instinctive. If I'd actually committed this forbidden act, why wasn't it accompanied by the smashing of stone tablets, the blast of Joshua's horn? Where was the manifestation prophesied in the seventeenth chapter of Revelation, one the entire borough of Queens would surely have witnessed:

"Come, I will show you the punishment of the great prostitute, who sits on many waters. With her the kings of the earth committed adultery and the inhabitants of the earth were intoxicated with the wine of her adulteries . . . I saw a woman sitting on a scarlet beast that was covered with blasphemous names and had seven heads and ten horns . . . This title was written on her forehead: MYSTERY BABYLON THE GREAT THE MOTHER OF PROSTITUTES AND OF THE ABOMINATIONS OF THE EARTH.*"*

But lo, the Earth did not shatter, and the sea did not swallow me up. The police had not knocked at my door, nor had the downstairs neighbors. There was nothing in the paper about it. I began to feel somehow both lighter and fuller, with the knowledge that there was no going back. As far as I could tell, God was fine. I was absolutely sure that I was too. My mother, however, was another story.

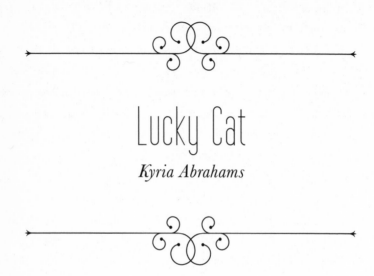

Lucky Cat

Kyria Abrahams

It's my first Halloween in Massachusetts and I'm doing what I imagine all twenty-seven-year-old ex–Jehovah's Witnesses do, wandering aimlessly through the streets of Cambridge and crying because I was never allowed to celebrate Halloween as a kid.

I'm dressed up as Maneki Neko, the Good Luck Cat with one paw in the air that sits on Chinese take-out counters and oversees your egg rolls. To illustrate: I am wearing a white sweater, a headband with ears, cat whiskers drawn on with eyeliner, and a red pet bell I bought at CVS. All I need is somewhere to be. Where's the party at?

When I first left "the Truth," I thought all worldly people ever did was get drunk and have parties. As it turns out, evil sinners are pretty low-key. Most adults don't even go out on Halloween. But me, I'm drinking brandy from a flask while dressed up like a

Japanese cat. It didn't occur to me this could be a disturbing sight, a grown woman with a bell around her neck, drunk and crying at other people's children.

I see girls dressed up as princesses and I want to write poems about them, how lucky they are to be "normal." Parents wrap their forearms around their kids and lead them away from me, never breaking my gaze. These reactions will make an even better poem. People probably think I'm a pedophile. Misunderstood, as always.

Despite the holiday, I like where I live here in Cambridge. I have hardwood floors in my $1,500-per-month apartment. I can afford this because I taught myself HTML and Photoshop and now I am a web designer. As of 1999, web design is becoming one of those jobs you actually need a college degree for. I never graduated high school, so I'm lucky. It seems I got in just under the wire. I got in on the ground floor.

Three years ago, I was disfellowshipped from the Pawtucket, Rhode Island, congregation of Jehovah's Witnesses for cheating on my husband. I was twenty-three at the time. We had been married for five years. I'd realized on our first anniversary that I'd made a terrible mistake. I told my husband I didn't love him anymore, but that didn't matter. As a Jehovah's Witness, you aren't allowed to get a divorce. What God has sewn together, let no man tear apart. We made a commitment before God, and so, before God, we stayed married for four more years. Eventually, I found a friend of a friend and quite unceremoniously fucked him in a hotel room. After that, I was free to get a divorce. I was also thrown out of the religion of my birth.

W HEN YOU'RE DISFELLOWSHIPPED IT means no one can talk to you or hang out with you anymore. If I'd wanted my friends back,

I could have gone to the Kingdom Hall three times a week and sat in the back, with my head down, looking repentant. But I didn't want them back, I wanted to be free. I wanted to be worldly. Now, I am worldly. I do the things I wasn't allowed to do as a good Jehovah's Witness. I listen to techno music, I smoke pot, I have sex with whomever I want. I refinish my own furniture, just like the artist I always was inside.

I am eccentric, naturally. My parents did not allow me to go to art school because Armageddon was coming. So I've decorated my home in a way that reflects my inner creativity. I am free to do all of this now. For example, my kitchen tabletop is a magazine collage. My bookcase is a wrought iron-bed frame. How did I turn it into a bookcase? Well, I just threw books on top of it. Instant bookcase! Who would do that? Someone who was never really a Jehovah's Witness, that's who. Someone who was always an artist.

> I AM:
> — A stand-up comedian.
> — A performance poet.
> — A pot smoker.
> — An artist.
> I AM NO LONGER:
> — Married to a Jehovah's Witness.
> — Stuck in a religion I hate.
> — A bored housewife.
> — Obligated to be a good Christian.

WHEN I TELL YOU that I don't remember marrying Dennis, a man who is twenty years older than I am and with whom I never have sex, I'm not exaggerating. We got married a few months ago, but I don't remember why. I do, however, remember *how* he asked me to marry him. It wasn't romantic, I admit. I had to double-check the next day to make sure he had really asked.

We had just left the Laugh Studio in Porter Square when he proposed. We were aimlessly walking home in silence. Suddenly—and he doesn't stop or look up or anything—Dennis blurts out, "So, are we getting married or what?" The next day, I confirmed that he had, in fact, asked me to marry him.

You would think I'd remember what happened after that. But the next thing I know, it's Halloween. I'm married for the second time.

My ex-boyfriend Leo spent money to see a therapist because he was sexually molested as a child. He was my second boyfriend, Dennis was my third—and is my second husband. I am sure I would have married Leo if he had asked, too. Leo explained to me once that "losing time" is actually pretty common for someone who has suffered trauma. But I don't think of what I've been through—leaving God and everyone I grew up with behind me—as trauma, I think of it as an escape. I was so bored in that stupid religion, so bored with my nerdy Christian husband who listened to Broadway musicals and wore polyester pants. I wanted to get out, so I did. Yes, I lost my friends and family, but I did what I needed to do. I did the right thing. I cheated, I was freed, and I left. How could that be traumatic? That's a good thing!

Dennis and I got married at city hall and my mother drove in from Rhode Island after I told her how much she'd love him because he reminded me of Dad. Dennis even has the same hat as my father, and I just can't get over it, it's like we were meant to be. We're both outcasts, weirdos, freaks. When we met last year, we said to each other: Let's be freaks together.

The only problem is, I don't want to be a freak anymore. And he doesn't seem to care.

After the ceremony, we had dinner at an Italian restaurant that gets all their ingredients from a local farm. The Italian restaurant also owns a holistic doctor's office diagonally across Massachusetts Avenue. This is the world I live in now. It's a grown-up, classy world! It's a world where regular people watch R-rated movies and use Ouija boards and sleep in on Sunday mornings instead of knocking on people's doors to tell them about Armageddon. This is how people who aren't Jehovah's Witnesses eat dinner after they get married at city hall.

I WORE A WHITE sweater and white pants for my wedding. Tonight, I put on the same white sweater to create my Good Luck Cat.

Dennis is a professional stand-up comic, out doing a Halloween show in Maine tonight, so I'm home alone. He headlines shows at clubs, but I'm just an open-miker. He's a closer, the main event. I go to the club four or five nights a week and hang out with my friends, all of whom are stand-up comics. We get drunk and make fun of everyone else.

Dennis and I made love twice before we got married. At this point, I think we've had sex about four times total. I have sex with some of my friends, instead. I worry that they think I'm the kind of girl who would cheat on her husband. I'm really not that kind of person, it's just that I made a mistake in getting married. Still, I think they judge me.

One time, this girl said to me: "You're like the only girl in this group of guys and they all want to fuck you and you don't know it." But I knew that wasn't true, because I was fucking only a few of them.

My husband is embarrassing, also called "gay" in Boston, which means he's retarded. I'm afraid people think we have sex just because we're married.

I THINK I KNOW how I ended up married to this weird old man. I know how I made such a terrible mistake. I started getting into Wicca shortly after I left the Jehovah's Witnesses, and I had experimented with a spell to bring on my one true love. It involved lighting candles and pouring salt on the ground. I did it in the kitchen. Now I am starting to think the spell is the reason my life is in shambles. I didn't know what I was doing and I hadn't believed it would work, so I had attracted black magic. The Jehovah's Witnesses had been right. Demons were out there, I shouldn't have toyed with them.

MY HUSBAND GOES TO Costco and buys a case of his favorite toothpaste and then lines up all the tubes on top of the door frames in his bedroom. The room has an ugly folding table instead of a desk, a bed, and all this toothpaste.

When my friends come over, I shut the door to his bedroom. When we get drunk and high, I open the door and make fun of how weird he is.

WHEN I FIRST LEFT the Witnesses, my new circle of friends was comprised entirely of performance poets, but I'm over that scene now. I'm a stand-up comic and I only hang out with other comics. Slam poets are even more retarded than improvisers, and improvisers are totally retarded. I've never really seen an improv show, but it seems cool to hate them. I see improvisers around town, anyway. I haven't really experienced much since I left the Jehovah's Witnesses, and sometimes I just pick random things to love or to hate.

I DO A LOT of speed-reading of important books like *Fear and Loathing in Las Vegas*. I fast-forward through John Cassavetes movies and watch *The Matrix*.

Comedy. This is where I belong. I want to be Bill Hicks or this new girl Sarah Silverman. I'm pretty outrageous with the things I say. I'm what you call a "cerebral comic." I rant and stuff. All I have to do is catch up on politics and history and then I'll be able to really let 'em have it. I just need to watch *The Matrix* again, figure out what else I don't know about the world, and fill in the holes before someone figures me out.

I'm so damn close to being normal.

INDUSTRY PEOPLE COME TO the Comedy Studio and they watch our sets, which means they watch us perform and they don't go to the bathroom. I'm learning phrases like "television clean" and "the perfect seven-minute set," because seven minutes is what you'll get if you go on Conan.

The club has Conan auditions and it's blowing my mind how close I am to being what I always wanted to be. Three years ago, I was in a cult; now I have the chance to be on television.

When I first came into the comedy scene, I felt like I was doing a good job at making people like me. They couldn't really tell I was different, maybe just quirky. I hid the fact that I had only been to one rock concert in my life, that I had never done mushrooms, and that I'd never voted.

I was doing such a great job that some of the more successful comics invited me to the studio where they recorded *Dr. Katz* and all the Squigglevision cartoons. Even Oprah was getting a cartoon. My friends were all getting jobs doing voice-overs and I thought maybe this was the answer to everything.

I left the Jehovah's Witnesses, now I would work for Oprah.

But then I had to go and do something really stupid, like find a Wicca voodoo spell on the Internet and throw salt on my kitchen floor and marry this weird guy who was twenty years older than I am. After that, no one invited me back to the *Dr. Katz* studio again. Now people were standoffish; they said things like "I couldn't believe it when I first heard you two got married," or, even worse, "I don't care what anybody else thinks, I just think it's so great that the two of you got together. Love knows no bounds."

And that's when I knew I'd fucked everything up and nothing would ever be okay again. All because of that salt, because of demons. I never should have left the Jehovah's Witnesses.

So I take a razor and I carve ALONE into my arm. It hurts me that they judge me.

The main problem is it's Halloween and I have no party to go to. I'm drunk and crying and I hate my husband and Conan hasn't called and, anyway, *where's the party at?*

I call my other ex-boyfriend Dave, I tell him I'm bored because it's Halloween and I'm all dressed up like a Maneki Neko but my husband isn't paying any attention to me, seeing as how he is in Maine. So Dave comes to pick me up. I wrap bandages around my arm so the blood doesn't seep into my white sweater. I am disappointed it isn't bleeding very much. I didn't cut deeply enough.

Dave picks me up with a brand-new bottle of whiskey in the

car. It is ten at night, which seems impossibly late, and I am sure everything will be closed. All the clubs will be shut down by now. We drive through Lexington, through a sleepy Colonial town, with everything shut up tight and dripping with very expensive Halloween decorations. "We'll find some club or party," he tells me. But we find only driveways.

After about two hours of going nowhere, we pull to the side of the road and I put his dick in my mouth. My red cat bell jingles as he comes in my mouth.

So we talk about how great things are, and how different things are now. I say I am so happy in my new apartment, now that I'm not a Jehovah's Witness anymore. I like that we broke up but we can still be friends, still have sex.

Things can only get better, I tell him. I'm finally free to live life however I choose. I can make all my own decisions now, and I never was allowed to make any decisions before in my entire life. What more could you ask for? How could anything possibly go wrong when you can finally make all your own decisions?

The Church of the Snake

Carolyn Briggs

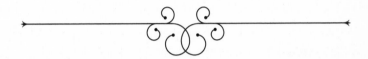

I t was in an elevator in Istanbul that God made His first move. I had hoped the small freight elevator at the back of the international terminal would take me to the domestic terminal where I would catch a connecting flight to Ankara. I entered it alone with two suitcases and my overstuffed carry-on. Two books fell from my bag as the door slid closed. I picked them up and then tried to make sense of the buttons on the wall—none with numerals. I decided the bottom button was the most likely and was about to push it when the lights went out.

I gasped and slammed my hand against the concrete doors, calling for help. No doubt I had probably ignored signs in Turkish that said the elevator was out of commission. I thought instantly of my ex-husband, his loving-kindness, his eagerness to fix my problems, to kneel in prayer with me, to take me before the Lord in supplication. But he wasn't here and would never be here again. I was just about to reap what I had sown when I had turned my back on God and left both Him and my devastated husband behind. For twenty years I had toed the line, and then, one day, I stepped over.

So this was it: my long-deserved demise, a slow suffocation in a dark corner of a foreign country. Why hadn't I followed other people to the correct elevator? Why had I struck out on my own?

But following other people is what got me into this mess in the first place. I had been a follower all my life, taking my cues from parents, preachers, deacons, elders, and my husband, and I followed them right into a place as small and confined as this elevator. I swore and slammed my hand down, pressing all the buttons. The elevator hummed and jerked into motion. When the doors opened, I lunged into the terminal and reached back in to pull out my luggage. After I took a deep breath, smoothed my hair, and retied shoes that did not need tying, I merged with the other passengers.

I asked strangers questions in English, waved ten-dollar bills, and finally a taxi sped me to what I hoped was the domestic terminal. Then I gratefully sank into my seat on the Turkish airliner headed for Ankara, the capital city deep in the heart of Turkey. I accepted a piece of bread and a small greenish orange from the flight attendant who wore a hat like a 1950s Pan Am stewardess. The man beside me pulled out a cigarette and lit up. I listened to the announcements from the pilot and the flight attendants and assumed they were saying basically the same things such people always said. *"We're happy you're flying with us today. Fasten your seatbelt. Your cushion is also a flotation device. We hope you're not running from God because our Allah doesn't suffer fools gladly."*

The other passengers smoked and read the paper while I looked out the window, closed my eyes, and pleaded with God to not kill me before I saw Thom one more time. I loved how this man was dramatically different from my ex-husband and all the men I had known in the church. I met Thom at the university where we were both graduate students in a writing program. I was newly single and scared about a lot of things, but Thom, a handsome Irishman, was an older man of the world, a man of drink and irreverence and literature, and I sought refuge in all those things, especially him. And I was a novelty to him, a woman who had slept with only one man in her entire life, a woman in love with poetry and literature, an almost-virgin in the shark tank of graduate school. He was fascinated with me and my reinvention and regretted my youth in a religious community far more than I did. While I loved his nonconformity, I was taken aback when he defended his thesis and promptly accepted a job in Turkey. His breezy willingness to leave me behind had been one more reminder that he was not the kind of man I had always known: devoted, committed, trustworthy. No, Thom was mysterious and exciting. Sexy. His last email was a steamy anticipation of our being reunited after three months apart. I had to shift in my seat thinking about it.

And the anticipation only built until two hours later when I was starring in my own romantic movie, sprinting when I saw him—actually parting people in my path. Thom was taller than everyone around him, so regal, so erect in his trench coat, and his gray-green eyes burned like I had never seen them before. We kissed deeply, an island of passion in the midst of shorter and duller people. I felt sorry for them and so glad to have left ordinariness behind.

"There's a *dolmus* out front. Let's hurry," he said, pulling me out to a shuttle bus. The van was filled with people shoulder to shoulder; I leaned against his chest.

"This is the happiest day of my life," Thom said, stroking my upper arm and kissing my hair. I didn't say anything, stunned to be in Turkey, to be driving past red-tile-roofed houses built on the sides of hills. Rebar everywhere I looked. Construction, cars, a haze of petrol vapors.

"Tomorrow, I'll show you the city proper. You are not going to believe your eyes, darling. We'll go to Kocatepe," Thom said into my hair.

"Caught-cha what?" I asked.

He laughed. "It's the largest mosque in Ankara. Oh, God, can the driver go faster?"

Thom's university was as modern as any I had ever seen, an oasis in the landscape of rusted steel and hovels. Carefully groomed gardens, an artificial waterfall, marbled pillars. And the brand-new faculty condos were pristine, white stone and sparkling windows, vines with pink flowers and swept paths leading to the campus. Thom's apartment was bare, with plastered white walls, ceramic-tiled floors, a large window in the living room that I tried to look out of as he swept me toward the bedroom. My luggage never made it past the threshold of the apartment. I didn't see the bathroom or the kitchen or anything else. He undressed me in the hallway, and we sank to the cold floor.

That next morning when I woke I realized the light was different in Turkey. The source was still the sun, but it was an older sun, indifferent to me. I lay in bed after Thom had left to teach his class. I stretched in his bed, feeling damp and sore, but I didn't care. Sometime in the long night, we had made our way to his bed. I had pulled the coverlet to my chin and suddenly thought of my mother on the other side of the world. About that time, Mom would be spreading raspberry preserves on her toast, brewing coffee, and making a grocery list for later that morning. I saw it clearly, that pensive way she had about her, the sorrowing self-righteousness I had always felt heir to. Not now. Not in Thom's arms, not thousands of miles away from that coffee-scented Iowa kitchen. I didn't want my mother's life. I never had, but then I found myself living it, year after year after year.

I WANTED TO SEE everything and all at once. Thom took me to downtown Ankara right away. Walking was dangerous with the uneven sidewalks with twelve-inch curbs, streets a rubble of potholes and gravel. The traffic was unrelenting, constant, honking. Beggars with missing limbs and women wearing tight jeans and boots strode between women covered from head to foot. A woman in a dark green chador wept as she held out a black-and-white photograph of a man in uniform and told me something in Turkish. Only her eyes showed, and they were dark with sorrow.

There was street food everywhere. Ears of corn boiled in pots and chestnuts roasted over blue jets of gas, kebobs of lamb sizzled on grill pans, and white paper bags of *simet*, a pretzel-like bread covered with sesame seeds, were stacked in precariously tall piles. We bought fresh figs and doner kebabs of spicy meat shaved off a giant whirling side of beef, stuffed into warm yeasty rolls. It was a dervish of gluttony. I was famished and kept reaching for lira, more lira.

Kocatepe was a wedding cake rising with tier upon tier of narrow stained glass windows. I unfolded the scarf I had brought for this purpose and tied it under my chin. We slipped off our shoes and placed them in the massive parking lot of footwear. The mosque was empty of furniture, no pews, no pulpit that I could see, only acres of rugs spread side by side. Far above stretched a series of domes tiled in blue and red where a huge chandelier hung, a crystal ball with tiny lights so bright in the dark interior it had the brilliance of a swallowed sun. Men prayed with their faces pressed into the carpet. I stayed back from them, nervous and uneasy. Light wavered through the tiny windows, making them glow red and blue in the late afternoon, and this thin illumination suddenly exhausted me. I wanted to sit down. I tugged Thom's sleeve and nodded toward the door.

Thom told me that he had students who struggled with Islam; one had dared to write about it in his composition class.

"He finally rejected his Islamic faith, the whole code, the dress, the patriarchy, the praying five times a day, washing up and all that nonsense. His family took him to a holy man who told him it was the Evil One who made him question holy things," Thom said slowly.

"What happened?"

"He left Islam anyway, turned his back on the whole lot of them, but he says it's hard to no longer belong to something bigger than himself. Rather like you."

"Yes. Like me," I said. "I don't know where the hell I belong."

"Do you feel lost?"

"Sometimes," I said. "Not this minute."

"I hate those motherfuckers who kept you scared and small."

"I was born scared," I said. "I just took the first way out I came to, I guess."

"We should put some of your Bible indoctrination to good use—we could go to Cappadocia—there's a valley there with cave churches. It's ancient as hell. Saint Paul and all those guys escaped there once when Rome started to hunt them down."

"Really? Is it a long way away?"

"A morning's drive. It's secluded, but you like a retreat, don't you? To remove yourself from the world?" he smiled while he said this, but I heard the subtext. I had navigated the world with the crutch of faith for a very long time, a cowardly thing for an educated person to do, according to Thom.

He thought he knew everything about me and my history, even the history of my faith, but there was much that had escaped him. I valued the things he overlooked—this was perhaps the biggest difference between us and why we could never spend a lifetime together. He was enamored with literature and writers but clueless about people like me who had resigned ourselves to our factories and fields, to white clapboard churches where we sorted clothing to ship to the missionaries. Sometimes I saw his distaste for me and my faith—it would flit across his face until he composed his features into benign tolerance. Taking me to the Ihlara Valley would be a concession, a nod to my primitive nature, a token gesture Thom was willing to dispense.

I SPENT A LOT of time alone in Thom's whitewashed apartment, and I began to think it was the emptiest place I had ever been in. The deep blue prayer rug I had bought to take home was the only bit of color in the neutral rooms. There wasn't even a picture of me, despite the fact that I had framed two and given them to Thom for a going-away present. I opened a few drawers to try to find the pictures, but was scared I'd find something I didn't want to find: pornography, a picture of his ex-wife, newspaper clippings of a hit-and-run accident, still unsolved. My heart could be broken in a thousand well-deserved ways. Each afternoon I sat on the sofa with my hands folded on the pile of books Thom recommended, but I didn't move, didn't read. I just watched the clock until he came back home.

The first weekend, we took the Blue Train to Istanbul where I hired a guide to show us Tokapi Palace. The gentleman wore a long double-breasted coat and horn-rimmed glasses. Even though it was I who handed him the lira, he had kept his eyes on Thom. "Secretary?" he asked and nodded toward me. He smiled broadly.

"Friend," Thom said.

"Yes, secretary," the man said and winked. "Not wife."

I walked ahead. I had questions to ask the sexist guide and I intended to ask them. I knew what I was worth in his eyes: forty-one million lira, or about twenty-five bucks for a half-hour tour of a sultan's palace. I walked through the harem quarters and saw the golden cage where concubines were once enclosed high above the rest of the room. I knew what that was like, the feeling of being a captive, the angst of knowing life continued below. We drank fresh-squeezed orange juice at a sidewalk café. When I finished I asked for another, and Thom laughed at my greediness.

A few days later, we were on the bus to Cappadocia and beginning to pass strange rock formations, conical rocks stretched twenty feet into the air. Some of the cones and towers had carved windows and doorways, hobbit houses. It could have been created in Hollywood, a strange valley of volcanic deposits with the occasional fairy chimney, a cap of hard rock on top of a rock cone.

Thom said, "There's historical evidence that Saint Paul visited here. Actually some biblical reference to this area—surely you know it?"

"No," I said. "I know about Ephesus. That's in Turkey, too, I think."

"It is. A pity we won't be going there. But the chapels I want you to see are a bit later—they've dated the frescos from the ninth and tenth centuries. They built monasteries in the face of a cliff.

Looks like a wasp nest cut of stone. And then you'll see over thirty of these rock chapels or cave churches, rustic but magnificent."

The bus pulled into a village and parked and became the only noticeable marker of the modern century. Hay and muck littered the pathways, no sidewalks to speak of, no yards, no fences. Chickens wandered in and out of living areas. A goat munched on the grass roof of a house. I smiled at the women who wove cloth in their front yards and at the children who rode burros. The men in the village gathered around outdoor tables drinking cups of chai. One young woman jumped up with a scarf of muslin she had beaded with tiny drops of amber and draped it over my hair. The beads glistened in the Hittite sun as we faced each other, only our eyes and lips showing. "Beautiful," she said.

I bought the scarf, digging out wads of lira and pressing them into her hand. I joined Thom, who was studying some bit of a Roman ruin.

"Pretty," he said. "How much?"

"Twenty million," I said.

"You got robbed."

"I like it," I said. I folded it and carefully put it in the bottom of my backpack. I pulled out the brochure the guide on the bus had passed out. It was a map of the valley with the churches labeled. Kokar Kilise, the church of the sweet smell. Sumbullu Kilise, the hyacinth church. Agacalti Kilise, the church under the tree.

The Melindiz Suyu ran through the valley, gray-blue, crystal clear. As we began walking, the cliff faces stretched on both sides with doorways and windows carved at all heights. Tall, thin poplars, silent forests with fluttering silver and green leaves. The guide picked small golden berries and handed them to us. We ate the cherrylike fruit and tongued the pits into our palms as we walked deep into the valley.

The first cave was covered with frescos, the paintings remarkably preserved, especially on the ceilings and upper walls where tourists weren't able to rub or chip. Angels brandishing crosses. Saints lined up like judges looked down at the scruffy tourists, who stared back with wide eyes and flashing cameras. Christ was everywhere and as primitive as I had ever seen Him. No gentle Jesus meek and mild here; this angular Byzantine *glared*.

The colors were amazing, centuries old but vibrant gold and azure and red. The artists must have worked on these for years— the detail, the flowers, rosettes, checkerboard patterns, everything layered and ornate, on stone, in a cave with windows chiseled for light. The Garden of Eden. The Red Sea. Daniel in the lions' den. Everywhere I looked was another story and another truth and I had believed them all. God made a way in the wilderness if you were his true daughter. But impostors were struck with boils and lightning and turned to salt. I felt dizzy. Centuries ago my forefathers had lived and worshipped here and were now buried beneath me. The very air condemned me. I was breathing their bones. These dead saints had persevered, unlike me. I suddenly remembered the winter mornings my sisters and I would meet before light in the morning. We'd leave our warm beds to start reluctant cars and wade through drifts of snow for prayer before our husbands and children woke for the day. Our faces were bare, still creased with sleep, as we held each other's cold hands and sought the face of God. I was willing to sacrifice sleep, time, comfort, anything that would keep me from being in His presence.

"Are you all right?" Thom asked.

"No," I said after a pause and suddenly I wanted to go back to the bus. "May I have some of your water?"

I took a long swallow from his bottle and handed it back to him. I led the way out of the cave and stood, uncertain, at the door.

"Can we go sit by the river?" I asked.

Thom tried to subdue his impatience with me. "We've only started," he said. "Later, we'll take a break, okay?" He was intent, knowledge his aphrodisiac; I knew that. His gray eyes deepened. "Come on. The next cave is fucking fantastic—Yilanli Kilise."

We entered the arched doorway and stepped into the domed room. The frescos were even more intact. An enormous spotted snake writhed over the walls, a woman caught in its grip here and there. Saints gasped in horror as this snake attacked. It was primitive and ridiculous, such an obvious threat I wanted to laugh, but I was afraid if I did, I'd cry instead. Thom launched into lecture mode.

"Some say this is the dragon that Saint Michael wrestled, but it could be a snake sent to punish sinners. Or is it the devil, straight from the Garden of Eden?"

"It's rather misogynistic, wouldn't you say? Why is it the women who are being punished?"

"Eve, of course," Thom said. "It was all her doing, the fall from grace. Poor Adam, minding his own business, and next thing you know, he's naked."

I focused on one of the women in the painting. She stood still as the snake approached her. She wasn't screaming or running like the others. It was as though she knew this moment would come. God would not be mocked. I took Thom's hand to pull him away. He squeezed my hand.

"Stop it," I hissed.

"What's the matter?" he asked.

"You crushed my hand," I said, and couldn't stop myself from crying. My defenses were down, and I was suddenly aware of how much I had lost, all that confidence in an ordered universe, an approaching day of reckoning, a settling of accounts, and justice for all. I couldn't make myself believe in any of it any longer.

"Ah, this is too much for you. I'm sorry," he said and put his arms around me. I let him hold me.

"Would you mind if I waited for the guide? I have to hear more about this," he said as he wiped the tears off my face with the back of his hand and kissed the top of my head. "A fucking anaconda in a church, good God." He looked up at the snake with obvious admiration.

I told him it was fine if he wanted to stay and that I'd find him later. I made my way back down the hill and sat by the river with my back to the cave churches. A woman knee-deep in the Melindiz Suyu carried a log on her back. Though it wasn't large it looked heavy. It made my own shoulders ache in sympathy. How many years had she been gathering wood in this river? I wondered if she resented this task or if it had become automatic and not worth thinking about anymore.

I threw little stones into the river and imagined floating down the Melindiz, away from these small rooms carved from rock, past the minarets with their loudspeakers insisting on prayer, past the whirling dervishes lost in ecstasy, past the glimmer of stained glass, the whiff of incense, until I arrived somewhere I could breathe again.

A light step nearby made me turn around. A little girl, probably about seven, brown hair and eyes, stood nearby. She was dressed in a plain brown tunic and wide cotton pants. She pointed to her lips and then to my purse.

"Lipstick?" I asked, miming the tube across my lips. She nodded, happy. A first-rate germophobe who had only reluctantly shared a lipstick in the past, I unzipped my purse, fumbled for the tube, and rolled it out. I held her chin and carefully applied Dusky Mauve to her solemn mouth. Then I watched her climb toward the chapels on the hill, her tiny feet picking through the roots and rocks and scrambling for balance.

What could she be looking for up there? I wondered. I hoped it was lira and lipstick, a handful of berries, something she could taste or touch, anything she could see. You couldn't go far wrong in loving things like that. But I had stopped doing exactly that when I was eighteen years old, when I'd wrapped myself in a cocoon of scripture and sermons and tattered hymnals.

I had spent a lifetime bending knee to that which I could not see, and I wasn't ready to say that was a waste or a tragedy or anything of the sort, but now I wanted to praise the threescore and ten, the running water and poplar trees, that singular ride from the airport through Istanbul leaning into the side of a man I loved, his lips on my hair, the apple tea we sipped as we cruised the Bosporus, the canvas bags of spice that filled the market. I took a deep breath. It wasn't too late for me, after all, and it certainly wasn't too late for her. I dug through my purse for an extra tube of lipstick, and then I went hunting for the girl.

The Imperceptible Head Shake

Julia Scheeres

I was thirteen the first time I doubted Christianity.

My family had just finished eating dinner, and, as usual, Dad was reading to us from the Bible. He would read a chapter at a time, usually from the New Testament, as he sipped his sugared coffee and my brothers and I silently urged him to finish already so we could get back to our kid business.

His scriptures-reading voice was a soporific drone; he may as well have been reading the list of ingredients off a box of cornflakes. While he spoke, I'd usually zone out until he bent his head to pray, the cue that we were about to be released from our familial obligation. But for whatever reason, on that particular day, this passage caught in my ear:

I do not permit a woman to teach or to assume authority over a man; she must be quiet. For Adam was formed first, then Eve. And Adam was not the one deceived; it was the woman who was deceived and became a sinner. But women will be saved through childbearing—if they continue in faith, love, and holiness with propriety.

That's 1 Timothy 2:12–15.

I felt slapped. Angry. Disturbed. I don't know what struck me more—my father's nonchalance as he read the passage, or the words themselves, which brimmed with injustice. (At thirteen I wasn't familiar with the term *sexism*.)

I do, however, remember my reaction. I looked down at the plastic white tablecloth and shook my head in disagreement. Mind you, this headshake was imperceptible to anyone but me. My father was a violent patriarch who brooked no disagreement, especially with his beloved scriptures. But it mattered to me, this headshake. I was taking a stand. I wasn't going to passively sit there and be told I was worth less than my father and brothers because I was born with a vulva instead of a penis. *Why should I be punished for something a woman did six thousand years ago?* I remember thinking.

There was no gendered division of labor at our house, as far as we kids were concerned. I shoveled snow from the driveway and chopped logs for the wood stove beside my brothers; they took turns peeling potatoes at the kitchen sink. I prided myself on my toughness, on swinging an axe as capably as they did. Why didn't this same equality extend to our roles in church? On that evening, I looked across the table at them with great resentment. I imagined a smugness blooming in their chests as Dad read the Apostle Paul's sexist screed, but in reality the passage probably didn't even register with them. They tended to zone out just like I did.

SHORTLY AFTER MY RUN·IN with Paul, I had a run-in with the head usher at our church.

My brothers, who were roughly my age, took great pride donning their wide-lapel suits and leading families through the hushed sanctuary to their pews. Like all the other girls, I volunteered in the church nursery, which was in the basement. But once the novelty of bottle-feeding and diaper-changing wore off, I decided I wanted to take a turn at ushering as well. I approached the head usher. Our exchange went something like this:

Me: "I'd like to usher."

Head Usher: "Yes, well. All the ushers are male."

Me: "My brothers are ushers."

Head Usher: "Yes, well. They're male."

Me: "So I can't do it?"

Head Usher: "All the ushers are male."

Me: "I know."

Head Usher: "You're better off helping in the nursery."

With a condescending pat on my shoulder, he walked away. End of conversation.

The entire dialogue was spoken through polite, albeit tight, smiles, mind you. But another log had been tossed onto the growing fire of my resentment. Sitting in the pews afterward, I looked around. The preacher was male. The deacons were male. The elders were male. None of those positions was open to women. During the offertory, I watched the deacons, so officious and self-important, march in unison to the altar to distribute the brass collection plates. I began to hate what they stood for.

I now read the Bible with a new awareness, stung by the anti-female sentiment in so many passages. A sampling:

1 Corinthians 14:34–35. Women should remain silent in the churches.

They are not allowed to speak, but must be in submission, as the law says. If they want to inquire about something, they should ask their own husbands at home; for it is disgraceful for a woman to speak in the church.

That explained why women who volunteered in my church were relegated to the basement child care.

Genesis 3:16. Unto the woman he said, "I will greatly multiply thy sorrow and thy conception; in sorrow thou shalt bring forth children; and thy desire shall be to thy husband, and he shall rule over thee."

That explained why the wives in my church seemed so listless and mute, forever deferring to their husbands.

Of course, all this sexism is rooted in Eve. The Bible establishes women's second-rate status in chapter 2 of Genesis. Eve is an afterthought, created from Adam's rib to become his "helpmeet." In chapter 3, a snake tempts the weak-willed Eve with an irresistible apple, and therefore *all* female kind, from the first to the last, shall suffer her disobedience. Consider the injustice of this story. Then consider its absurdity. I mean really, people—a talking snake? If some dude told you that story today, you'd think he was nuts. There are many equally absurd moments in the Bible, and I find it stunning that otherwise lucid people would believe these stories, post-Enlightenment.

The apostles were male. Jesus Christ was male. God the Father is male. Even the Holy Ghost is presumed male, but how can a disembodied spirit be one sex or the other? It was a mystery to me. But hey, if the Bible says so, it must be true. Right?

In my teenage mind, the seeds of doubt kept growing.

I WAS BROUGHT UP fundamentalist. By that, I mean that I was made to believe that the Bible was the inerrant word of God. It was all fact, all true. There was no innuendo or nuance. Jonah *was* swallowed by a whale. Balaam's donkey *did* talk . . . as well as that damn snake in the Garden of Eden. When you're six years old, the Bible is entertaining. Such imaginative morality plays! Good versus Evil! Magic tricks! All great material for Sunday School coloring books. But when you're thirteen and starting to develop a healthy skepticism, the Bible becomes a natural target.

My family was Calvinist—that dour, hellfire-obsessed denomination embraced by the Puritans. I attended church twice on Sunday, catechism on Wednesday nights, and Calvinettes on Saturday mornings. I went to a private Christian grade school run by Calvinists. We were a tribe and socialized, almost exclusively, with other members of our tribe. We believed we were the chosen people, far superior to the idolatrous Catholics and the babbling Pentecostals. They weren't going to heaven. *We* were. And we surely wouldn't let them drag us to hell by associating with them.

At thirteen, I was a budding "women's libber"—that most hated and denounced creature among conservative Christians— although I didn't know it yet. There was no way I could talk about my growing skepticism with my mother. She was a firm believer in her secondary role, a woman who retreated into a wounded silence whenever my father barked at her for interrupting a slow-forming thought or suggesting he obey traffic signs.

My questing adolescent brain collided smack-dab with the biblical dictate of not questioning. "Our brains are too finite," I was often told, "to understand God's infinite wisdom." In church we sang the nineteenth-century hymn "Trust and Obey," whose refrain was "Trust and obey, for there's no other way, to be happy in Jesus, but to trust and obey." I was not happy in Jesus.

THE LOGICAL CONCLUSION TO my thirteen-year-old epiphany played out four years later, when, at seventeen, I committed the worst possible offense for a young Christian woman: I lost my virginity, that "most precious gift" that I was expected to pack away in mothballs for my future husband. While my parents were away on a mission trip, the woman staying with me witnessed my boyfriend climbing from my window at six in the morning.

Deuteronomy advocates stoning women to death for having premarital sex. I was sent to a Christian reform school in the Dominican Republic instead.

At Escuela Caribe, where I spent my senior year of high school, I saw extreme examples of Christian sexism and hypocrisy. The Christian staff routinely brutalized students, and the housefather of my group home lorded his chosen-male position over us girls on a daily basis. It was during the year I spent at this isolated, miserable place that my resentment for Christianity and its practitioners fully blossomed. To survive, I played the part of the repentant teen, parroted their Jesus mumbo-jumbo, and got out as quickly as possible.

Twenty years later, I wrote about all this in a memoir, *Jesus Land*. Some folks are offended by the title. So be it. I meant it as a pointed reference to the fake, plastic atmosphere of a Disney theme park. A place where the surface is all pasted-on smiles and welcome mats, but the pith is a putrid hairball of oppression, exclusion, and malevolent superstition.

I also joined forces with other Escuela Caribe alumni to create a website warning parents away from the so-called Christian therapeutic boarding school, and convinced dozens of former students to complete surveys about their experiences. They wrote about the Christian staff slamming them into walls, whipping them with a leather strap until their skin broke, and molesting them while they slept. As a result of our activism, enrollment dropped, and the school, which had been operating for forty years, charging a monthly tuition of $6,000 a month, closed. I'll praise my alumni sistren and brethren for making this happen—not any god. God enables child abuse. To paraphrase Proverbs 13:24: "Spare the rod, spoil the child."

Today the sight of any religious symbol—be it a twenty-four-karat gold pendant dangling from a woman's neck in the shape of a cross or a Star of David; be it a turbaned cab driver or televised footage of a woman in a burka—makes me cringe. For me, these symbols signify all the things I was subjected to in my youth: ignorance; a sect that values superstitious dogma over basic human kindness; a system that believes I'm inferior because I don't have a scrotum. The bile rises in my throat when I hear "Christianese," that intellect-numbing vernacular riddled by *Jesus* this and that, *He* and *His* and *Him* and sporadic Bible verses. It brings me right back to that genteel sexism of my youth: All the ushers are male.

Ancient misogynists used the Bible to establish male domination, and today, Abrahamic religions oppress women on every continent. Why would any woman participate in her own subjugation by believing such crap?

Once in a while, people try to lure me back to Christianity. They'll email me asserting that the Christians I knew in my youth weren't "real" Christians and that they know other Christians who are the "real" Christians, and that I really should check them out before giving up on "God" altogether. I scoff. Yes, I do. I find this Christian compulsion to out-pious other Christians endlessly amusing. Furthermore, their threats of hellfire fall flat on my ears. I no longer believe in an afterlife. I believe I am like a zinnia, a plant that sprouts, grows, blooms, then dies, and provides mulch for next year's garden. My daughters will be so much freer than I was.

I never respond to these email pleas. I've wasted too much of my life to superstition. I just jab the delete key, sometimes with my middle finger.

End of conversation.

Duct Tape and Baling Wire

Valerie Tarico

I can't recall his name—the small boy who severed the final strands of my faith—just a vague image of soft brown hair, pale velvety limbs, and trusting eyes. I was twenty-six, in the last stage of my PhD, which required a year-long internship at the University of Washington. In one of my rotations, at Children's Hospital, interns provided mental health consultation for families of patients on the medical wards. The child was two, in the first phase of treatment for a spinal cord tumor that would leave him paraplegic even if the nightmare course of chemotherapy were successful. I don't know how long he survived.

Maybe it was his eyes, or his inability to comprehend why he couldn't walk anymore, or why people who looked kind kept hurting him. Maybe it was the unbearable tenderness of his parents, who simply wanted to take their child home and love him rather than watch him suffer inexplicable months of "treatment"—for a long shot at extending his life. But something inside me broke.

For years I had been holding together the last remains of my evangelical Christian faith with duct tape and baling wire. As far back as grade school, I had struggled with the idea that my friend Kay, a Mormon-not-Christian, was going to be tortured in hell forever. I had inherited my own salvation. My father's family of Italian immigrants had been saved from Catholicism by door-to-door Pentecostals. My sisters and brothers and I were raised in an independent Bible church. At the time, I didn't even recognize Catholics as Christians. Dad's childhood stint as an altar boy was a curiosity to us, almost as peculiar as Grandma's stories about playing meat market with captured frogs next to *her* grandmother's stone cottage in the hills above their village.

MY FAMILY HAD COME far from Italy and Catholicism, and yet in some ways we were as culturally isolated as my grandmother had been in her small village. My sisters and brothers and I didn't butcher the frogs we raised from pollywogs. But, like Grandma, we were taught that the Bible was the literally perfect word of God, a blueprint for this life and the next. Being Protestant, our church didn't have altar boys, but it did have altar calls. With bowed heads the congregation listened to organ music as the pastor implored the unsaved among us to make our way to the front and confess our sins. I responded on more than one occasion, each time asking Jesus to be my savior, because, inherited or no, I never took my salvation for granted. I was acutely aware of my own imperfections, and hell, with its tortured hoards of burning souls, was a scary place.

Now, a decade later, having journeyed from my childhood

evangelical community in Arizona to attend Wheaton College of Billy Graham fame, then on to an ecumenical Christian commune for graduate school, and finally to Seattle, I was faced with hell in a different form. Each morning I pedaled my bicycle to the beautiful green campus of Children's Hospital, then made my way through halls bright with art—fantastical animals and clowns, clusters of balloons, whimsical landscapes—to a pediatric oncology unit where children were suffering unto death. I walked past wards of kids with broken bones and babies with birth defects, past little wheelchairs or stretchers in the halls and elevators, past the occasional murmur of voices or muffled crying and soothing sounds—with huge heavy silences in between.

Some people think that when sick or wounded children are silent they are comfortable. I knew better, thanks to intense headaches that had started when I was not much older than the small boy with the tumor. Shortly after I learned to talk I told my mother my head hurt, and then I threw up. Throughout childhood my parents took me for consultations and tests. In one clinic I lay perfectly still while a nurse stuck little blobs of gummy cotton in my hair and attached electrodes, and then waves appeared on an unfamiliar machine. I picked gooey bits out of my hair the next day. The doctors could offer no solution; along with my salvation I had inherited a family pattern of migraines. When I could do nothing but be in pain my parents gently put hot cloths on my head. When I could think of nothing but pain they rubbed my feet. When I could be nothing but pain, they prayed for me. And then I would lie in a bath of hot water or with my face pressed against a pillow, waiting, waiting for the pain to fade—silent when I wasn't writhing and sometimes even then. By the time I arrived at the oncology ward, I had no illusions about how much a child can suffer in silence.

I looked at that beautiful, trusting two-year-old boy and my mind conjured up fragments of a Pat Benatar song, "Hell is for Children": *"Be a good little boy and you'll get a new toy. Tell Grandma you fell off the swing . . . Love and pain become one and the same in the eyes of a wounded child . . . It's all so confusing, this brutal abusing."* Benatar's song is about child abuse, but for me, as a believer in an omnipotent, omnibenevolent, interventionist God, the line between abuse and cancer was getting blurry. Child abuse or child cancer, little brains damaged by shaken baby syndrome or damaged by the birthing process, bones broken by angry parents or by car accidents: If God is our heavenly Father, is there a difference?

Despite my growing sense of doubt, it was my job to offer comfort and practical support, not questions. So I listened as medical staff and family members struggled to make meaning out of the unavoidable tortures that abound in a hospital for children. I kept my skepticism to myself. Maybe, still, I could shore up my belief in an all-loving, all-powerful God and find comfort in those beliefs.

Through many years of sermons and Bible studies, my Christianity had offered two justifications for what some call "the problem of pain." These justifications of suffering had been part of my spiritual arsenal for as long as I had been old enough to find myself troubled by nature and humanity. Now I tried on the first of them: Suffering is because of sin. Someone, somewhere has done wrong—either the person who is suffering, or his parents or our collective parents Adam and Eve, and so we (implicitly) deserve to be punished. The wages of sin is suffering unto death and eternal suffering thereafter. We all deserve to suffer, and any reprieve is simply a sign of God's mercy.

I looked at the small beings around me, the peaked faces, some with fuzzy postchemo hair; some with wan smiles and dark circles under their eyes, hooked to IV drips; and I saw them in a way that I had never been able to see my child-self. Innocent. Hurting. Deserving more than this. Justification One wasn't working. To my mind, it excused abuse. It made God contemptible. It let Him off the hook by making a mockery out of justice.

I tried out Number Two: What seems bad to us is actually good. "We know that all things work together for good to those who love God, to those who are called according to His purpose" (Romans 8:28, NKJV). My pastor would say things like: Pottery must be fired to become beautiful; metal must be forged—suffering has a higher purpose, even when we cannot see it. God's ways are beyond our comprehension. The thought had offered some comfort when I battled with headaches.

But now the words rang hollow. These children were dying. There was no way to argue that their suffering would bring benefit into their own lives. Nor was it moral to make them suffer without their consent for the benefit of someone else. All the *justification* in the world couldn't make it *just*. Nor could it fix the problem—the illness and injury that wracked those little bodies. Unlike the eternal lake of fire that I had been taught awaited the unrepentant sinners, a simple prayer couldn't make this kind of real-world hell go away.

A kind chaplain at the hospital tried to patch up what was left of my crumbling belief. He offered me a copy of a best-selling book, *When Bad Things Happen to Good People*. The author, Rabbi Michael Kushner, suggests that there is suffering in the world because God is not all-powerful. Even God is constrained by the rules of nature. He grieves along with us when cancer strikes a two-year-old. Sometimes, Kushner said, tragedy has no meaning. It just is. That part sounded right, the "it just is." But I couldn't accept the benign-yet-limited deity that Kushner offered as a replacement for my own dubious

God. Kushner's argument seems to be grounded more in a need to believe than in any real-world evidence that a tender, heavenly Father grieves with us. To paraphrase Richard Dawkins, "The spinal cord tumors we observe have precisely the properties we should expect if there is, at bottom, no design, no purpose, no evil, no good, nothing but blind, pitiless indifference."

Over the course of a few weeks, things got worse. After two decades of warping my feelings, my perceptions, and my intellect in order to defend the absolute goodness of the Christian God, I was mad. As I walked the halls of the hospital or bicycled home, arguments erupted in my mind. *"His eye is on the sparrow."* What in the world does that mean anyway? Sparrows live short, hard lives. *"Whosoever shall offend one of these little ones that believe in me, it is better for him that a millstone were hanged about his neck, and he were cast into the sea."* So we shouldn't harm little children, but God can? Even the most benign passages of the Bible appeared in a new light. A Jesus who would make one lame man walk or one blind man see? Was that the best God could do? They were impressive tricks for a magician, to be sure, but not at all impressive for a deity who with equal ease could simply do away with all blindness—or with all cancer that leaves two-year-olds paralyzed and dying.

One day I found myself struck, viscerally, by the contrasts of the hospital—the part that humans controlled and the part that was the domain of God. Outside, thanks to the labor of patient gardeners, flourishing beds of hosta and iris and hydrangea soothed anxious parents. Inside, in the waiting rooms tanks of bright tropical fish distracted achy children, and the elevators offered glimpses of whimsical art balloons and whales for those riding in wheelchairs. Through it all moved men and women who had dedicated their imperfect, finite life energy to the well-being of children, to having there be a bit less suffering in this world. All this stood against the deeply imperfect handiwork of my perfect God: genetic disorders, birth canals that damaged little brains, cell division gone awry, and worse. God was visible in the hospital in the silences, in the small soft bodies with faces staring or whimpering or buried in pillows, waiting.

Abruptly, I said to the god in my head, *I'm not making excuses for you anymore.* I quit conjuring a long-dead spirit in the swirling smoke of my own mind, and just like that, God was gone. All that was left was the empty frame of tape and wire: excuses, rationalizations, and songs of worship that sounded oddly flat.

And me.

I walked away and didn't look back.

Nun Hands

Mary Johnson

The other day, after a reading, I was signing a book when a woman told me, "Nothing about you is nunnish anymore—except your hands."

That stung. I'd taken care to set my curls, had applied a little makeup, had my toenails polished, and had even chosen my most colorful silk tunic. I'd consciously cultivated my "I'm not a nun anymore" look—and I'd been betrayed by my "nunnish" hands?

Hadn't the woman noticed my decidedly unnunnish wedding ring? Sure, my fingernails were short and unpolished, but at a certain point I just can't be bothered.

Even if I'd lavished hours on my nails, the wrinkles on my hands might still have given me away. Twenty years of laundry scrubbed by hand, twenty gloveless winters, daily wringing of an old potato sack in cold water so that I could then squat and pass the wet sack over the floor in the Missionaries of Charity's version of mopping—in the fifteen years since I've been out, I haven't yet found a lotion that can soothe that history from my hands. Or from my heart.

THE SISTERS INTRUDE MOST frequently when I'm most defense-less. Nuns invade my dreams, and it's not usually the friendly ones who show up.

Usually, I appear first, and it's like those time-travel movies where the actor looks down and is startled to find herself in unfa-miliar clothes—except that the white sari with a blue border is all too familiar. I know I'm not meant to be wherever the dreams put me—church, convent, bus, train. I want to get out, but the sisters won't let me, repeating that I don't have permission to leave until next week or next month or just simply "till later." In my dream I do all the nun things—say the prayers on the bus, do the chapel housework, wash my clothes, eat in the refectory—but my heart isn't in any of it. Some nights I try to run away. Sisters chase me, several at a time, sometimes twenty or thirty of them, down long corridors and through secret tunnels and on staircases that go up and up and up and end nowhere.

When Mother Teresa appears, she is nearly always alone, and silent. She doesn't give chase. She just looks at me. She seems to want to say something, but I sense that she still doesn't know how, that she'd like to speak to me as a peer but can't lose the sense that she's sup-posed to be my mother and has failed. I want to hug her and tell her it's okay, but one doesn't hug Mother Teresa, even in dreams.

NOW THAT I LIVE in the world, I wash my clothes once a week, in a machine in a little room off the kitchen. While that might not seem remarkable to some, to me it's a welcome reminder of how far I've come. No more daily scrubbing of clothes by hand in a bucket on a stretch of concrete under the open sky. No more chapped hands during winter, no more futile attempts to stretch the weekly ration of laundry soap. I am now a twenty-first-century woman with a washer and drier—at least until the drier broke and we decided to go green. For the past month or so, I've lugged my wet laundry to the backyard, where I hang my clothes on a clothesline.

I pull a blouse or a pair of jeans from my laundry basket, fix it to the line, and the feel of the wood, the snap of the clip, recalls other clothespins, each etched with a cross and an ID number—mine was 985. After a while, most pins sported a wrapping of twine or a smidgen of glue because each sister was allowed only six clothespins and it wasn't easy to get a replacement if you lost or broke one. You had to "speak your fault" for destroying the property of the community or for being careless and having lost the property of the community. Then you had to write in the garment book, "Please, sister, may I have a clothespin? Thank you, sister." Then you waited until Thursday to see if the superior thought you really needed a clothespin, if you deserved a clothespin, if you'd expressed adequate sorrow for not having taken care of the pin you had abused or neglected, and maybe she gave permission for you to be given another clothespin, or maybe she decided to make you wait.

All that returns to me now as I clip skirts and socks to a line in New Hampshire. I haul the empty laundry basket inside and the sisters climb the back stairs with me. Sometimes they stay all day.

Perhaps it's true that memories return to everyone, memories summoned by little things like laundry or the smell of baking bread or the way a stranger's shoulders slump as you pass her on the street. Perhaps my memories of the sisters seem particularly pernicious because I so yearn to be free of their taunts, their unspoken accusations, my unfinished business.

Perhaps the sisters miss me when they sing one of the hymns I wrote or study the notes I left. Perhaps.

A FEW WEEKS AGO I met with several women who had read my book. We gathered in the cafeteria of our town's Catholic college, invited by a sister in a veil and orthopedic shoes. We were a small group: three sisters, three former sisters, five women from the community, and me. I knew only one woman, from her flower shop downtown.

I was nervous about the nuns. What would they think of my tell-all tale? How could I let them know that I considered their work and their lives valuable, even though I'd turned my back on their lifestyle?

Our discussion was intense, but not hostile. One of the women congratulated me on writing such a readable book. One of the sisters interrupted: "That book was hard to read, painful." She didn't elaborate. Others commented on how mean the sisters in my book had been—and I tried to explain that I hoped readers wouldn't dwell on anyone's faults but could see how, by denying simple human pleasures to its members, even a well-intentioned system could produce monsters. Another of the sisters said, "If only you'd joined a more liberal congregation, one that believed in education." After an hour, the sister with the veil called intermission and we broke for tea and cookies.

Round two began with one of the ex-sisters, who'd already said quite a bit, but whose look of determination and absence of cookies led me to suspect that she'd spent the break steeling up the courage to say something important.

"There's nothing like the life of a sister," she began. "Nothing to equal the camaraderie, the devotion, the sense of purpose." This woman had to be at least sixty-five, and she spoke with so much wistfulness that it broke my heart. She told us that back in her twenties, she had left the convent—more than once. A year after her first departure, she'd returned, then left again. She'd even joined a third time, determined to stick it out, but before too long the sisters sent her home, claiming she wasn't suited for the convent. "I wanted it so badly," she said.

I'd wanted it, too, had never wanted anything so badly in my whole life: to dedicate myself completely, to be of service, to share my life with those good women. I'd envisioned a life where each sister's gifts were respected and nourished, where we encouraged and challenged each other, all working together for a common goal. I hadn't bargained that two power-hungry sisters would enmesh the Missionaries of Charity in right-wing church politics, that they would substitute intimidation for inspiration, confuse loyalty with integrity, and pull the group so far to the right that I would hardly recognize it. I hadn't imagined that my own human needs for intimacy would clash so dramatically with rules demanding the denial of every human desire. I hadn't realized what a toll obedience would take.

I still stumble to find words with which to think and talk about my leaving. Had I failed, betraying God and my vows, or had I simply outgrown a tragically stunted community? When I left, I had the audacity to believe that God was calling me out. I'd heard the words of Jesus, "I came that you may have life, and have it to the full," and

I knew that my life in the convent was not full.

But I'm not sure my present life is full, either. I'm not sure I even know what *full* means. I do feel freer to search for fullness and for purpose, if they're to be found.

I want to stop chasing phantoms.

AT ANOTHER BOOK DISCUSSION, a woman reminded me that I'd done a lot of good for the sisters, that I'd been a positive influence while in the convent. She asked why that hadn't been enough for me. She seemed to imply—at least in my mind—that it *should* have been enough for me.

Sometimes I think of the sisters and I get this hard, tight feeling in my chest, like I want to cry. But I don't cry. I tell myself that crying would be foolish and ungrateful. It's good that I left the sisters and their nunnish ways. It's good that now I can think for myself, that I'm in a wonderful marriage, and that I've created communities of various sorts where people can be themselves. I feel that tightness in my chest and I defy it. I *shouldn't* miss the sisters. I *shouldn't* regret not having been able to tough it out. No regrets.

But I do regret.

Why couldn't we have had it all? What stopped us from being a group where both community and individuals mattered? Couldn't we have created something truly beautiful? Couldn't we have been allowed to think for ourselves and make our creative contributions within that system?

But you can't change one part of a system without affecting the entire system—and Mother Teresa had always made it clear that we didn't enter the Missionaries of Charity to change the community, but to accept it. She told us that if we didn't like the

MC way of doing things, we should pack up and go home, right now. That's what she said: *Right now.* She wagged her finger at us and she told us that if we didn't want life in the convent exactly as it was, we should go through the door—because she wasn't changing anything.

For Mother Teresa, a sister proved her fidelity to God by accepting things as they were and doing things exactly as they were meant to be done, according to the Rules. Why couldn't she see that living creatures grew, that as they grew they changed, that institutions only remain vital when free to respond in new and creative ways to the challenges before them?

I've heard that Missionaries of Charity these days, when faced with a decision, ask themselves, "What would Mother do?" I'd like to tell the sisters that answering that question will never result in more than a guess anyway, that they need to take responsibility, that they might consider asking, "In this situation now, what is the most loving thing to do, the action that will bring about the most good?"

Perhaps, when the knot in my chest tightens, I should let the tears flow. Perhaps crying is the only possible release in the face of such futile loss.

A friend who also happens to be a family therapist once told me that the hardest relationships to heal are those in which love and trauma are closely entwined.

IN THE MIDST OF struggling with the issues in this essay, I take a break to walk my sister's dog. I'm visiting her in West Virginia, and the hills we stroll are, for me, unfamiliar territory. The dog, a Bernese mountain dog my sister calls a puppy but I call a bear, pulls hard on the leash and drags me from one side of the road to the other. We approach an enormous tree that had been ripped from the earth in a recent storm and I feel a lump rise in my throat. I've been uprooted more times and in more ways than I care to count. I've spent decades trying to figure out what to be and how to be. I've lived in shacks and farmhouses, in towns and cities, have mingled with the famous and the destitute. I devoted decades of my life to a group in which I'd never really fit.

I want to belong somewhere.

The bear-dog, seemingly oblivious to my struggle, fully engaged in the adventure of a walk that has taken him beyond any place my sister had yet brought him, pulls hard and tugs me over yet another hill.

I don't want to live in the past, caught in the pain of longing for what might have been. Here, today, I have friends who care about me, parents who don't condemn me for having abandoned the God they taught me to love, and a husband with whom I share everything. I've known deep faith and deeper doubts. I've learned to give myself with honesty and openness. I've been vulnerable and strong. I've tried and I've failed and I've tried again.

At the crest of yet another hill, the bear-dog pauses, panting. A hawk flies overhead, dark wings unfurled against a sky that stretches over hills and valleys, and as I gaze upon that blue sky, the world fills me, fills me with a love so immense that I want to burst and spill it across the countryside.

There it is—that same impulse that impelled me into the convent in the first place—the irresistible urge to love the whole world.

As I look across the hollow, I realize that I do have a place to call home. My home is the Earth. My family has been here for generations. I don't know everyone, but we are one in important and mysterious ways that I may never grasp, but have experienced once again.

PERHAPS THE NUNS WILL continue to chase me in my dreams and haunt me at the clothesline. Perhaps I will learn to stop resisting that. Perhaps my sisters will always be part of me. I may never know if I did the right thing by choosing to leave, but I know I did the necessary thing, and sometimes that's all anyone can do.

Unpolished fingernails, tightness in the chest, tears, a dog panting at my side, and sisters far away and close by—for the moment, I don't need anything more.

Acknowledgments

This being my first anthology, I was pleasantly surprised by how much I *loved* working with authors to help them shape their stories. So first and foremost, I want to thank the many women we've had contact with throughout the process of putting this book together. Both to those whose pieces ended up in this collection and the many who submitted stories that just didn't quite fit: Thank you for sharing your sacred stories with us! I know it takes courage to speak unpopular, difficult, or partially discovered truths.

And then I must say a huge thank-you to my coeditor, Susan Tive, for working tirelessly and sharing the vision of this passion project with me. Pamela Malpas, my wonderful agent, who is all encouragement, common sense, and warm e-hugs when needed . . . Thank you! A huge "You rock!" to Brooke Warner, my friend and our acquiring editor at Seal, and to Laura Mazer, who stepped in and made my heart sparkle with her "I love this book."

And then, there aren't any words for how grateful I am to have a community of people around me who love me and cheer me on in every endeavor I embrace, whether it's running a marathon or working on a book. Bill Pech, my best friend and husband, thank you. I'm grateful, too, for my pals who wait patiently for me to return to them when I'm in the middle of a project, who forgive me for missing important events in their lives or skipping happy hour so I can work. You know who you are, and you know I love you.

Finally, this project never would have come about had Susan and I not taken a nine-month course called Writing the Modern Memoir taught by novelist and really superb person Laura Kalpakian. Hugs to Laura for fostering my eye for a good narrative arc and interesting scenic depiction.

This anthology has been a gift to me because it has combined my work as a therapist with my commitment to writing. For a long time in my practice, I've nurtured the telling of difficult stories. Now I've discovered a new way to foster tellings—through helping writers do what they do: write.

—Cami Ostman

B*eyond Belief* began as a spark of recognition that was flamed by conversation, friendship, and trust. This collection represents a group of writers whose stories, generously written, strive to create new opportunities for discussion and reflection. I am deeply grateful to each and every one of our contributors. Thank you for trusting us with your stories, for your carefulness in revisiting difficult times and places, and for your willingness to share your lives.

Cami Ostman, my coeditor, deserves more credit than I can

express for listening to me talk for years about this crazy idea for an anthology even after we were told that no one would care.

Thank you, Pamela Malpas, Brooke Warner, and Laura Mazer, for your genuine enthusiasm, guidance, and support throughout the entire process of making this book a reality.

Thank you to my longtime friend Judy Moore, who listened to me (and believed me) at a time when no one else would, to Julie and Damon DeFoer for keeping me laughing when the editing would not stop, and to Paula Gilman for all the long walks that helped remind me why this project is so important.

I am especially grateful to my husband, Michael Falter, whose love and encouragement has not only brought humor and compassion to my story, but also given it a happy ending I would never have imagined possible.

—Susan Tive

About the Contributors

KYRIA ABRAHAMS is the author of *I'm Perfect, You're Doomed: Tales of a Jehovah's Witness Upbringing* (Touchstone, 2009). She writes a weekly column for *Street Carnage*, most notably "The Myth of Hipster Racism," which landed her an interview on NPR. She makes a lot of YouTube videos in characters that people think are real. *Gawker* once called her an "angry neocon." She is neither angry nor conservative, but is often misunderstood. She lives in Queens with her artsy husband, Marcus, and a dog and cat who actually seem to like each other. She's currently trying her hand at photography.

HUDA AL-MARASHI is an Iraqi American at work on a memoir about the impact on her marriage of her dual-identity. Excerpts from this memoir have appeared in the anthologies *Love Inshallah: The Secret Love Lives of Muslim American Women, Becoming: What Makes a Woman,* and *In Her Place.* She is the recipient of a 2012 Creative Workforce Fellowship, a program of the Community Partnership for Arts and Culture, made possible by the generous support of Cuyahoga County citizens through Cuyahoga Arts and Culture.

YOLANDE BRENER is an English writer living in New York. She is the author of the memoir *Holy Candy.* She has worked as an actress, a filmmaker, a singer in an all-girl band, and a disciple of an alleged Messiah. Her essays have been published in *New York Press, Nerve,* and *Strange Angels,* and her film scripts have been funded by the British Film Institute and the Arts Council of Great Britain. She won the 2010 NYC Department of Parks & Recreation Poems in the Park competition. Currently Yolande works as a teleprompter operator and plays at training in pole fitness. She believes that all religions contain wisdom and is grateful to the Unification Church for teaching her to see all things as holy.

CAROLYN BRIGGS holds an MFA in Creative Writing from the University of Arkansas. Her 2002 book, *This Dark World: A Memoir of Salvation Found and Lost* (Bloomsbury USA), was reissued in 2011 as *Higher Ground: A Memoir of Salvation Found and Lost* (Rowman & Littlefield) to coincide with the release of the film adaptation, *Higher Ground* (Sony Pictures Classics), for which she also wrote the screenplay. She currently writes for *Religion Dispatches* and has begun a new screenplay exploring one woman's journey into Eastern mysticism. Carolyn is an associate professor of English at Marshalltown Community College in Iowa.

CAITLIN CONSTANTINE is a journalist, blogger, and writer whose work has appeared in *Bitch*, *Creative Loafing*, and *The Huffington Post*. She is working on a memoir based on her much-loved zine, *I Was a Teenage Mormon*. When Caitlin isn't writing, she's training for marathons and duathlons. She lives in Clearwater, Florida, with her husband, greyhound, and two cats.

ELISE BRIANNE CURTIN is a writer and editor who hardly lets a day go by without putting pen to paper and fingertips to keyboard. After spending six years of her young adult life as a hardcore devotee of the International Church of Christ in Staten Island, New York, she walked away from her member-owned marriage and churchly obligations to rediscover the authentic voice within. She now finds her sanity in artistic expression, as a writer, and as a bluesy soul-folk song-stress. She recently set foot on a new path of sharing her passion for inner artistry in a variety of healing workshops geared toward women. Though far from her original home, she's happily nesting these days with her best friend and loverman in Bellingham, Washington.

STEPHANIE DURDEN EDWARDS knew since she was in second grade that her mission in life was to become a writer. Today, she lives that dream as a small-town journalist, freelance writer, and aspiring novella author. She shares her home in West Central Missouri with her husband, three growing children, a stubborn horse, and a loud beagle. Stephanie spent the majority of her adulthood as a devout and active member of the Church of Jesus Christ of Latter-day Saints until her faith was shaken in late 2006. Within months, her beliefs came full circle, beginning a paradigm shift that changed her life forever. Taking the journey a day at a time, Stephanie continues to rebuild and redefine her life. She finds peace in long walks along country roads near her home. She is convinced that happiness can be found at the bottom of a steaming cup of good coffee sitting alongside her husband and best friend of twenty years.

ELISE GLASSMAN lives and works in Seattle. She studied fiction writing with Laura Kalpakian and others at the University of Washington Extension, and with Marilynne Robinson at the Iowa Summer Writers' Workshop. Her work has appeared in *Colorado Review, Neon Beam, The Summerset Review, Main Street Rag, The Portland Review, Tawdry Bawdry,* and *Switchback.* Her story "The Shabiby Express" was a Top-10 Finalist in the Dylan Days Creative Writing Contest.

LUCIA GREENHOUSE is author of *fathermothergod: My Journey Out of Christian Science,* published by Crown in August 2011. *fathermothergod* was recommended by such publications as *O, The Oprah Magazine; Marie Claire* magazine; and *The Atlantic.* Lucia lives with her husband, four children, and dog in Westchester County, New York. She is a graduate of Emma Willard School and Brown University. She is a big fan of the Writing Center at Sarah Lawrence College.

COLLEEN HAGGERTY is a writer of personal essays, with stories published in *The Spirit of a Woman: Stories to Empower and Inspire* (Santa Monica Press), *He Said What?: Women Write About Moments When Everything Changed* (Seal Press), and *Dancing at the Shame Prom: Sharing the Stories That Kept Us Small* (Seal Press). She is currently working on a memoir about being a disabled mother. You can read about her journey as she walks through life as an amputee at www.mymilewalk.com.

PAMELA HELBERG is something of an expert at living two lives: fundamentalist Christian/closeted lesbian; Catholic school employee/mostly out lesbian; writer/computer geek; lesbian mom in the not-so-gay nineties. She received her MA in Creative Writing from Western Washington University where she studied under award-winning novelist Laura Kalpakian. Pam founded and operated Fremont Place Books in Seattle and taught English composition for many years at Whatcom Community College, before succumbing to her inner geek and launching a career in IT. Pam currently works in IT by day, writes whenever she can, and is at work on her memoir. She lives with her partner, Nancy, in Bellingham, Washington, where she works at making her life more congruent. She blogs on a variety of topics at www.pmbgp.blogspot.com.

MELANIE HOFFERT grew up on a farm near Wyndmere, North Dakota, where she spent her childhood meandering gravel roads, listening to farmers at church potlucks, and daydreaming about impossible love. She has an MFA in Creative Writing from Hamline University, where she was awarded the 2008 Outstanding Nonfiction Thesis Award. Her work has appeared in several literary journals. She received the 2005 Creative Nonfiction Award from *Baltimore Review* and the 2010 Creative Nonfiction Award from *New Millennium Writings*. Her memoir, *Prairie Silence* (Beacon Press), is forthcoming in 2013. Melanie lives in Minneapolis where—on a daily basis—she plots her escape from all actions that do not feed her soul.

DONNA M. JOHNSON is the author of *Holy Ghost Girl*, a critically acclaimed memoir awarded a 2011 Books for Better Life Award and the Mayborn Creative Nonfiction Prize for a manuscript-in-progress.

Donna has written about religion, family, and culture for *Huffington Post*, the *Psychology Today* blog, *The Dallas Morning News*, *The Austin American-Statesman*, *Austin Monthly*, and other publications. She lives in Austin with her husband, poet and author Kirk Wilson.

MARY JOHNSON is the author of *An Unquenchable Thirst*, named one of the best memoirs of 2011 by *Kirkus Reviews*. At age nineteen, Mary joined the Missionaries of Charity, also known as the Sisters of Mother Teresa of Calcutta. During her twenty years as a sister, she spent fifteen of those in Rome, where she lived and worked with Mother Teresa. After leaving the sisters in 1997, she completed a BA in English at Lamar University and an MFA in Creative Writing at Goddard College. Mary's work has been widely featured in *O, The Oprah Magazine*; *Salon.com*; *The Washington Post*; *Poets & Writers*; *Bloomberg View*; *Los Angeles Times*; National Public Radio; and *The Rosie Show*, among others. She currently serves as Creative Director of Retreats for A Room of Her Own Foundation.

LEILA KHAN (pen name) was born in Pakistan and lived in various countries in Asia and Europe before settling in the United States at the age of eleven. A lawyer by training and profession, her writing has largely been academic, in the form of book reviews, law review comments, and chapters in books. A few years ago, she joined a writing group and started writing about her life experience of searching for belonging as a Pakistani Muslim woman who spent most of her life in the West. Her story "Rerouting" was recently published in the anthology *Love Insh'Allah: The Secret Love Lives of Muslim Women in America*. She lives in Northern California with her husband and daughter.

LEAH LAX holds an MFA in Creative Writing from the University of Houston. She has published prose, poetry, award-winning fiction, memoir, essays, and the libretto for a major opera and produced a world-traveling exhibit. She is currently working on a memoir of her thirty years among the Hassidim as a covered woman and a closeted lesbian, an excerpt of which appears in this book. Another excerpt was included in the 2010 anthology *Keep Your Wives Away from Them: Orthodox Women, Unorthodox Lives.* Her book *Not from Here: New Houstonians and Their Journeys* will be published by Bright Sky Press in 2013. Leah lives in Texas with her partner and their Airedale, Maggie.

GRACE PETERSON is a writer and blogger. She has published in several anthologies and blogs about the writing craft and recovery topics. She is working on a memoir that goes into much more detail about her experience with Brock, including the events that led up to it and her recovery process out of it. She is also an avid gardener. When the weather is unsuitable for weed pulling, she can be found in front of her laptop, working on her garden column, her garden blog, or her forthcoming garden book.

JOSHUNDA VICTORIA SANDERS is a writer, journalist, and poet. Her writing has appeared in *San Francisco Chronicle, Publishers Weekly, The Texas Observer, The Dallas Morning News, Bitch* magazine, and many other publications. Her work has been widely anthologized in Seal Press anthologies like *Secrets and Confidences: The Complicated Truth About Women's Friendships, Click: When We Knew We Were Feminists,* and *Madonna and Me.* She lives with her adorable dog, Cleo, in Austin, Texas, and is working on her first book. She blogs at www.thesingleladies.wordpress.com and www.jvictoriasanders.com.

ERIN SEAWARD·HIATT is a writer, editor, and designer who left small-town Illinois at seventeen for an elite Latter-day Saint education in the reddest of red states. After earning an English degree, she began her career as an enthusiastic but underpaid editor for a Christian press and fell in love with liberalism after a lefty novel slipped through the cracks and ended up on her desk. Erin edited a stack of books and wrote a handful of articles before landing face-first in graphic design, which consumes most of her life. Her artwork has gained prominence at national conventions and delights mixed-media artists and paper crafters worldwide. Erin spent ten years as a devout woman of faith before taking the leap into agnosticism. In her rare free time, she wrestles with a decorating scheme based on floor-to-ceiling bookshelves and periodically cruises the Western landscape with her filmmaker husband.

JULIA SCHEERES is the *The New York Times* best-selling author of *Jesus Land*, a memoir, and *A Thousand Lives: The Untold Story of Jonestown*. She lives in Berkeley, California, with her husband and children.

NIKKI SMITH has always been an initiator—from starting the first health-education program on the island of Guam to developing recruitment, retention, and student affairs departments for universities to being an assistant professor in public health. She has written for academic publications, held public office, and lectured for both local and national educational organizations. Her positions within the Seventh-day Adventist Church included Sabbath School teacher, elementary church school instructor, Loma Linda University professor, and missionary in both South Korea and Guam. She now resides in Southern California with her husband and is working on a memoir.

VALERIE TARICO is a psychologist and writer in Seattle, Washington. Valerie is the founder of www.WisdomCommons.org, an interactive library of quotes, poetry, stories, and essays that "elevate and celebrate humanity's shared moral core." As a writer she tackles the intersection between religious belief, psychology, and politics. Her books include *Trusting Doubt: A Former Evangelical Looks at Old Beliefs in a New Light* and *Deas and Other Imaginings: Ten Spiritual Folktales for Children*. Her articles, which have appeared at *Truthout, AlterNet, Jezebel, Slate*, and *The Huffington Post*, can be found at www.awaypoint.wordpress.com.

ELIZABETH TAYLOR-MEAD was born in New York during the baby boom generation. Moving to London at age twenty, she formed Metropolis Pictures, a documentary film company. Her Jehovah's Witness background provided great training for a producer: making cold calls without fear and conducting evangelical pitch meetings. Metropolis built a reputation for provocative award-winning films and was part of the emerging independent film movement in the United Kingdom Returning to the United States after eighteen years, she raised movie-worshipping daughters while working on PBS documentaries, followed by ten happy years as a director of a fine art house cinema. While she is currently planning her next adventure, she is pretty certain it will not include warning people to prepare for the Apocalypse.

NAOMI J. WILLIAMS'S short fiction has won a Pushcart Prize and appeared in numerous literary journals, including *One Story, A Public Space, The Southern Review, Ninth Letter*, and *The Gettysburg Review*. She has an MA in Creative Writing from UC Davis and lives with her family in Northern California.

About the Editors

CAMI OSTMAN IS A life coach, marriage and family therapist, and author of *Second Wind: One Woman's Midlife Quest to Run Seven Marathons on Seven Continents* (Seal Press). Cami holds a Bachelor's of Education in English in Theater from Western Washington University and a Master's of Science in Marriage and Family Therapy from Seattle Pacific University (both in Washington State). She has a special interest in helping women live more authentically and freely. She is also a dog lover, a wine connoisseur, a runner, and a blogger. Her blogs can be found at 7marathons7continents.com and psychologytoday.com/blog/secondwind. Cami hasbeen appeared in *O Magazine*, *Adventures Northwest*, *Fitness Magazine*, *The Mudgee Guardian* (Australia), and *La Prensa* (Chile). She lives in Bellingham, Washington with her husband and for-legged creatures.

SUSAN TIVE IS A writer and editor for a variety of academic, film, and women's studies projects as well as non-fiction book titles including *Faith and Feminism* and *Rachel's Bag*. She is currently the grant-writer and Development Director for Salt Lake Film Society. A former stay at home mom, she raised three, now grown, children in a small orthodox Jewish community in northern New Mexico. Along the way she completed her Bachelor of Science degree and earned her Masters of Liberal Arts from St. John's College. Susan is currently writing her memoir, *Woman of Valor,* the occasionally humorous tale of a twenty-something wife and mother who bid farewell to her fashionable freedoms and blue jeans to become a religious Jew. She now lives with her agnostic husband Michael in the Pacific Northwest where she is learning to brave the rainy weather and play in her garden, delighting in the fruits no longer forbidden in her life.